JOURNAL FOR THE STUDY OF THE OLD TESTAMENT SUPPLEMENT SERIES

38

Editors
David J A Clines
Philip R Davies

JSOT Press
Sheffield

SLEEP, DIVINE & HUMAN, in the Old Testament

Thomas H. McAlpine

Journal for the Study of the Old Testament
Supplement Series 38

Published by JSOT Press
JSOT Press is an imprint of
Sheffield Academic Press Ltd
The University of Sheffield
343 Fulwood Road
Sheffield S10 3BP
England

Typeset by Sheffield Academic Press
and
printed in Great Britain
by Billing & Sons Ltd
Worcester

British Library Cataloguing in Publication Data

McAlpine, Thomas H.
Sleep, human and divine, in the Old Testament.
—(Journal for the study of the Old
Testament supplement series, ISSN 0309-0787; 38).
1. Bible O.T.—Criticism, interpretation,
etc. 2. Sleep—Biblical teaching
I. Title II. Series
220.8'612821 BS1199.S5/

ISBN 1-905774-98-1
ISBN 1-905774-99-X Pbk

CONTENTS

CHARTS

TABLES

PREFACE

I wish here to acknowledge the counsel and encouragement of the Old Testament teaching group, Professors Brevard Childs, Lansing Hicks, Bonnie Kittel, and Robert Wilson. Particular thanks go also to the staff and occupants of the Yale Babylonian Collection, particularly Professor William Hallo.

Only a pattern of sacrificial decisions on the part of my colleague and supervisor, Mark Lau Branson, and my wife and friend, Elvice Strong McAlpine, made the completion of this work possible.

ABBREVIATIONS

AASOR	*Annual of the American Schools of Oriental Research*
AB	Anchor Bible
AfO	*Archiv für Orientforschung*
AHw	*Akkadisches Handwörterbuch*. See von Soden 1965-81.
ANET	*Ancient Near Eastern Texts*. See Pritchard 1969.
AnOr	Analecta Orientalia
AnSt	*Anatolian Studies*
AO	Tablet number in Louvre Museum, Paris.
AOAT	Alter Orient und Altes Testament
ASKT	*Akkadische und sumerische Keilschrifttexte*. See Haupt 1881-82.
b.	Babylonian Talmud
BA	*Biblical Archaeologist*
BARev	*Biblical Archaeology Review*
BDB	*A Hebrew and English Lexicon of the Old Testament*. See Brown, Driver, and Briggs 1951.
BHS	*Biblia Hebraica Stuttgartensia*
BJRL	*Bulletin of the John Rylands University Library of Manchester*
BKAT	Biblischer Kommentar: Altes Testament
BO	*Bibliotheca orientalis*
BRM	*Babylonian Records in the Library of J. Pierpont Morgan*. See Clay 1912-23.
BSAE	British School of Archaeology in Egypt
BZAW	Beihefte zur *Zeitschrift für die alttestamentliche Wissenschaft*
CAD	*The Assyrian Dictionary*. See Gelb 1956–.
CBQ	*Catholic Biblical Quarterly*
CT	*Cuneiform texts*. See British Museum. Dept. of Egyptian and Assyrian Antiquities. 1896–.

CTA	*Corpus des tablettes en cunéiformes alphabétiques*. See Herdner 1963.
EI	*Eretz Israel*
FRLANT	Forschungen zur Religion und Literatur des Alten und Neuen Testaments
Gil	'The Epic of Gilgamesh'
GKC	*Gesenius' Hebrew Grammar*. See Cowley 1910.
HAT	Handbuch zum Alten Testament
HGŠ	*Sumerisch-babylonische Hymnen und Gebete an Šamaš, I*. See Schollmeyer 1912.
HR	*History of Religions*
HUCA	*Hebrew Union College Annual*
IEJ	*Israel Exploration Journal*
IVR	*The Cuneiform Inscriptions of Western Asia. IV*. See Rawlinson 1891.
JAOS	*Journal of the American Oriental Society*
JBL	*Journal of Biblical Literature*
JCS	*Journal of Cuneiform Studies*
JSS	*Journal of Semitic Studies*
K	Tablet number in Kouyunjik Collection, British Museum, London
KAI	*Kanaanäische und aramäische Inschriften*. See Donner and Röllig 1971.
KAT	Kommentar zum Alten Testament
KB	*Hebräisches und aramäisches Lexikon*. See Koehler and Baumgartner 1953, 1967–. Where available, the third edition has been used. —Keilinschriftliche Bibliothek
LLA	*Lexicon Linguae Aethiopicae*. See Dillmann 1865.
SS	Leipziger Semitische Studien
LXX	Septuagint
m.	Mishnah
MDP	Mémoires de la Délégation en Perse
Midr.	Midrash
NAB	*New American Bible*
NEB	*New English Bible*
NICOT	New International Commentary on the Old Testament
OECT	Oxford Editions of Cuneiform Inscriptions

Or	*Orientalia*
OTL	Old Testament Library
OTS	*Oudtestamentische Studiën*
RA	*Revue d'assyriologie et d'archéologie orientale*
RSV	*Revised Standard Version*
SANE	Sources from the Ancient Near East
SBH	*Sumerisch-Babylonische Hymnen*. See Reisner 1896.
TCL	Textes Cunéiformes. Musée du Louvre.
tm	translation mine
trans.	translation by
translit.	transliteration by
UF	*Ugarit-Forschungen*
UMBS	The University of Pennsylvania, the Museum, publications of the Babylonian Section
UT	*Ugaritic Textbook*. See Gordon 1965.
VAB	Vorderasiatische Bibliothek
VAT	Tablet number in Berlin Museum
VT	*Vetus Testamentum*
VTSup	*Vetus Testamentum*, Supplements
WUS	*Wörterbuch der ugaritischen Sprache*. See Aistleitner 1974.
ZA	*Zeitschrift für Assyriologie*
ZAW	*Zeitschrift für die alttestamentliche Wissenschaft*
ZDPV	*Zeitschrift des deutschen Palästina-Vereins*
ZNW	*Zeitschrift für die neutestamentliche Wissenschaft*
ZThK	*Zeitschrift für Theologie und Kirche*

Chapter 1

INTRODUCTION

The writers of the Old Testament, and those they wrote about, spent approximately one third of their lives sleeping. But as this fact is quite unremarkable, they did not remark on it. They, and those studying their writings, were far more interested in time spent awake. Thus sleep as a topic has received little attention. Nevertheless, there is an intriguing set of issues here, some of which go beyond the boundaries of this particular topic. As an introduction to these, I will sketch out first the sorts of contexts in which sleep was remarkable, survey the research that has been done up to this point, and describe the focus of this study.

1. *Remarkable sleep*

References to sleep occur throughout the Old Testament. And these references occur in an apparently wide variety of contexts. Only rarely is sleep itself the topic; in the bulk of cases, sleep is mentioned in connection with some other topic. Thus references to sleep can most easily be grouped by grouping those topics whose discussion elicits the mention of sleep. And review of these topics will allow us also to indicate what work has been done relevant to sleep in particular contexts.

a. *Sleep as occasion of vulnerability*

People are vulnerable during sleep, and thus when safety is an issue, sleep may be mentioned. In fact, the safety/vulnerability topic is the one which most frequently includes mention of sleep. The problem is set forth in a programmatic way in Ecclesiastes 5.11: 'Sweet is the sleep of a laborer, whether he eats little or much; but the surfeit of the rich will not let him sleep'.[1] The father's commandment and mother's teaching are commended because

> When you walk, they will lead you;
> when you lie down, they will watch over you;
> and when you awake, they will talk with you (Prov 6.22).

Similarly Proverbs 3.24. But more often it is YHWH who is spoken of as protecting one during sleep:[2]

> I lie down and sleep;
> I wake again, for the Lord sustains me (Ps 3.6).

> In peace I will both lie down and sleep;
> for thou alone, O Lord, makest me dwell in safety (Ps 4.9).

Likewise Psalms 57.5; 91.1 and Job 11.18-9. Probably relevant here are the problematic references to waking in Psalms 17.15 and 139.18. Jonah's sleep is perhaps a negative example (Jonah 1.5-6).[3]

In narrative, this vulnerability is made use of in Delilah's attempts to neutralize Samson's strength (Judg 16), in the switching of babies (1 Kgs 3), in the deaths of Sisera (Judg 4), Ishbosheth (2 Sam 4), and in the near death of the sleeping Saul (1 Sam 26). In response, people take precautions. During Absalom's rebellion the location of David's camp is an issue (2 Sam 17). Nehemiah makes provisions for guarding Jerusalem at night (Neh 4).

In cities of dubious reputation one must be careful. Both in the divine visitation of Lot and the Gibeah outrage the danger of sleeping in the streets and the relative safety of sleeping in a home are contrasted (Gen 19; Judg 19, 20). Job cared for the traveler:

> if the men of my tent have not said,
> 'Who is there that has not been filled with his meat?'
> (the sojourner has not lodged in the street;
> I have opened my doors to the wayfarer) (31.31-32).

And the vulnerability of travelers appears to be the basis for the poignant questioning in Jeremiah 14.8-9a:

> O thou hope of Israel,
> its savior in time of trouble,
> why shouldst thou be like a stranger in the land,
> like a wayfarer who turns aside to tarry for a night?
> Why shouldst thou be like a man confused,
> like a mighty man who cannot save?

On a national level, safety during sleep becomes a standard way of talking about peace: 'And I will give peace in the land, and you shall lie down, and none shall make you afraid; and I will remove evil beasts from the land, and the sword shall not go through your land' (Lev 26.6). Similarly Hosea 2.20 and Ezekiel 34.25.

But evil beasts and people are not the only threats during sleep. There are tantalizingly brief references to the *pḥd lylh*:

> You will not fear the terror of the night,
> nor the arrow that flies by day,
> nor the pestilence that stalks in darkness,
> nor the destruction that wastes at noonday (Ps 91.5-6).

> Behold, it is the litter of Solomon!
> About it are sixty mighty men
> of the mighty men of Israel,
> all girt with swords
> and expert in war,
> each with his sword at his thigh,
> against alarms by night (Cant 3.7-8).

And God may bring death during sleep. Thus Job 36.20:

> Do not long for the night,
> when peoples are cut off in their place.

Other examples are found in Job 27.19; 34.20,25 and Proverbs 20.20. The death of Egypt's firstborn (Exod 12 and in subsequent references) and the death of the besieging Assyrians (2 Kgs 18-19 // Isa 36-37), neither of which mentions sleep, also occur at night.[4] If a reading like *The New American Bible*'s is adopted (hereafter NAB), Psalm 90.5 (discussed in the next chapter) belongs here. While these examples perhaps focus as much or more on night as on sleep, Elijah's curious behavior during his flight from Jezebeel redresses the balance:

> But he himself went a day's journey into the wilderness, and came and sat down under a broom tree; and he asked that he might die, saying, 'It is enough; now, O Lord, take away my life; for I am no better than my fathers'. And he lay down and slept under a broom tree (1 Kgs 19.4-5a).

b. *Dreams*

While dreams or visions are often referred to without mention of sleep, some dream accounts include references to sleep: Abimelech

(Gen 20), Jacob (Gen 28), Joseph (Gen 37), Pharaoh's chief butler and baker (Gen 40), Pharaoh (Gen 41), Balaam (Num 22), a Midianite (Judg 7), Samuel (1 Sam 3), Solomon (1 Kgs 3), Job (Job 7), and Nebuchadnezzar (Dan 2).[5] Generally these are quite brief references, and thus Genesis 28.11 is unusual in the circumstantial detail given: 'And he came to a certain place, and stayed there that night, because the sun had set. Taking one of the stones of the place, he put it under his head and lay down in that place to sleep.' This is probably the rule-proving exception, for the stone has nothing to do with the dream, but does figure in the narrative of the next morning's events (v. 18). In other cases the references to sleep may be part of a particular dream report form (Gnuse 1982). In addition, there are the generalized accounts in Isaiah 29, Job 4 and 33. Perhaps Jeremiah 31.26 is to be added to this group: 'Thereupon I awoke and looked, and my sleep was pleasant to me'.

Somewhat more complex are references to sleeping and waking within the context of visions as in Zechariah 4.1: 'And the angel who talked with me came again, and waked me, like a man that is wakened out of his sleep' (compare also Dan 8.18; 10.9). Experience with dreams or visions may further be used metaphorically:

> He will fly away like a dream, and not be found;
>   he will be chased away like a vision of the night (Job 20.8).

Potentially relevant here are Psalms 39.7 and 73.20, where Gunkel ([1929] 1968, 163,311) and Kraus (1978, 451,663) take *ṣlm* as 'Traumbild'. Thus Gunkel renders Psalm 39.7:

>   nur als ein Traumbild wandelt der Mann dahin.
> Um nichts häuft er 'Reichtümer' auf
> und weiss nicht, wer sie einheimst.

c. *Preferred activities*

Sleep and most activities—notably work—are mutually exclusive. Predictably, Proverbs takes the most interest in this antithesis, and commonly uses sleep as an example of sloth (6.9-11; 10.5; 19.15; 20.13; 24.33-4; 26.14). Thus Proverbs 6.9-11:

> How long will you lie there, O sluggard?
>   When will you arise from your sleep?
> A little sleep, a little slumber,
>   a little folding of the hands to rest,
> and poverty will come upon you like a vagabond,
>   and want like an armed man.

Appropriate behavior will sometimes involve foregoing sleep. Sometimes this involves regular activity, as in the description of the good wife:

She rises while it is yet night
and provides food for her household
and tasks for her maidens (31.15).

That not all were early risers is at least suggested by another proverb:

He who blesses his neighbor with a loud voice,
rising early in the morning,
will be counted as cursing (27.14).

Other times particular circumstances call for foregoing sleep, as when one is involved in a bad business deal:

Give your eyes no sleep
and your eyelids no slumber;
save yourself like a gazelle from the hunter,
like a bird from the hand of the fowler (6.4-5).

This exhortation is formulaic, for it appears in different circumstances —and in the first person—in Psalm 132.3-4. The narrative reflex of the activity/sleep choice appears in cases where activity is begun during the night (Gen 32.23; Judg 16.3; Neh 2.12). Thus Genesis 32.23: 'The same night he arose and took his two wives, his two maids, and his eleven children, and crossed the ford of the Jabbok'. But common to these three texts is the use of *qwm* 'rise', which does not necessarily imply prior sleep. This illustrates the difficulty of drawing precise boundaries around the topic.

The desirability of particular activities over sleep also becomes an issue in contexts which are military (in a narrow sense) or (more broadly) concerned with guarding. Thus part of the terror of the advancing army is its excellence as an army:

None is weary, none stumbles,
none slumbers or sleeps,
not a waistcloth is loose,
not a sandal-thong broken (Isa 5.27).

And it is here that the references to divine sleep belong. On the one hand, YHWH's competence as a guardian is affirmed by stressing that he stays awake on the job (Ps 121.3-4). On the other, severe difficulties may suggest divine sleep, whether YHWH's (Pss 35.22-23; 44.24-25; 59.5b-6; 78.65) or Baal's (1 Kgs 18.27).

d. *Travel*

Sleep also becomes worthy of note when people are not at home. Special arrangements must be made. The examples from the Old Testament cluster in three groups. The first group contains bivouacs. In the early chapters of Joshua attention is paid to the temporary encampments of the Israelites (chs. 3, 4, 6, 8). 'So he caused the ark of the Lord to compass the city, going about it once; and they came into the camp, and spent the night in the camp. Then Joshua rose early in the morning, and the priests took up the ark of the Lord' (Josh 6.11-12). In a later context Joab warns David (2 Sam 19.8):

> Now therefore arise, go out and speak kindly to your servants; for I swear by the Lord, if you do not go, not a man will stay with you this night; and this will be worse for you than all the evil that has come upon you from your youth until now.

To this may be added a verse from a description of an advancing army (Isa 10.29):

> they have crossed over the pass,
> at Geba they lodge for the night;
> Ramah trembles,
> Gibeah of Saul has fled.

Common to all of these examples is the verb *lwn/lyn* 'spend the night'. Bivouacs are not always planned, thus the thankfulness shown in recording the provisions (including bedding) provided for David during Absalom's rebellion (2 Kgs 4).

The second grouping can be covered under the rubric 'houseguests', who range from family (Gen 24; Judg 19) to state officials (Num 22) to soldiers (Josh 2; Judg 18). Thus Genesis 24.54: 'And he and the men who were with him ate and drank, and they spent the night there. When they arose in the morning, he said, "Send me back to my master"'. It is here that this group overlaps with the larger 'sleep as an occasion of vulnerability group', and relevant examples from that group could be included here as well (Gen 19; Judg 19; Jer 14; Job 31).

The third grouping is composed of sleep recorded at apparently 'neutral' encampments when covenants are made. In the accounts of the covenants made between Abimelech and Isaac (Gen 26) and between Jacob and Laban (Gen 31) the action is spread over one day and the next. Thus Genesis 31.54-32.1:

> and Jacob offered a sacrifice on the mountain and called his kinsmen to eat bread; and they ate bread and tarried all night on the mountain. Early in the morning Laban arose, and kissed his grandchildren and his daughters and blessed them; then he departed and returned home.

Is the overnight stay an integral part of the covenant making, or simply the result of other realities (customary time for feasts and the dangers of night travel)? Up to this point studies have not recognized encampment as an element in covenant making per se (Pedersen 1926-40, 1.305-306; Buis 1966; Nicholson 1974), but if more evidence becomes available, it could be worth pursuing.

In addition to these groups, sleep away from home is also noted in contexts of sexual activity (Cant 7.12-13, which activity is played off against in Ruth 3), and/or cultic activity (Isa 65.3-5). In addition, it becomes an issue when merchants encroach on the Sabbath (Neh 13), and for the gatekeepers (1 Chr 9).

e. *Sleeplessness*

Descriptions of sleeplessness generally serve to stress the severity of whatever it is that is troubling the person. Again, the cases tend to cluster. Sleeplessness appears in descriptions of illness (Isa 38; Ps 102; Job 3; 7; 30). Thus

> I lie awake,
> I am like a lonely bird on the housetop (Ps 102.8).

One might mention here also the description of the sleeplessness that comes with old age (Eccl 12).

Sleeplessness also occurs in passages where 'anxious care' is being described, although it should be noted that there is no particular lexical correlate to this phenomenon. The cases include Psalm 127.2; Proverbs 4.16; Ecclesiastes 2.22-23; 5.11 (previously cited in the discussion of vulnerability); and 8.16-17. Thus: 'What has a man from all the toil and strain with which he toils beneath the sun? For all his days are full of pain, and his work is a vexation; even in the night his mind does not rest. This also is vanity' (Eccl 2.22-23).

And sleeplessness becomes an issue in descriptions of poverty broadly speaking, that is, descriptions of powerlessness or dependency. And the middle term here may well be cold: without adequate clothing or coverings, sleep flees. Jacob complains 'Thus I was; by day the heat consumed me, and the cold by night, and my sleep fled from my eyes' (Gen 31.40).[6] The same theme appears in Job's description of the poor: 'They lie all night naked, without clothing, / and have no covering in the cold' (24.7). Finally, the threat of cold to sleep may form part of the background to the law requiring the return of the pledged cloak at nightfall (Exod 22; Deut 24).

f. *Other*

Finally, there are a number of texts spread over a wide variety of situations. These include Eve's creation (Gen 2), instructions for handling 'leprosy' (Lev 14), instructions for teaching one's sons (Deut 6.11), the David-Bathsheba story (2 Sam 11), a proverb built on the experience of short beds and narrow coverings (Isa 28), a *rwḥ trdmh* poured out in judgment (Isa 29), a city struck by famine (Isa 51), an obscure reference to a baker (Hos 7), a warning against sharing secrets (Mic 7), Ruth's promise to Naomi (Ruth 1), a description of sleeping with the heart *'r* 'awake' (Cant 5), and a discussion of strength in numbers (Eccl 4).

2. *Prior studies*

As a topic in Old Testament studies, sleep has received little attention. In fact, a survey of entries for 'sleep' in biblical encyclopedias and the like suggests a certain deterioration of interest. In Huré's *Dictionnaire universal de l'Ecriture Sainte* (1715, 2 vols.) sleep is treated by noting in a general way some of its different senses. Thus 'lethal' sleep (death described as sleep) is noted, but not divine sleep. Since discussion is confined to the Greek, the Hebrew lexical group is not treated.

In Calmet's *Dictionnaire historique, critique, chronologique, géographique et littéral de la Bible* (1722, 2 vols.) an entry under sleep does not appear. But in the two volume *Supplément*, a four-paragraph entry appears under 'dormir'. In the first, the natural, moral (sleep as unresponsiveness or stupidity), and lethal senses are noted. The second provides examples of the lethal sense, states that God does not sleep, and notes sleep's causal relationship to poverty (Prov 23.21). The third takes up the theme of incubation, citing Vergil and Strabo in the discussion. The fourth notes the use of 'sleep' for 'le commerce d'un homme avec une femme: Génes. xix.33'

(1728, 3.214-15). The word involved in the commerce is, of course, *škb*, which has the more general sense of 'lie down', sex, sleep, and death all being contexts in which it is characteristically employed. Thus the Hebrew text is still not influencing the discussion.

Braus's *Biblisches universal Lexikon* (1806, 2 vols.) starts with the physical sense of sleep, and offers a scientific definition: 'der natürliche ist gleichsam eine Abspannung der äusserlichen Sinne vom Joche ihrer gewöhnlichen Verrichtungen, und entsteht von Abmattung der Kraft' (1806, 2.574). This is followed by noting supernaturally induced sleep as well as the sleep-poverty relationship (as above) and the attested tendency of worry or riches to impede sleep. Finally, the moral and lethal senses are noted—as 'verblümten'. Later, Schenkel's *Bibel-lexikon* (1869, 5 vols.) is primarily concerned with sleep in the moral sense (New Testament). Divine sleep (Old Testament) is noted, as is the 'euphemistisch' use of 'sleep' for death (1869, 5.221-22).

Before proceeding, the course of the discussion and its possibilities up to this point may be summarized. Calmet noted the role of choosing places to sleep in relation to dreams, and the sleep-poverty relation. The latter is present in Braus, who also notes the sleep-riches/worry relation. These observations about the place of sleep in Israelite experience could be pushed considerably further, but in general they tend to be absent from the later entries. Thus the entry for sleep in the one-volume abridgment of Calmet (Robinson 1832, 858) notes only the different senses of sleep.

Further, the discussion of the senses of sleep shifts in a subtle way. For Luther, the senses 'sleep' bears and the senses of the texts, e.g. the Psalms, in which it occurs are intertwined in an organic and complex fashion. It is a truism that in a given body of literature the senses of a word are governed by that literature. And in the case of sleep the interrelationships of sense in and established by the varied contexts are engaging, *so long as the figural way of reading Scripture is intact* (cf. Frei 1974, 17-50). Once that way of reading has broken apart, the senses of 'sleep' become simply senses of 'sleep' ('verblümt' or 'euphemistisch') and rapidly lose interest. Thus entries under 'sleep' are simply absent in Winer's *Biblisches Realwörterbuch* (3rd edn, 1847, 2 vols.), Kitto's *The Cyclopaedia of Biblical Literature* (10th edn, 1857, 2 vols.), and *Fairbairn's Imperial Standard Bible Encyclopedia* (1891, 6 vols.).

Both the varying roles of sleep and the varying ways 'sleep' can be used (in the Old Testament) do not lend themselves to elucidation by travellers' reports. This may also have had something to do with the eclipse of sleep as a topic, for in the following works the interest has decisively shifted towards describing the cultural realia, first with travellers' reports, and later also with data from excavations. And thus whereas up to this point the entries under 'sleep' and 'bed' have been of roughly equal length, 'bed' and related entries now take the lion's share.

An early stage in this process is represented by Taylor's revision of Calmet (1797-1801, 3 vols.), the last volume entitled 'Fragments: being illustrations of the manners, incidents, and phraseology, of the Holy Scriptures: principally selected from the most esteemed and authentic voyages and travels into the east . . . '. Entries under 'On the mode of sitting in the east' (1797-1801, 3.25-28) and 'Beds of the east' (1797-1801, 3.28-30) occur. Already here we are introduced to the divan, which will have a long life in the discussion.

Here McClintock and Strong's massive *Cyclopaedia of Biblical, Theological, and Ecclesiastical Literature* (1894-96) is a prime example. In it are contained entries under 'bed', 'bedchamber', 'bedstead', 'bolster', 'couch', 'divan', and 'sleep'. As the engravings in the entries suggest, the primary influence is current ethnography. And the entry under 'sleep'? One sentence covers the three senses, and discussion of the third sense (death) is pursued in the next paragraph via a discussion of early Christian inscriptions. But the bulk of the article is devoted to the various accouterments (bolsters, mattresses, etc.), most of which duplicates material in other entries. Only in the last sentence is there a recognition of other ways of handling the subject: 'To be tormented in bed, where men seek rest, is a symbol of great tribulation and anguish of body and mind ([references])' (1894-96, 9.807).

After McClintock and Strong, 'sleep' is simply absent as an entry in the *Encyclopaedia Biblica* (ed. Cheyne and Black, 1899-1903, 4 vols.), *A Dictionary of the Bible* (ed. Hastings, 1903, 5 vols.), *Dictionnaire de la Bible* (ed. Vigouroux, 1895-1912, 5 vols.), Galling's *Biblisches Reallexikon* (1937), Barrois's *Manuel d'archéologie biblique* (1939, 2 vols.), and the *Interpreter's Dictionary of the Bible* (ed. Buttrick, 1962, 4 vols.).[7] The entry in the *International Standard Bible Encyclopaedia* (ed. Orr, 1915, 5 vols.) simply confirms the judgment that the subject is not on the cutting edge:[8]

> Represents many words in Heb. and Gr. For the noun the most common are [list]; for the vb., [list]. The figurative uses for death (Deut 31.16, etc.) and sluggishness (Eph 5.14, etc.) are very obvious. See Dreams (Easton 1915, 4.2817).

Thus when the Hebrew is brought into the discussion it does not influence it significantly.

And this lack of interest is not confined to the encyclopedias. Pedersen's *Israel: its Life and Culture*, which has so much to say on so many topics apparently has nothing to say about sleep. The closest Pedersen comes to discussing sleep is in his discussion of the nature of dreams: 'Just because the dream so utterly rises from the depths of unconsciousness it is particularly significant' (1926-40, 1.134). And that is not very close.[9]

However, since World War II the subject has begun to reappear, both in Kittel (Balz 1972, Oepke 1965), its Old Testament counterpart (Schüpphaus 1982), in Bible dictionaries, and Thomson (1955). Neither of the treatments in the *Theological Dictionary of the New Testament* breaks new ground, although Oepke's work is preferable to Balz's.[10] Schüpphaus offers in the *Theological Dictionary of the Old Testament* primarily a linguistic study in which both *yšn* 'sleep' and *yšn* 'be old' are covered together with related words.[11] *Nwm* is taken to be 'das dichterische Synonym' to *yšn*, and *rdm* is taken to be 'der besonders feste Schlaf'. The author considers both positive and negative evaluations of sleep, and sketches out—through a consideration of *rdm*—its relationship to dreams. Sleep functions as a way of viewing death, 'wodurch der Gedanke des Wiederaufstehens zum Leben bereits vorgegeben ist'. Finally, the question of divine sleep is addressed, and—whether for Baal or YHWH—Schüpphaus judges that the language is being used metaphorically (1982, 1033-35).

The treatment in the Bible dictionaries varies widely, and in some cases entries are lacking (*Encyclopaedia Biblica* [Hebrew], *Encyclopaedia Judaica*, *Interpreter's Dictionary of the Bible*).[12] In the *Biblischhistorisches Handwörterbuch* (1966, 4 vols.), 'Schlaf' receives a one-sentence entry, which notes the 'physisch' and 'geistig' uses (Reicke 1966, 3.1699). In the *Bibel-Lexikon* (2nd edn, 1968), Schilling provides a one-paragraph entry, which in addition to noting the standard senses, observes ways in which sleep has ethical significance, and ways in which it is used by God (1968, 1539). In the *Calwer Bibellexikon* (5th edn, 1959) Frohmeyer devotes a paragraph each to the Old and New Testaments. For the former, both the 'eigentlichen' and 'übertragenen' sense are noted, and the references to divine sleep noted. But in addition there is an attempt to indicate the range of situations in which sleep is mentioned, without, however, any grouping or indication of frequency (Frohmeyer 1959, 1175-76).

Thomson's study, 'Sleep: an Aspect of Jewish Anthropology', starts with a lexical discussion of the three Biblical Hebrew roots characteristically employed for sleep: *yšn*, *nwm*, and *rdm*. Comparative semitic and Septuagint evidence is offered for the meanings 'to sleep', 'to be drowsy or to slumber', and 'a heavy or deep sleep' respectively (1955, 421).

But at bottom the study is an apologetic piece. We are told that

> in respect of sleep and dreams the Old Testament is amazingly modern. This is the more astonishing when one recalls the Assyrian, Babylonian and Egyptian attitudes to sleep; and the vagaries of the Greek mind in its view of sleep; and also the hesitancy with which medical science approaches the same subject to-day (1955, 427).

and

> ...the Hebrews regarded dreams pretty much as men of good sense regard them to-day (1955, 431).

What is this Hebrew/Old Testament (the two are regarded as synonymous) view of sleep? '(1) Sleep is the result of a Divine intervention... (2) Closely related to the notion that sleep is divinely induced is the idea that sleep is a state of death' (1955, 423). Not surprisingly, most of Thomson's evidence for the first point consists of texts using *rdm* or *trdmh*, which generally do speak of divine intervention. But on the basis of Psalm 127.2 ('for he gives to his beloved sleep') Thomson apparently thinks that normal sleep is regarded as the result of divine intervention.[13] Thomson interprets the second point by appealing to cases in which death is spoken of as sleep. The argument becomes difficult to follow at this point, particularly when Psalm 139.18 ('When I awake, I am still with thee') is introduced: 'The psalmist seems to be speaking of sleep, and on waking from sleep he finds that he is still with God; implying, tacitly at least, that during sleep he had been in the presence of God' (1955, 424). But Thomson does not take Psalm 139.18b to be representative of the Old Testament, and so the bottom line appears to be that sleep is a sort of death, but not in the sense that it involves a separation of soul and body.

There are other points, but the remainder of the article is concerned chiefly to describe three points at which Jewish anthropology developed in response to Hellenism. First, while the Old Testament does not work with a dualistic view, later Jewish thought (rabbinic citations and Philo) does, and so speaks of the soul leaving the body during sleep. Second, in regard to individual eschatology, 'Judaism modified Greek dualism by insisting on the resurrection of the body' (1955, 430) and the experience of waking was taken as an earnest of resurrection (rabbinic citations, prayers, Dan 12.2). Third, whereas the Old Testament understood dreams in light of its 'unitary view of personality', the later Jewish view spoke of the soul leaving the body as the mechanism for dreaming (1955, 432-33).

In summary, sleep has received little attention, and often the attention given has been governed by concerns extrinsic to the Old Testament. One thinks of the disproportionate space given to incubation in Calmet (conditioned by the classical world) or to beds, divans, and the like in Taylor's edition of Calmet (conditioned by current ethnography). Nor have effective ways been found to bring the Hebrew text into the discussion. While this state of affairs is understandable given corresponding deficiencies in the treatment of other, presumably more important, subjects, it does not need to continue.

3. *The purpose and limits of this study*

While both the contexts in which sleep is remarked upon and prior work regarding sleep suggest particular questions, the precise set of questions addressed in this study are only partially determined by the material presented up to this point.

The study starts at the lexical level. Here the concern is to offer—with the aid of developing linguistic methods, particularly those concerned with a variety of word fields—more precise descriptions of the words employed in connection with sleep than have hitherto been available. Here, for example, Thomson's lexical proposals will be examined. This is not the first such study in Biblical Hebrew to utilize particular understandings of word fields. Barr (1968), Donald (1963), Reisener (1979), Sawyer (1972, 1973, 1980), are studies from which I have learned—if only in part—and Honeyman (1939), Kennedy (1898), Scharfstein (1964), and Strack (1929) are representative of earlier studies which pushed many of the same issues. In addition to exploring the ways different notions of lexical groupings can be used productively with words used for human sleep, the question of the behavior of these words when used in different contexts will be pursued.

Attention then turns to the immediate cultural correlates of sleep: where did people sleep, on what, when? Here the evidence in the Old Testament is extremely limited, and so archaeological and ethnographic data is introduced to provide additional perspectives from which to interpret the material. Not only evidence regarding domestic architecture and furniture is brought in, but also information regarding Palestinian burial practices. Given the close lexical links between sleep and death, it is worth exploring to what degree burial practices might be suggestive of sleeping practices, and this in turn will give us a running start in taking up the question of the meaning of these lexical links.

Attention then moves to Israelite understandings of sleep.[14] Here questions such as the identification of different varieties of sleep, possible physiological or psychological correlates to sleep (compare the sleeplessness group earlier identified), the possibility that sleep may have been interpreted in terms of activity of the (separable) soul, the meaning of the linkage—in various ways—between sleep and death, and the valuation of sleep (compare the earlier preferred activities group) will be addressed. In this chapter the comparative net is spread rather more broadly, taking in not only ancient near eastern, but also classical and rabbinic materials as well.

In various situations sleep was understood as a locus of divine activity. The situation most familiar to us is that of the sphere of intermediation, for it was during sleep that people dreamed. Because this is a relatively self-contained sphere, and because the problems it poses have more to do with other sorts of intermediation than with sleep per se, this set of questions has in general not been addressed in this study (but cf. chs. 4 §3; 5). But sleep was also understood as a locus for other sorts of divine activity. A group of texts speak of YHWH's knowing and guarding during sleep, and these will be examined via the question of sleep as part of a sacral-judicial process. Here is where a number of the texts grouped under sleep as an occasion of vulnerability will be treated. Further, some texts speak in a rather undifferentiated way of divine activity during sleep, and these also will be noted.

Finally, there is the question of sleep as a divine activity. For the

Old Testament, the problem is the proper positioning of the language about YHWH's sleep vis-à-vis language about divine sleep employed by Israel's neighbors. Thus the first order of business is a survey of Egyptian and Mesopotamian usage, followed by a fresh study of the relevant Old Testament passages.

Chapter 2

LEXICAL STUDIES

A good number of the questions introduced in the last chapter are, or can be posed as, lexical questions. And one way of organizing this chapter would be simply to list these questions and then address them seriatim. But this approach could well leave undescribed the relationship of the words to each other, the lay of the lexical landscape, so to speak. Within a set of studies on lexical patterning, used—minimally—as a heuristic device, the particular questions will be addressed.

1. *Lexical Fields*

Discussion of lexical patterning is complicated by two characteristics of this century's discussion. First, the discussion has been intertwined with the question of the relationship between language and culture. Thus Trier's *Der deutsche Wortschatz im Sinnbezirk des Verstandes* created a 'bombshell effect' by virtue of 'the unique combination of breathtaking ideas of W. von Humboldt with ultramodern razor-sharp formulations by Saussure' (Malkiel 1974, 274). Second, a wide variety of patterns has been recognized. Generally referred to as 'fields', these patterns are as often viewed as mutually exclusive as complementary (Oehman 1953, 125-26).

In this study the language-culture relation will periodically become an issue, as, for instance, in the use of sleep language for death. And the relationship will be decided on a case-by-case basis, rather than assuming a direct link (with Barr 1961, 21-45).

A variety of patterns, i.e. fields, are recognized, and their description occupies the bulk of this section. I am not concerned here with the question of whether a hierarchy of patterns can be established. The descriptions of different sorts of patterns or fields have different uses, and answer different questions.

a. *The Activity Field*

The first type of field is simply constituted by all the words associated with a particular activity, designated by Ipsen as a *Bedeutungsfeld* (Oehman 1953, 125). One might, for instance, assemble a field having to do with farming (the farming field), and include such words as chicken, plow, silo, rain, debt, and, to anticipate the next paragraph, ox. Nor would it matter if many of the words in the field never occurred in the same paragraph together. The words in this chapter, more precisely, those which are used in association with sleep, form this sort of *Bedeutungsfeld*. I will refer to fields of this type using an English word, e.g. the 'sleep field'.

b. *The Associative Field*

Ipsen's *Bedeutungsfeld* is defined by an activity. Thus 'the words do not all belong together etymologically nor are they related by association' (Oehman 1953, 125). A second type of field likewise casts a broad net, although centered on a particular word: 'a particular word is like the center of a constellation; it is the point of convergence of an indefinite number of co-ordinated terms' (Saussure [1915] 1966, 126). It is usually designated—following Bally—as an associative field (Ullmann 1972, 368). Bally spoke of associations which surround certain terms 'like a halo' and described the associative field for 'bœuf' as setting in motion three types of association.

> 1. with *vache*, *taureau*, *cornes*, *ruminer*, *beugler*, etc. (associations affecting the ox as a ruminant); 2. with *labour*, *charrue*, *joug*: *viande*, *abattoir*, *boucherie*, etc. (associations with the work performed by the ox and with butchering); 3. with the ideas of strength, endurance and patience, on the one hand, with those of heaviness and passivity, on the other (associations suggested by the qualities and faults of the ox) (Spence 1961, 89).

In this type of field all parts of the field are related semantically to its center. Other definitions—less appropriate for this study—include other sorts of relations (e.g. Saussure [1915] 1966, 122-23).

Coseriu and Geckeler properly criticize the process of identifying associative fields as being uncontrolled (1974, 113). That is, the edges of the fields are extremely fuzzy, and it is not clear precisely what one is describing. Here the associative fields will be identified on the basis of collocation. Further, the requirement that collocations have to be attested more than once allows focus on characteristic collocations and eliminates much marginally useful information. While these two decisions in the direction of control have the effect of limiting the number of words in associative fields, they also make it feasible to chart a number of associative fields simultaneously.

c. *Lexical Groups*

A third type of field employed in this study is the lexical group. Description of this field properly starts with Trier's *Der deutsche Wortschatz im Sinnbezirk des Verstandes*, in which Trier by analyzing changes in the group of words used for 'understanding' in Old and Middle High German was able to argue for a corresponding change in the cultural understanding of understanding. Oehman gives a concise summary of Trier's hypothesis:

> The linguistic field . . . is no isolated sphere in the vocabulary, even if this at first appears to be the case. Just as sections of a lexical field border on one another and form a whole, corresponding to the conceptual field, so do the lexical as well as the conceptual fields . . . join together to form in turn fields of higher orders, until finally the entire vocabulary is included. The fields of lower order 'articulate' (*ergliedern sich*) to form those of higher order, while the fields of higher order 'resolve' (*gliedern sich aus*) into those of lower order (1953, 127).

A formal expression of Trier's theory is provided by Lyons.

> the vocabulary, *V*, of a language is a closed set of lexemes . . . which can be partitioned into a set of lexical fields . . . i.e. divided into subsets, such that (i) the intersection of any two distinct fields is empty (no lexeme is a member of more than one field), (ii) the union of all the fields in *V* is equal to *V* (there is no lexeme which does not belong to some field) (1977, 1.268).

Trier's theory has been hotly debated (bibliography in Ullmann 1972, 372 n97). First, although Trier is well aware that in diachronic change the field can be quite fluid (Spence 1961, 95), he does not seem to have taken sufficient account of the amount of disorder this would cause. That is, it would be surprising if at any period there were not holes and cases of overlapping in at least some fields. And the literature on the various sorts of overlapping possible shows that this phenomenon is well-attested (discussion and bibliography in Baldinger 1968 and Collinson 1939).

Spence argues that Trier's account is faulty because one doesn't need to know all the words in a presumptive field to know one of them. Thus 'I can know the Russian for 'to walk (habitually)' without knowing the Russian verbs for 'run', 'hop', 'skip', or 'jump' (habitually or otherwise)' (1961, 92-93). True. But one cannot know that one has the correct Russian word without knowing what at least some of the adjacent words are. That is, in at least some cases, full appreciation of the value of a particular word depends on knowledge of other words in the same field, e.g. in the contrast between 'to' and 'at' ('First I will throw the chalk *to* you . . .').

Spence further notes that where we would expect on Trier's account to find well-organized fields we may be disappointed. Thus he cites Scheidweiler, who has argued that Trier's fields (*kunst*, *wist*, etc.) show less organization than Trier claimed, and Betz, whose request to university students to write down the (current) German terms in the 'field of knowledge' demonstrated that—in Spence's words—'their usage was full of semantic overlapping and outright contradictions' (1961, 96).

Nevertheless, there are gains in Trier's work, of which Ullmann (1972, 372) provides a convenient summary:

> (a) in sharp contrast to the atomism of traditional semantics, the field theory is more interested in the structure of lexical systems than in the elements of which these are composed . . .
> (b) The field theory has considerable heuristic value in that it enables the linguist to formulate problems which would otherwise have passed unnoticed.
> (c) It provides a new method for studying the influence of words on conceptualization and on thinking in general . . .
> (d) The field theory has succeeded in extending the structural approach to diachronic problems . . .

In this study the first and second points will be in evidence. In particular, the use of lexical fields will be heuristic in the sense that in each case the degree of synonymy or presence of 'holes' will have to be independently evaluated.

The definition of a lexical field given by Coseriu and Geckeler provides convenient entry into the problem of identifying lexical groups. Coseriu defines the lexical field as 'a primary paradigmatic structure. *Paradigmatic* means that the lexemes which can be chosen at a specific point in the *chaîne parlé* make up a paradigm, i.e. a system of oppositions' (1974, 148; see chart 2.1). The advantage of this definition is that it appears to imply a highly rigorous methodology (chains differing only in one position are collected, and the variants form the lexical field). But this is also its drawback, first because the chains available would generate too many fields, and second because it is not obvious what chain would produce precisely the variants listed in chart 2.1. 'You're too _________ to do that' would generate heterogeneous fields, and one wonders whether the only solution would be to accept only sentences which have the desired semantic requirements built in, for instance, 'In terms of age, he's too _________ to do that'.

Chart 2.1
Chaîne parlé and paradigm

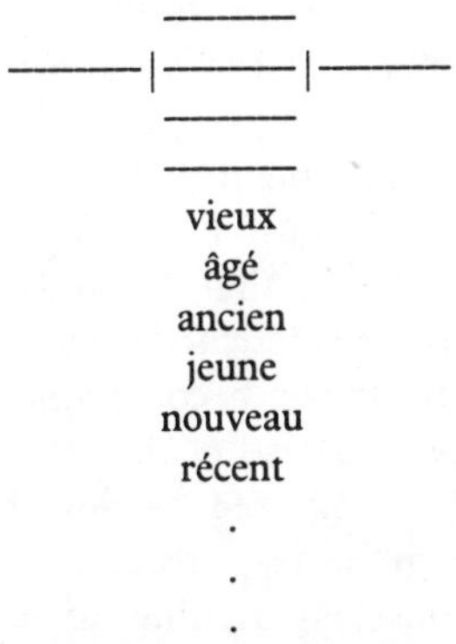

Source: Coseriu and Geckeler 1974, 148 [adapted].

Here Lutzeier's recent study is helpful (1982). He notes that the string 'Victoria was pleased about her _________' yields a paradigm including such disparate elements as 'weight', 'singing', and 'income'. To create manageable paradigms, he invokes the notion of aspect,[1] and thus can generate a set of paradigms which group these elements under 'appearance', 'activity', and 'financial income'. Lutzeier emerges with the following definition (1982, 13):

> Lexical fields are special types of words-paradigms because they fulfill at least two conditions in addition to the ones for words-paradigms, namely a syntactic one and a semantic one. The syntactic one says: There is a syntactic category in the fragment

> such that all elements are members of this syntactic category; and the semantic one says: There is an aspect such that all elements fall under this aspect.

Note that by this definition there are as many lexical fields as there are aspects, which is to say that every word is a member of an indeterminate number of lexical fields. Thus rather than a picture of lexical fields neatly dividing up the vocabulary, one gets a picture of an interlocking grid.

This definition of a lexical field appears to be workable. In a language where there are native informants, it should be possible to test easily the acceptability of the strings (fragments) used to establish the lexical groups. When working with a language without native informants, the situation is more difficult. There is simply not enough text. Thus here the procedure of deriving lexical groups from fragments has had to be weakened to the demand that members of lexical groups are members of the same syntactic category (verb, noun, etc.).

In some studies the requirement that lexical groups be composed of only one part of speech is neutralized by appeal to transformational grammar. That is, it is asserted that the study will be more accurate if it takes into account a hypothetical deep structure (which, through a set of regular transformations becomes the surface structure, i.e. the text) in addition to or instead of the texts at hand. Thus nouns which have been long recognized as deverbal in origin may be analyzed as being verbs in the deep structure. Sawyer takes this route (1972, 65, transliterations his), arguing, for example, that *lišu'atka qiwwiti* YHWH (Gen 19.18) is generated from two 'kernal structures' which separately could generate **hošia'* YHWH *'et*-[Noun Phrase] and **qiwwiti lă*YHWH. Without prejudicing the question of the status of the various versions of transformational grammar, this procedure appears to be a dubious one to adopt in dealing with a language known only through texts, for it assumes that deverbal nouns, e.g. *yšw'h*, have not developed characteristics of their own. That is, the strictures Barr applied to the etymologizing fallacy appear to apply also to this procedure (1961, 107-10). Therefore here the procedure will be to analyze, for example, *yšn* and *šnh* separately, and then to see how much they have in common. To avoid confusion, roots will be capitalized. Thus two groups and their members can be identified: the *yšn* group (*yšn, nwm, rdm, škb*) and the *Yšn* group (*yšn*, *šnh*, *nwm*, *tnwmh*, *rdm*, *trdmh*, *škb*, *mškb*).

There are other sorts of fields which will occasionally come into view in this study. Thus Porzig introduced the notion of 'elementare Bedeutungsfelder', which are binary fields characterized by '"essential semantic relationships" between verbs and nouns or between adjectives and nouns' (Oehman 1953, 129). The pair *trdmh* and *npl* would be an example of a field of this type.

d. *Methodological notes*

Prior to defining a lexical field, Coseriu and Geckeler set forth seven preliminary distinctions, one of which is diachrony/synchrony (1974, 143). Citing Coseriu, 'la lengua funciona sincrónicamente y se constituye diacrónicamente', they argue that study of lexical fields is properly based on synchronic study. This is the approach taken here, which means that attention to the etymology of the various words is subordinated to concern for their interrelationships.[2]

The decision has also been made here to treat the Old Testament texts as coming from a single period. It is of course possible to assign some texts with relative certainty to particular periods (Robertson 1972, Polzin 1976). But because there are enough texts whose assignment is tentative at best, systematic assignment of all the texts involved to particular periods would introduce too many guesses too early in the study.

Which Old Testament text? Sawyer articulates the following procedure in his study of *Yš'*:

> For present purposes, then, it has been decided that the final form of the text as preserved in masoretic tradition and transmitted to us in the Codex Leningradensis, should be the literary corpus in which the terms to be discussed occur, and that how the masoretes themselves understood the text should be the subject for semantic analysis (1972, 11).

This study follows Sawyer, though, like Sawyer, construing the second half of the statement to refer to the pointing, rather than to the traditions preserved in sources such as the Mishnah and targums.

2. *Activity Fields*

The first step was the isolation of the relevant material, and this was a two-sided process. On the one hand, it involved the identification of a group of texts in which the situation was human sleep. On the other hand, it involved identifying characteristic vocabulary in that group of texts. The results of this step are given in table 2.1, Sleep situations: texts, and table 2.2, Sleep activity field.

In many cases identification of texts and vocabulary was unproblematic. Most cases of texts using *yšn* would fall into this category. But two groups of cases presented problems. In the first group of texts, it was a question of the interpretation of a passage. These cases are handled in the notes to table 2.1.

The second group of texts pushed towards greater precision in method. The verb *škm* is a good case in point. Its characteristic collocation with *lyn* suggests that it may imply prior sleep. Should all of these cases in which this implication is likely be included? No, because implication is not sufficient grounds for inclusion. To borrow an image, sleep needs to be within the scene.[3] Thus *wyškm 'brhm bbqr wyḥbš 't-ḥmrw* (Gen 22.3) is not included, because in the narration it is not marked as being continuous in time with the preceding action. This despite the ease with which the previous conversation between God and Abraham could be construed as a dream or night vision (so Lindblom 1961, 97). In contrast, *wyškm 'bymlk bbqr wyqr' lkl-'bdyw* is included because it continues the narrated night vision (Gen 20.8). In most of these cases, collocation with other words has been a convenient way of deciding inclusion, and information on this procedure is provided in notes to table 2.2.

Table 2.1
Sleep situations: Texts

Gen	2.21; 15.12; 19.2-4,15; 20.3-8; 24.23-25,32-33,54; 26.30-31; 28.11-18; 31.40,54–32.1; 32.14,22-23; 37.5-10; 40.5; 41.1-8, 11,15,17-22
Exod	12.30; 22.25-26
Lev	14.47; 26.6
Num	22.8,13,19-21
Deut	6.7; 11.19; 24.12-13
Josh	2.1,8; 3.1; 4.3; 6.11-15; 8.9-10,13-14
Judg	4.21; 7.13-15; 16.3,14,19-20; 18.2; 19.4-27; 20.4
1 Sam	3.2-9,15; 26.5-12
2 Sam	4.5-7,11; 11.2-13; 17.8,16; 19.8
1 Kgs	3.5,15,19-21; 19.5-9
2 Kgs	4.11
Isa	5.27; 10.29; 28.20; 29.7-8,10; 38.15; 51.20; 65.4

Jer	14.8; 31.26
Ezek	34.25
XII	Hos 2.20; 7.6; Jonah 1.5-6; Mic 7.5; Zech 4.1
Ps	3.6; 4.9; 17.15; 39.7; 57.5; 90.5[a]; 91.1,5; 102.8; 127.2[b]; 132.3-4[c]; 139.18
Job	3.26; 4.13; 7.3-4,13-14; 11.18-19; 20.8; 24.7; 27.19-20; 30.17; 31.32; 33.15
Prov	3.24; 4.16; 6.4,9-10,22; 10.5; 19.15; 20.13; 23.21; 24.30-3; 26.14; 27.14; 31.15
Ruth	1.16; 3.2-4,6-8,13-14
Cant	3.7-8; 5.2-5; 7.12-13
Eccl	2.23; 4.11; 5.11; 8.16; 12.4
Esth	6.1
Dan	2.1-3; 8.18[d]; 10.9
Neh	2.12; 4.16; 13.20-21
1 Chr	9.27

a. *zrmtm šnh yhyw*. One is inclined, with Kraus (1978, 795) and the *Biblia Hebraica Stuttgartensia* (hereafter BHS) to take the Septuagint (hereafter LXX) and Syriac as indicating an original *šānāh* for *šēnāh*, which, assuming haplography, would have originally been *šānāh šānāh*, and to read *zr'tm* for *zrmtm*. The chief difficulty is that this reconstruction fits so nicely with the context that it is hard to see how it could have been lost! RSV's 'Thou dost sweep men away; they are like a dream' suffers from the fact that *šnh* is not used for 'dream', nor, with the probable exception of Jer 31.26, is it used to imply dreaming. NAB's 'You make an end of them in their sleep' is more promising, the adverbial use of *šnh* paralleled in Num 6.19, *wlqḥ hkhn 't-hzr' bšlh*, cited by Joüon ([1923] 1965, §126a). But then the picture does not fit particularly well with the succeeding image. NAB's understanding is provisionally adopted in further discussions.

b. *kn ytn lydydw šn'*. If *šn'* is taken as 'sleep', it is either the object of *ytn* or adverbial. Otherwise, a different etymology for *yšn* may be sought. All three interpretive options are ably reviewed by Emerton (1974, 15-31), although a different conclusion is reached here. The possibility of taking *kn* as the object of *ntn* is reviewed and rejected by Hamp (1972, 71-4).

The difficulty with taking *šn'* 'sleep' as the direct object of *ytn* is that the resulting statement is insufficiently motivated. This is Emerton's reason for rejecting this approach, and it is followed here.

Emerton uses a parallel argument against taking *šn'* 'sleep' as adverbial: 'The problem is to find a convincing explanation of the reason why God should be said to give things while men sleep' (1974, 20). But is this a real problem? Verses 1a-2a portray effort without reward, and v. 2b contrastively—hyperbolically—portrays reward without effort. Emerton objects that it would fit poorly with 'the ethos of Israelite wisdom literature'. There is some tension here, but it is a tension internal to that literature whose flavor Wolff expresses well (1974a, 134):

> Sleep can be praised provocatively as being the opportunity through which Yahweh supplies his friends with the bread (Ps. 127.2b) which the over-zealous only enjoy with a great deal of trouble, without reaching their aims in spite of many self-torturing extra hours of work (vv. 1-2a).

Further, the picture of God providing during sleep is evocative, resonating with other OT narratives (Solomon's sleep, the manna).

Against the adverbial interpretation Hamp (1972, 75) argues that because *šnh* is not a temporal noun, for a temporal use to be recognized 'die temporale Funktion notwendig und unzweideutig gefordert wäre'. But the interpretation adopted for Ps 90.5 (above) together with Num 6.19 are two counter-examples.

Hence it is unnecessary either to emend the text or to seek for other meanings of *šn'*. In regard to the latter, Emerton (1974, 23-4) adequately deals with Bussby's suggestion (1934) that 'sleep' is here a euphemism for intercourse. Both Dahood's later suggestion, 'prosperity', and Emerton's suggestion, 'high estate' or 'honor' are possible, but neither fits as well as *šn'* 'sleep'. The form is to be identified as an Aramaism (Cowley 1910 [hereafter GKC] §80h).

c. The form *šĕnat* occurs only here, and with it may be compared other occurrences of the old *-at* feminine ending (cited in Joüon [1923] 1965, §89n). The close parallel to this verse in Prov 6.4 argues for simply treating *šnt* with *šnh*, and this has been the practice here.

d. *wbdbrw 'my nrdmty 'l-pny 'rṣh*. Hartman (Hartman and DiLella 1978, 227-28) suggests that *nrdmty* is an incorrect translation of an original Aramaic *dĕmak* on the grounds that 'nothing in the context implies that the seer was unconscious or even asleep; the angel does not awake him, but merely raises him to his feet', and thus *dĕmak* would here function in the sense of 'to lie down', not 'to sleep'. But this line of argument is unnecessary in that the angel's actions do not prejudice the question of whether Daniel was awake or asleep at their inception, and thus it makes more sense to take *rdm* here in the sense of 'swoon'.

If Hartman wishes to weight *rdm* too lightly here, translations which employ 'trance', e.g. 'I fell to the ground in a trance' (NEB), weight it too heavily. Daniel is already 'in' a vision which began in v. 2 and is still occurring in v. 18, as the repeated mention of the site in v. 16 confirms.

Table 2.2
Sleep activity field

Word	Frequency	Word	Frequency
'kl	14	*'yp*	1
bṭḥ	3	*'lh*	1
bqr	18	*'p'p*	1
gg	3	*'ṣl*	3
ḥdr	1	*'ṣlh*	1
ḥzwn	1	*'rb*	2
ḥzywn	1	*'rś*	2
ḥlwm	25	*pḥd* [v]	1
ḥlm	8	*pḥd* [n]	2
ḥrd	3	*p'm*	3
y'p	1	*pqḥ*	2
yṣw'	1	*ṣlm*	1
yqṣ	15	*qwm*	26[d]
yšb	2	*rdm*	6
yšn	15[a]	*rḥṣ*	3
kswt	2	*ślmh*	3
lylh	37	*šḥr*	2
lyn	45[b]	*škb*	59[e]
mṭh	3	*škm*	16[f]
mṣ'	1	*šlwm*	3
mškb	7	*šmš*	4
mtq	1	*šnh*	21
ndd	4	*šqd*	2
nwḥ	1	*šqṭ*	1
nwm	1	*šth*	7
'wr	3[c]	*tnwmh*	5
'yn	6	*trdmh*	7

Note: See Appendix A for texts in which words in this table appear.

a. In this study the nine occurrences of *yšn* which can be classified as participles (Mandelkern 1971) or adjectives (Brown, Driver and

Briggs 1951 [hereafter BDB], Koehler and Baumgartner 1953, 1967 [hereafter KB]) are treated as participles, i.e. together with the (obviously) verbal forms. The issue is one of historical grammar, in that the stative verbs (*kābēd, qāṭōn*) can be regarded as originally adjectives (Joüon [1923] 1965, §41b).

b. Texts in which *lyn* has the sense 'lodge', with human subject and without temporal markers, have not been included (Isa 21.13; Pss 49.13; 55.8; Prov 19.23; Cant 1.13).

c. These occurrences of *'wr* collocate with *yšn* or *šnh*.

d. These occurrences of *qwm* collocate with *yšn*, *lyn*, *rdm*, *škb*, *šnh*, with the exception of Exod 12.30; Prov 31.15; Eccl 12.4; Neh 2.12, all of which are borderline (but are included).

e. While in some cases the inclusion of cases of *škb* is made clearer by collocation with *ḥrd*, *yqṣ*, *yšn*, *lyn*, *rdm*, *šnh*, etc., in the majority of cases one relies on context.

f. Occurrences of *škm* are included in the sleep field on the basis of collocation with *ḥlwm*, *lyn*, *šnh*, with the exception of Gen 26.31 and Prov 27.14. These borderline cases collocating with *lylh* were not included: Judg 6.28, 38, 40; 9.33; 2 Kgs 6.15; 19.35. For a discussion of the etymology of the word, see von Soden (1981).

In the process of assembling the sleep texts, all occurrences of many of the high-frequency words were checked, and it was found that a number of situations were regularly occurring. A number of these situations were checked systematically, and table 2.4, Activity fields, presents the results. Only those words are listed which in more than fifty percent of their occurrences in the OT occur in the situations listed. Further, only those words are listed which occur in the (human) sleep situation. Thus words used only in situations of death would not appear.

Table 2.3
Situations lexically related to human sleep

Situation	Definition	Code
divine sleep	sleep in which the sleeper is taken to be divine (includes YHWH, other gods, idols)	DS
animal sleep	sleep in which the sleeper is an animal (non-human)	AS
(human) sleep	unconsciousness (except that produced by alcohol) and inability to sleep	S

Situation	Definition	Code
infirmity	individual or group bedridden (hence code) due to sickness, injury, or age, with sleep(lessness) not an issue	B
death	death, but not including dying or murder	D
intercourse	sexual activity	I
mourning	formal mourning	M
nocturnal activity	breaking off sleep to praise YHWH, also meditating, lamenting, planning evil (all in bed)	N
drunkenness	drunkenness	W
	situations not defined	Z

There is obviously overlapping in some of these fields. Where words could be assigned to more than one activity field, they were assigned to the more specific, thus intercourse over drunkenness, drunkenness over sleep, and mourning over nocturnal activity. The situation may be represented by a set diagram. Here the largest circle (barely visible) indicates that the situation is located in bed, although in each case the situation was given a more specific designation.

Chart 2.2
Activity Fields

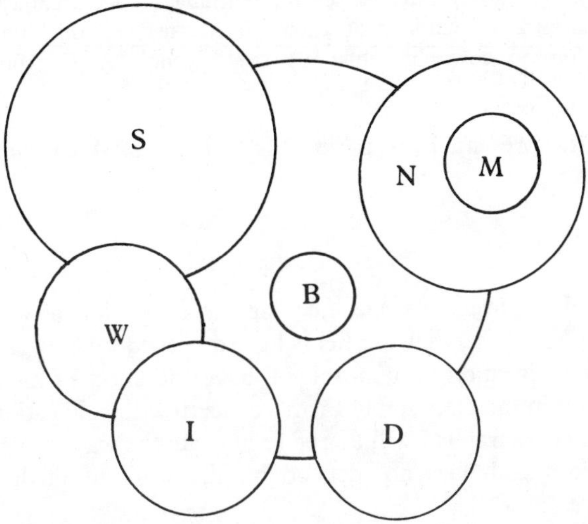

Table 2.4
Activity fields

Word	Codes										Total
	DS	AS	S	B	D	I	M	N	W	Z	
ḥlm			18							10	28
yṣwʿ			1		1	2		1			5
yqṣ	7		15		6				3	2	33
yšn	4		15		6						25
lyn		5	45				2			19	71
mṭh			3	10	4	1		2	1	8	29
mṣʿ			1								1
mškb			7	5	3	14		6		11	46
nwm	2	1	1		2						6
ʿrś			2	1	2	2		1	1	1	10
pʿm			3					1		1	5
rdm			6		1						7
škb		2	59	6	64	55	4	1	3	18	212
šnh			21		4						25
tnwmh			5								5
trdmh			7								7

Notes: Codes: DS, divine sleep; AS, animal sleep; S, (human) sleep; B, infirmity; D, death; I, intercourse; M, mourning; N, nocturnal activity; W, drunkenness; Z, unidentified situations. For the texts in which these words appear (broken down by situation), see Appendix A, Concordance by fields.

The data presented in table 2.4 will be used in subsequent chapters.

3. *Associative Fields*

The dual requirements specified for the discussion of associative fields in §2.1, viz., that the fields be established by collocation and that the collocation be non-unique, have the effect of moving this discussion in the direction of Firth's concern with collocation. In the following paragraphs I will therefore indicate the ways in which this study does and does not depend on the work of Firth and his followers.

Firth's account of language starts from its function as maintaining social relations, not simply, for instance, as communicating information: 'normal linguistic behavior as a whole is meaningful effort, directed towards the maintenance of appropriate patterns of life' (Firth [1951a] 1957, 225). Firth recognizes a number of levels of language, all of which he sees as contributing to meaning, using the analogy of light being divisible into a spectrum of colors, including 'phonetic, phonological, grammatical, lexical and semantic' (Lyons 1966, 296). Given language's function in maintaining social relations, Firth can claim that 'it is part of the meaning of an American to sound like one' ([1951b] 1957, 192). And part of a complete description of what sounding like one involves is a description at the lexical level, which would include an account of which words tend to collocate with which others—and with what frequency.

As an example, Firth suggests

> part of the meaning of the word *ass* in modern colloquial English can be by collocation:
> (i) An ass like Bagson might easily do that.
> (ii) He is an ass.
> (iii) You silly ass!
> (iv) Don't be an ass.
> One of the meanings of *ass* is its habitual collocation with an immediately preceding *you silly* and with other phrases of address or of personal reference ([1951b] 1957, 194-95).

Firth has a point. Language learning involves also some attention to collocation if one wishes to use the language, and great attention if one wishes to pass as a native. But will his account do as a full-fledged account of meaning? With Lyons (1966, 290-94), no. Neither reference nor meaning-relations (antonymy, synonymy, etc.) have an adequate place in this account. What we do have is a tool for (1) providing clues to the meaning of words, and (2) describing the particular groupings of words, i.e. a stylistic or comparative tool. This latter is not surprising, in that stylistics is an explicit concern—perhaps even the dominant one—of Firth's study from which most of the preceding quotations have been taken. The first use of this tool will appear in following sections in the discussion of the *Yšn* and *mškb* groups, and the second in a subsequent chapter covering Israelite understandings of sleep.

Firth's references to collocation are general, and it has been left to his followers to operationalize the concept. One such attempt is Sinclair's adaptation of the notion for computer analysis. To do this, he gives the following definitions:

> We may use the term *node* to refer to an item whose collocations we are studying, and we may then define a *span* as the number of lexical items on each side of a node that we consider relevant to that node. Items in the environment set by the span we will call *collocates* (Sinclair 1966, 415).

Thus

> we measure both the way in which an item [node] predicts the occurrences of others . . . and also the way in which it is predicted by others. Then we choose the second of these measurements for our statement of the lexical meaning of the item. This statement is called a 'cluster' and is derived from the total environment tables.
>
> Firth said, 'One of the meanings of *night* is its collocability with *dark*', and we can go from there to say that the *formal meaning* of an item A is that it has a strong tendency to occur nearby items B, C, D, less strong with items E, F, slight with G, H, I, and none at all with any other item (Sinclair 1966, 417).

But, as Sinclair notes, this method is crude. The length of the span to be considered is highly problematic, as his illustrations of the collocations of 'post', 'letter', and 'pillar-box' indicate:

> I posted the letter in the pillar-box
>
> he flipped the letter with careless elegance into the pillar-box
>
> the letter in his hand, that strangely anonymous, insignificant monument to his dreadful toils of composition, he posted, with a careless elegance which belied the gnawing terror he felt at the thought of whose cruel hands might open it. Then he continued past the pillar-box into the engulfing night (Sinclair 1966, 413).

The method further depends on a large text (Halliday, without documentation, suggests that a twenty million word text is necessary for statistically interesting results [1966, 159]). For these reasons, the decision was made here to work with spans of indeterminate, rather than determinate, length.

With this discussion as background, the remainder of this section is based on chart 2.3, Sleep field collocations (2x and up). The decision to treat different words from the same root separately adds a degree of precision to the chart. Thus *yšn/šnh*, *ḥlm/ḥlwm*, and *škb/mškb* appear as the only pairs. *Trdmh* appears, but *rdm*, although

Chart 2.3
Sleep field collocations (2x and up)

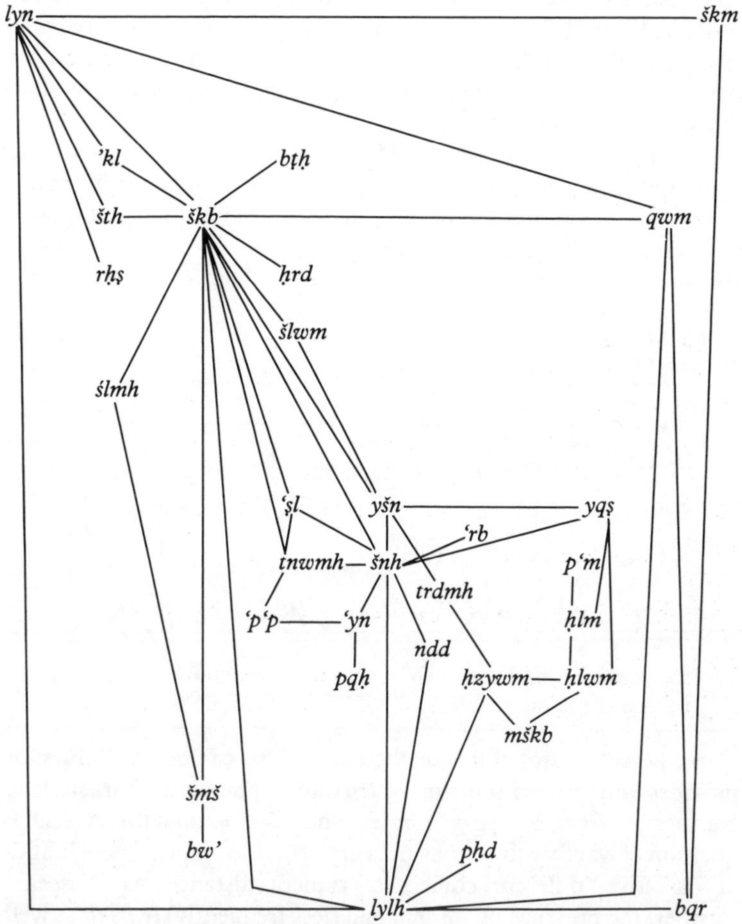

Note: See appendix B for documentation.

appearing six times in the sleep field, has no characteristic (non-unique) collocations. Of the pairs, both *yšn/šnh* and *ḥlm/ḥlwm* collocate within the pair as well as commonly with third words (*yšn* and *šnh* with *yqṣ* and *škb*, *ḥlm* and *ḥlwm* with *yqṣ*). This is perhaps evidence for common meaning in the pairs. On the other hand, *škb* and *mškb* do not characteristically collocate. Given the high frequency of both in the sleep field (*škb* 59, *mškb* 7), this is perhaps surprising, but throws into sharp relief the specialization in meaning *mškb* has undergone. Only one time does it simply denote *škb*-ing (*mšbk hṣhrym*, 2 Sam 4.5, which may be a case of a bound phrase). Elsewhere it either denotes the place of *škb*-ing, 'bed', 'couch', etc., or particular sorts of *škb*-ing (in death, or sexual, both sorts also often denoted by the verb).

The behavior of *yšn/šnh* and *ḥlm/ḥlwm* suggests the possibility of combining their nodes and redrawing the chart. Another refinement is desirable. As inspection of the data in appendix B indicates, there is a range of frequency of collocation (2 to 9 times). Choice of collocations of five times or more produces chart 2.4.

Chart 2.4
Sleep field collocations (5x and up)

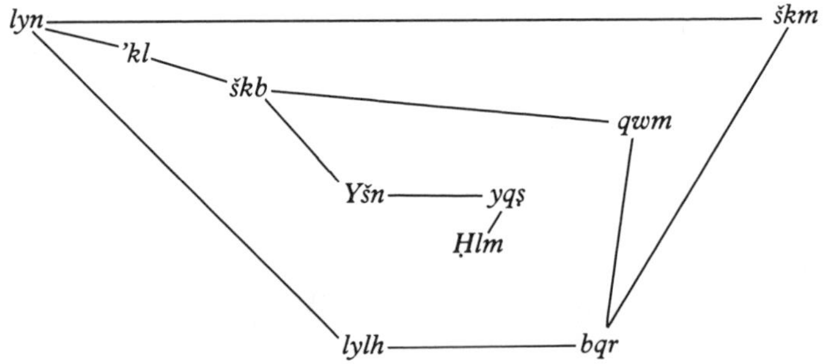

Three potential uses of this method of analysis can be noted. First, it provides entry into discussion of narrative. There are characteristic pairings: *lyn/škm, škb/qwm, Yšn/yqṣ*, and *Ḥlm/yqṣ*, and this raises the question of whether these may not correspond to different possibilities of narrative, different choices of camera distance, so to speak. Further, the presence of *škb/Yšn* and (less frequently) *lyn/škb* as well as the greater density of the left side of the charts, suggests that in the narrative tradition there are more possibilities of varying the description of the evening activities than the morning activities. Further, the absence of words such as *rdm* indicates that these have no fixed place in narrative—or any sleep-related discourse.

Collocation mapping reveals holes, and a second use of the mapping is the exploration of these apparent holes. For example, the charts lack any fatigue/sleep-like collocation. Does this collocation exist?

There are some occurrences. The Hebrew term involved is *'yp* 'weary'. Of twenty-two total occurrences, six describe states alleviated by food,[4] and in six others the condition is alleviated by drink.[5] In other situations one speaks of rest (*nwḥ*, Isa 28.12) or refreshment ([niph'al] *npš*, 2 Sam 16.14). In other cases particular causes are evident: age (2 Sam 21.15), stress (physical: Isa 46.1; otherwise: Jer 4.31). But there are some texts in which it is connected with sleep—with varying degrees of probability.

The prose account of Sisera's death records that 'Jael the wife of Heber took a tent peg, and took a hammer in her hand, and went softly to him and drove the peg into his temple, till it went down into the ground, as he was lying fast asleep from weariness. So he died' (*...whw'-nrdm wayyā'ap wymt*; Judg 4.21). Although the form *wayyā'ap* has caused difficulties,[6] taking it from *'yp* 'be weary', and therefore as an example of a tired-sleep collocation, seems the most straightforward solution.

2 Samuel 17.28-29, set in Absalom's rebellion, records that Shobi, Machir, and Barzillai 'brought beds (*mškb*), basins, and earthen vessels, wheat, barley, meal, parched grain, beans and lentils, honey and curds and sheep and cheese from the herd, for David and the people with him to eat; for they said, "The people are hungry and weary and thirsty in the wilderness" (*h'm r'b w'yp wṣm' bmdbr*)'. Here the preponderance of food items and the lack of anything specifically associated with quenching thirst suggests that *mškb* not be associated with *w'yp*. In fact, since the same group is earlier described simply as *'ypym* (2 Sam 16.14), the series *r'b w'yp wṣm'* here may well serve as a more precise specification of that earlier *'ypwm*.

In the description of an advancing army (Isa 5.27) we find *'yn-'yp w'yn-kšwl bw / l' ynwm wl' yyšn*. As will be argued later, *nwm* is probably best translated by 'doze off' or 'fall asleep'. And thus there is here a clear progression: weary, stumbling, dozing off, sleeping.

Finally, this collocation might be relevant to the vexing Jeremiah 31.25-26. Jeremiah 30–31 contains a series of oracles whose structure and redaction are far from clear. Jeremiah 31.23-25 is a relatively self-contained oracle:

> Thus says the Lord of hosts, the God of Israel: 'Once more they shall use these words in the land of Judah and in its cities, when I

> restore their fortunes: "The Lord bless you, O habitation of righteousness, O holy hill!" And Judah and all its cities shall dwell there together, and the farmers and those who wander with their flocks. For I will satisfy the weary soul, and every languishing soul I will replenish' (*ky hrwyty npš 'yph wkl-npš d'bh ml'ty*).

This is followed by v. 26:

> *'l-z't hqyṣty w'r'h wšnty 'rbh ly*
>
> Thereupon I awoke and looked, and my sleep was pleasant to me.

Then follow a series of oracles introduced by 'Behold, the days are coming, says the Lord' (vv. 27, 31, 38 [*qĕrê*]), in the midst of which is found another poetic oracle introduced by 'Thus says the Lord' (vv. 35-37). Bright writes of v. 26:

> Some see it as the ejaculation of one who, as it were, wakes refreshed from a beautiful dream; others see the dejection of one who awakes from a beautiful dream to confront the hard realities. Still others (cf. Rudolph, Weiser), translating 'For this reason (it is said), "I awoke . . . ,"' believe it to be a citation, perhaps of a well-known song. I confess I am baffled (1965, 282-83).

And Thompson, sharing Bright's uncertainty, suggests that it is perhaps a marginal comment or an incompletely preserved editorial framework (1980, 577). Perhaps a step towards explaining the placement of this verse—if not its presence—is to recognize here another case of a *'yp*/*Yšn* collocation.

To summarize, *'yp* sometimes functions as the first term in a fatigue/sleep collocation. But it is not often used for a state remedied by sleep, and the particular words it collocates with when it is remedied by sleep are quite varied.[7] But it is this sort of examination of a hole in the associative field of *Yšn* that collocation mapping can spur.

Third, these mappings can be used for comparative purposes. While the Ugaritic corpus is much smaller, it can provide an example of this use. In the literary texts collocations are found among *ḏrt, ḥlm, yšn, lyn, ndy, nhmmt, nšmt, 'ly, qmṣ, škb*, and *šnt*.[8]

For comparative purposes this information can be charted on the analogy of the previous charts. It should be noted, however, that this may skew the evidence because (a) evidence from texts which, if Hebrew, would be assigned to other activity fields are included (5.5.19-21, intercourse; 17.1.5-6, 15, mourning), (b) a high percentage of the words are involved in parallel constructions.

Chart 2.5
Ugaritic collocations: sleep and related fields

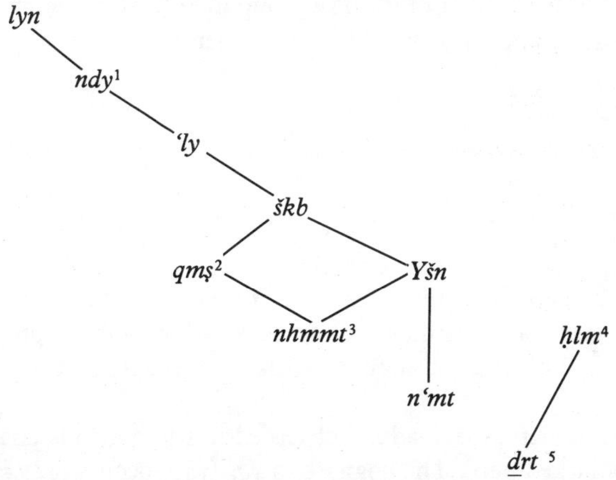

1. *UT* 442 cites *ndy* 'throw down' (Pyramid texts); *WUS*, Akkadian *nadū* 'werfen'.

2. *wyqmṣ*, 14.1.35 has been problematic. Virolleaud, followed by Albright and Pedersen, solved the problem by reading *wyqm gg* (Herdner 1963, 73 n. 5). Sauren and Kestmont (1971, 195) translate 'et il ferma les yeux', citing post-Biblical Hebrew *qmṣ* (qal passive participle 'closed' [of eye] in Jastrow [1903] 1967). Greenfield (1962, 296) argues that *qmṣ* 'in most semitic languages has a meaning centering around the concept "to draw together, contract"' and cites Hebrew, Ugaritic (here, and elsewhere in the sense '"to strangle", i.e. shut the hand'), Arabic, Aramaic, and Akkadian *kamās/ṣu*. This interpretation is followed by Caquot, Sznycer, and Herdner (1974, 509) 'et il se *pelotonne*'. The definition ('aufspringen, hüpfen') and translation of *wyškb nhmmt wyqmṣ* ('er lag unruhig u. schreckte auf') in Aistleitner 1947 (hereafter *WUS*) rests, inter alia, upon a mistaken analysis of *nhmmt*.

3. *nhmmt*, as Gordon (1965 [hereafter *UT*] 442) recognized, is to be associated with Hebrew *nwm*. To his examples of related CW/YC and CHC verbs may be added (Greenfield 1969, 62) Hebrew *nwr* and Aramaic *nhr*, Hebrew *ʿwd* and Arabic *ʿhd*, Hebrew *dwr* and Arabic *dhr*, Hebrew *dwk* and Arabic *dhk*. With Greenfield, *nhmmt*

may be taken as a *p'll*-type noun, compare Ugaritic *ṣḥrr* and Hebrew *'mll*, *r'nn*. The parallelism with *Yšn* argues for this derivation rather than *WUS*'s *hmm* 'Verwirrung, Sorge?'.

4. Although it would not be unreasonable to propose a collocation of *ḥlm* with some member of the *Yšn* group in 14.1.31-5, which word in that group to single out would be a problem:

> (31) *bm bkyh wyšn*
> (32) *bdm'h nhmmt*
> (33) *šnt tl'u'an* (34) *wyškb*
> *nhmmt* (35) *wyqmṣ*
> *wbḥlmh* (36) *'il yrd*
> *bḏrth* (37) *'ab 'adm*

5. Neither *UT, WUS*, nor Caquot, Sznycer, and Herdner (1974, 509) offer suggestions regarding the cognates, although the appropriate consensus is that the parallelism with *ḥlm* suggests 'dream' or 'vision'.

Note that the left side 'loading' observed in the previous charts is even more marked here. The cognate to *yqṣ* (*yqǵ*) occurs only in the context of preparing one's ears to hear (16.6.30, 42). The word *qwm* appears frequently, but not in situations of sleep. The verb *škm* does not appear, nor has an equivalent been identified.

Second, the ordering *lyn . . . škb . . . Yšn(. . . ḥlm?)* is common to both Ugaritic and Biblical Hebrew. In addition, particular cases of parallelism could be noted, e.g. Ugaritic *šnt/nhmmt* and Biblical Hebrew *šnh/tnwmh*.

But there are differences as well. First, note the absence of words corresponding to Biblical Hebrew *bqr* and *lylh*. Second, note the lack of 'horizontal' collocations particularly prominent in chart 2.4.

Obviously there are limitations imposed by the limited corpus. But comparison of vocabularies and collocation at this level may prove to be at least as important a tool as isolated comparisons of words or word pairs. For example, what are we to make of the references to Pbl's lack of sleep when Krt comes upon him (14.3.119; 5.222)? The Hebrew *yšn/šlwm* collocation suggests that the force of the references to Pbl's difficulty might be sought in this direction. That is, study of collocation provides another entry into the question of literary *topoi*.

4. *The Yšn Group*

The words treated in this section are *yšn*, *šnh*, *nwm*, *tnwmh*, *nwmh*, *rdm*, *trdmh*, *škb*, and *mškb*. They are initially divided into two groups composed of verbs (the *yšn* group) and nouns (the *šnh* group), and discussion starts with the human sleep field. Prior work on the two groups is evaluated, and the results of this study presented. At that point the relation between the two groups, i.e. the question of the identity of a *Yšn* group, can be addressed. Finally, discussion is broadened to include other activity fields.

In prior work, discussion has generally revolved around *Yšn*, *Nwm*, and *Rdm*. Here, *Škb* is also included in view of its close relationship to these, recognized, for example, by the RSV, which translates occurrences of *škb* in the human sleep field four times with 'sleep' (Exod 22.26; Deut 24.12, 13; 2 Sam 11.9).

Both Kennedy (1898) and Thomson (1955) address the question of the relationships between *Yšn*, *Nwm*, and *Rdm*. Kennedy suggests that two sorts of distinctions are involved. First, by type of sleep: *Nwm* refers to 'lighter slumbers', *Yšn* to 'sound sleep', and *Rdm* to 'deep or heavy sleep'. Second, while *Yšn* (and presumably *Rdm*) is neutral, 'the idea of blameworthiness appears to be nearly always distinctly associated [with *nwm*] . . . indolent self-indulgence in sleep, at a time when one ought to be awake and active, seems essentially implied in all these words' (1898, 26-28). Thomson confines himself to a distinction based on type of sleep: 'Properly speaking *nûm* means to be drowsy or to slumber; *yāšēn* signifies to sleep; while *rādham* is used to describe a heavy or deep sleep' (1955, 421). While noting that current sleep research is very much in flux, Thomson suggests that these Hebrew terms in fact reflect the phenomena currently under research:

> *Tĕnûmāh* answers to what the modern neurologist describes as the pre-dormitum stage of sleep; i.e., the period that precedes sleep proper when the flow of thought becomes modified. As conscious thought detaches itself increasingly from volition the sleeper slips imperceptibly into what the Old Testament calls *šēnāh*, and, on occasion, into *tardēmāh* where the flow of thought continues in dreams and figments of the imagination (1955, 421).

Both treatments have more the character of exposition than argument, so it is not always clear what is being used as evidence, or how much weight is being put on it. Kennedy illustrates his points with a wide variety of texts;[9] occasionally there is explicit argument.

> The comparative ease with which Jael slew Sisera (Jud. 4.21) is not surprising, 'seeing that he was fast asleep (*nirdam*)'; and sufficient explanation is given of the famous exploit of David and Abishai at the hill of Hachilah, when 'David took the spear and cruse of water from Saul's head, and they departed, without any one seeing, or knowing, or awaking; for they were all sleeping (*yĕšēnîm*), because a deep sleep from Jehovah (*tardēmat YHWH*) had fallen upon them' (1 Samuel 26.12) (1898, 28).

That is, the needs of the narration dictate the choice of words. But this argument is double-edged, and Kennedy does not consider texts where the apparent needs of the narration do not produce the word choice his account would predict.

Thomson appeals both to other semitic languages and to the Septuagint. For the *Yšn/Nwm* contrast, he cites Syriac *šentā'* 'sleep' and *naūmā'* 'slumber' and Ugaritic *yšn* and *nhm* 'to be drowsy' (1955, 422; all transliterations and definitions his). However, no texts are cited illustrating the presumptive differences in meaning in operation. As for *Rdm*, Thomson follows Ball (1922, 137), who suggested an original bilateral *Dm*, and offered the following evidence:

Aram	*dmk* 'sleep' (DAM + K 'closed-like' = sleep')
	'ṭm 'shut' (lips) 'stop' (ears)
Akk	*katāmu* 'close, shut' (mouth, lips, door, etc.)

To these Thomson adds (1955, 422-23):

Syr	*damkūthā'* 'deep sleep'
Arab	*radama* 'its original meaning, that of blocking up a hole, stopping a breach, patching a garment'

Of these, Aramaic *dmk* and the Syriac cognate are possible, and Arabic cognate quite probable. The rest involve the doubtful assumption that *d*, *t* and *ṭ*' can freely interchange, so that from the same root Hebrew would have *'ṭm*, *ktm*, and *rdm*, and Aramaic *'ṭm*, *dmk*, and *ktm*. But to reiterate a methodological point, even the authentic cognates do not *establish* the meaning of *Rdm* in Biblical Hebrew.[10]

In the Septuagint, Thomson notes that *nwm* is normally translated by *nustazō* or its derivatives, and *yšn* by *hypnos* or its derivatives. To establish that this is evidence for distinction in meaning, Thomson would have to have shown that *nustazō* and *hypnos* together with related words have distinct meanings. All he has demonstrated is that the translators used different words for translating *nwm* and *yšn*. Turning to *Rdm*, Thomson notes that of its fourteen occurrences in the Old Testament, 'nine different Greek words are used to translate it' (1955, 422).

In sum, Kennedy and Thomson are throughout assuming what they need to establish in their discussions of texts and related languages. As for the Septuagint, Thomson's analysis that '*rādham* puzzled the Greek translators to such an extent that they did not know quite what to make of it' (1955, 422) tells against his proposal for a relatively simple contrast in meaning between *Rdm* and *Yšn*.

Turning to the standard lexicons, we find

yšn	BDB	'sleep, go to sleep', and 'be asleep'
	KB	1. 'einschlafen', 2. 'schlafen', 3. 'v. Todesschlaf', 4. (Gott)
nwm	BDB	'be drowsy, slumber'
	KB	'slumber, be drowsy'
rdm	BDB	'be' or 'fall fast asleep'
	KB	'snore, be in heavy sleep, lie benumbed'

These entries make clear that there is a basic consensus to which Kennedy and Thomson have contributed. The one surprise is KB's treatment of *rdm*, which appears to be guided by the Septuagint.[11]

A different approach is taken by Schüpphaus (1982, 1032-35). He begins with the question of whether *yšn* 'to sleep' and *yšn* 'to be old' should be identified as one or two roots, noting, but apparently not convinced by, Ugaritic *yṯn* 'old', 'to become old'[12] alongside *yšn* 'to sleep'. Biblical Hebrew *Yšn* 'to sleep' is nicely summarized:

> Der Grundstamm des Verbums kennzeichnet ein 'träge, still sein, einschlafen' bzw. 'schlafen'... zu bestimmter Ruhezeit (nachts, mittags oder aus Anlass von Ermüdung), also den Vorgang zwischen dem Sich-Hinlegen bzw. Niederlegen (*šāḵaḇ*...) und dem Erwachen (*jqṣ*...) bzw. Aufstehen [(]*qûm*...) (1982, 1033).

Noting—but not explicitly arguing from—the distribution of *nwm* in the Old Testament, he states 'die parallel verwendete Wurzel.. "schlummern, schläfrig sein",... muss als das dichterische Synonym zu *jšn* aufgefasst werden'. Due, presumably, to a printer's error,

'*Rdm*' does not appear, though the discussion and text citations make clear that it is taken as sound ('fest') sleep, often due to divine influence.

Common to all these treatments is the judgment that *Yšn* is the neutral, or unmarked, term, and that *Nwm* and *Rdm* are variations or specifications of it. This has tended to be confirmed by the relative infrequency of collocations between *Nwm* and *Rdm*, and so characterizes the set of questions asked here.

a. *The yšn group*

The first major division within this group is that between prose and poetry (table 2.5). Thus *yšn* appears with roughly equal frequency in prose and poetry, *rdm* and *škb* tend to appear more often in prose, and the only occurrence of *nwm* is in poetry:

'yn-'yp w'yn-kšwl bw l' ynwm wl' yyšn

None is weary, none stumbles,
none slumbers or sleeps (Isa 5.27a).

The placement of *nwm* in parallel with *yšn* might suggest—as it did to Schüpphaus—that no distinction in meaning be sought, and in fact the evidence continues to point in this direction until other activity fields are brought into the discussion.

Table 2.5
yšn group: prose/poetry

Word	Prose	Poetry
yšn	8	7
nwm		1
rdm	5	1
škb	41	18

Note: Documentation for this and following tables is in appendix A.

This leaves *yšn*, *rdm*, and *škb*. The first topic is the *yšn/rdm* relationship. Then the varying uses of *škb* will be described, as an entry into the problem of the *yšn/škb* relationship.

The directly relevant evidence for the *yšn/rdm* distinction which prior discussions have produced may be exampled by Kennedy's argument that the correlation between demands of narrative and choice of words is evidence for his analysis of the *yšn/rdm* distinction. On this account, the distinction is physiological, *rdm* being particularly deep or sound sleep. But this account does not hold up. On the one hand, it does not explain the use of *rdm* in Proverbs 10.5:

> *'rg bqyṣ bn mśkyl nrdm bqṣyr bn mbyš*
>
> A son who gathers in summer is prudent,
> but a son who sleeps in harvest brings shame.

On the other hand, this proposal implies that *rdm* should appear when sound sleep is required by the narrative, i.e. when the narrative requires that the person is sleeping soundly enough that something can be done to them, or that they will not awaken in response to rousing stimuli. Now *rdm* does occur in two of these situations (Judg 4.21 [Sisera]; Jonah 1.5-6). But it is absent in three others (Judg 16.19; 1 Sam 26.5-12; 1 Kgs 3.20). Thus in 1 Kings 3.20, when the mother is arguing before Solomon that her child was removed from beside her (*m'ṣly*) and another substituted during the night, she says not **w'mtk nrdmh* but *w'mtk yšnh*. If *rdm* had the proposed force, it would have strengthened her case to have employed it here.[13]

Nor is the basis for the *yšn/rdm* choice aetiological, *rdm* indicating sleep as the result of exhaustion. Again, while Sisera's sleep in Judges 4.21 could have been caused by the narrated exhausting circumstances, these circumstances can only be read into the text in Jonah 1.5-6. And *rdm* would be expected after Elijah's flight from Jezebeel, when in fact the text reads simply *wyškb wyyšn* (1 Kgs 19.5).

Working only on the basis of the examples of *rdm*, one is tempted to simply identify two sorts of uses. On the one hand, it is used for involuntary sleep (Dan 8.18; 10.9). The connection with *trdmh* is clear. On the other hand, it is used when the narrator wishes to mark the sleep as inappropriate (unwise?): Sisera, Jonah, and the shame-bringing son (Judg 4.21; Jonah 1.5-6; Prov 10.5). But there are two problems also with this. First, if *rdm* is used to mark sleep as inappropriate, one would expect it in Judges 16.19, and perhaps Hosea 7.6. Second, there is no obvious link between the two uses. And, while both uses appear with *trdmh*, only Proverbs 19.15 evidences the second.

The general use of *trdmh* (to be explored in more detail below) for involuntary, divinely influenced sleep, sometimes in situations of revelation, prompts one to try taking this pattern as normative for *rdm*. This works, of course, for Daniel 8.18 and 10.9. But what of Judges 4.21, Jonah 1.5, 6 and Proverbs 10.5?

In Judges 4.21, *nrdm* appears to explain how Jael was able to kill Sisera: he was sleeping (*whw'-nrdm wy'p* 'as he was lying fast asleep from weariness'). But why *rdm* rather than *yšn* or even *škb*, as, e.g., in 2 Samuel 4.7a: *wyb'w hbyt whw'-škb 'l-mṭtw bḥdr mškbw wykhw wymthw wysyrw 't-r'šw*, 'When they came into the house, as he lay on his bed in his bedchamber, they smote him, and slew him, and beheaded him'. The clue lies in v. 9a: 'And she said, "I will surely go with you; nevertheless, the road on which you are going will not lead to your glory, for the Lord will sell Sisera into the hand of a woman"'. The choice of *rdm* integrates the narrative by recalling Deborah's warning. Sisera is victim of one of the weapons in the divine arsenal, sleep, used benignly in 1 Samuel 26.12, lethally in Psalm 76.6-7:

> The stouthearted were stripped of their spoil;
> they sank into sleep;
> all the men of war
> were unable to use their hands.
> At thy rebuke, O God of Jacob,
> both rider and horse lay stunned (*nrdm*).

The appearance of *rdm* in Jonah 1.5, 6 is intriguing, and there are at least two ways in which it might be playing off the more usual use of *rdm* for divinely induced sleep. On the one hand, the use of *rdm* may be heavily ironic. Jonah is a recipient of the *dbr yhwh* (v. 1). And roughly half of the occurrences of *Rdm* involve divine revelation. But Jonah + *rdm* does not equal revelation. Rather, as in Isaiah 29.10 (*trdmh*), the effect of the *(t)rdm(h)* is to render Jonah oblivious to YHWH's current action.

On the other hand, the text may be playing off the use of *rdm* or the *trdmh* as eternal sleep, or death. Here Landes's observation is suggestive: 'Just as Inanna required three days and three nights to complete her descent into the nether region, so also the fish needed the same time span to return his "passenger" from Sheol to the dry land' (1967, 12). Jonah does not know what awaits him, but perhaps the use of *rdm* is intended as a broad hint to the reader.

Finally, Proverbs 10.5: 'A son who gathers in summer is prudent, / but a son who sleeps (*nrdm*) in harvest brings shame'. This use—or both the uses in Proverbs (*trdmh* in Prov 19.15)—appears to be anomalous.

The conclusion: *rdm* is used for divinely induced, i.e. involuntary sleep, often associated with revelation. It is this aetiology, rather than physiology ('deep sleep', etc.) which is the distinguishing mark of *rdm*.

The uses of *škb* in the human sleep activity sleep field may be broken down as follows. While there is some overlap and some heterogeneity in these groups, the primary question has been the relationship between *škb* and the activity of sleep.

1. The easiest group to identify is one in which *škb* occurs in sequence with *yšn*, *rdm*, or *ḥlm*. One lies down, then goes to sleep:

Gen 28.11	*wyškb bmqwm hhw' wyḥlm*
1 Kgs 19.5	*wyškb wyyšn*
Jonah 1.5	*wyškb wyrdm*
Ps 3.6	*'ny škbty w'yšnh*
Ps 4.9	*'škbh w'yšn*

But sleep does not always follow *škb*-ing, as Job complains:

Job 7.4	*'m-škbty w'mrty mty 'qwm*

A moment's reflection suggests that also to be added to this group are the occurrences of *škb* in the listings of times to teach the law:

Deut 6.7	*wbškbk wbqwmk*
Deut 11.19	*wbškbk wbqwmk*

2. A second, somewhat overlapping group, might be called the *škb* in safety group:

Lev 26.6	*wškbtm w'yn mḥryd*
Hos 2.20	*whškbtym lbṭḥ*
Ps 57.5	*btwk lb'm 'škbh*
Job 11.18	*wḥprt lbṭḥ tškb*
Prov 6.22	*bškbk tšmr 'lyk*

The issue is safety in a vulnerable position, for which either *škb* or *yšn* would serve. In the following texts both occur:

Ps 3.6	*'ny škbth w'yšnh hqyṣwty ky yhwh ysmkny*
Ps 4.9	*bšlwm yḥdw 'škbh w'yšn*
Prov 3.24	*'m-tškb l'-tpḥd wškbt wšrbh šntk*

3. The largest group is one in which *škb* functions pars pro toto for *yšn*. The following texts are included:

Exod 22.26	*bmh yškb*
Deut 24.12	*l' tškb b'bṭw*
Deut 24.13	*wškb bślmtw wbrkk*
1 Sam 3.2	*w'ly škb bmqwmw*
1 Sam 3.3	*wnr 'lhym ṭrm ykbh wšmw'l škb bhykl yhwh*[14]
1 Sam 26.5	*'t-hmqwm 'šr škb-šm š'wl . . . wš'wl škb bm'gl*
1 Sam 26.7	*whnh š'wl škb yšn bm'gl . . . w'bnr wh'm škbym*
2 Sam 4.5	*whw' škb 't mškb hṣhrym*
2 Sam 4.7	*wyb'w hbyt whw'-škb 'l-mṭtw*
2 Sam 11.9	*wyškb 'wryh ptḥ byt hmlk*
2 Sam 11.13	*lškb bmškbw 'm-'bdy 'dnyw*
1 Kgs 3.19	*wymt bn-h'šh hz't lylh 'šr škbh 'lyw*
1 Kgs 3.20	*wtškybhw bḥyqh*
1 Kgs 19.6	*wy'kl wyšt wyšb wyškb*
Job 27.19	*'šyr yškb wl' y'sp*
Ruth 3.4	*wyhy bškbw wyd't 't-hmqwm 'šr yškb-šm*
Ruth 3.7	*wyb' lškb bqṣh h'rmh*

4. In this group *škb* is functioning only in the sense of 'rest'. Any reintroduction of the sense 'lie down' would create very odd pictures indeed:

Job 30.17	*lylh 'ṣmy nqr m'ly w'rqy l' yškbwn*
Prov 6.10	*m'ṭ ḥbq ydym lškb*
Prov 24.33	*m'ṭ ḥbq ydym lškb*
Eccl 2.23	*gm-blylh l'-škb lbw*

5. This group is defined by the temporal phrase *'d-ḥṣy hlylh* or *'d-hbqr*. The group may receive further attention in a later section, for in each case the reader is enticed to wonder about the sense in which *škb* is to be taken. Which is to say that the choice of *škb* rather than *yšn* creates a much more tensive text:

Judg 16.3	*wyškb šmšwn 'd-ḥṣy hlylh*
1 Sam 3.15	*wyškb šmw'l 'd-hbqr*
Ruth 3.13	*škby 'd-hbqr*
Ruth 3.14	*wtškb mrgltw 'd-hbqr*

6. In this group the relation of *škb* to sleep does not affect the narrative:

Gen 19.4	*ṭrm yškbw w'nšy h'yr*
Gen 28.13	*h'rṣ 'šr 'th škb 'lyh*

Lev 14.47	*whškb bbyt ykbs 't-bgdyw*
Josh 2.8	*whmh ṭrm yškbwn*
1 Sam 3.5	*šwb škb wylk wyškb*
1 Sam 3.6	*šwb škb*
1 Sam 3.9	*lk škb . . . wylk šmw'l wyškb bmqwmw*
Isa 51.20	*bnyk 'lpw škbw br'š kl-ḥwṣwt*
Mic 7.5	*mškbt ḥyqk šmr ptḥy-pyk*
Eccl 4.11	*gm 'm-yškbw šnym wḥm lhm*

7. In the following cases, the phenomenon of pars pro toto appears to push in a different direction, viz. *škb* as 'lodge':

Josh 2.1	*wylkw wyb'w byt-'šh zwnh . . . wyškbw . . . šmh*
2 Kgs 4.11	*wysr 'l-h'lyh wyškb-šmh*

In short, there are a wide variety of relations between the use of *škb* and the presence or absence of sleep in the narrated action. In two of the groups examined (nos. 1, 5), the choice of *škb* could be accounted for. But in the other groups the choice of *škb* rather than *yšn* is less easy to explain. It looks as though an explanation for these cases should be sought in the context of a discussion of style or narrative logic, rather than lexicon.

1 Samuel 3 may provide an example of narrative logic affecting word choice. Oppenheim (1956, 188-90) observed that that narrative had a number of elements characteristic of ancient near eastern dream narratives. Gnuse has attempted to show that the narrative conforms to the (form-critical pattern of the) message dream report, and has—minimally—demonstrated that many elements in the narrative can be explained in these terms. Thus, for instance, the notes regarding where Samuel was sleeping and the mention of the lamp correspond to the spatial and temporal specifications of the setting.

However, as Gnuse notes, there is an important twist given to the form in this case. Samuel does not understand what is happening, and repeatedly runs to Eli. Gnuse has not decided how to explain this twist, suggesting both 'literary artistry' evoking suspense and entertaining, and apologetic concern: Samuel was not incubating (1982, 382-83). But this twist seems to stretch the limits of a dream account, for although in dream accounts the awakening of the recipient is an element, the subsequent running off of the recipient to awaken some innocent bysleeper is not. Thus once this twist is introduced, YHWH's appearance may still be read as part of a dream

(Oppenheim 1956, 190), but the subsequent notice that Samuel 'lay until morning' now suggests inability to sleep rather than confirmation that 'the recipient was asleep, and therefore the dream is a valid message from the divine realm' (Gnuse 1982, 385).

This rather complex mix of sleeping, waking, and divine communication is perhaps reflected in (and smoothed over by) the word choice. Nowhere in the account is it said that Samuel (or Eli) slept (*yšn*). Only *škb* is used. Has this more general term been chosen as a means of smoothing over rough edges in the narrative or of expressing a different theology of visions? In either case, it would move us further away from the dream form described by Oppenheim and Gnuse.

b. *The šnh group*

Again, a clear pattern in use is seen in the distribution between prose and poetry (table 2.6). While *tnwmh* occurs only in poetry, *šnh* and *trdmh* appear in both, although weighted towards poetry. And there is only one occurrence of *mškb*: prose.

Table 2.6
šnh group: prose/poetry

Word	Prose	Poetry
mškb	1	
šnh	8	13
tnwmh		5
trdmh	3	4

For most of the words the breakdown of functions is straightforward. In the sense of 'sleep' or 'nap' *mškb* occurs only in the phrase *mškb hṣhrym*. The general word for sleep is *šnh*. In four of its five occurrences *tnwmh* is the B-word for *šnh*. In the fifth occurrence (Job 33.15), it appears to be the result of poetic play, forcing a rescanning of the lines from Eliphaz's earlier speech (Job 4.13). The *trdmh* is characteristically said to *npl*.[15] But description of the referent(s) and functions of the *trdmh* is less obvious, and this is the chief problem of this section.

The occurrences of *trdmh* can be broken down in two ways. First, by agent. In six of the seven occurrences the explicit agent is divine. The clearest cases:

Gen 2.21	*wayyappēl yhwh 'lhym trdmh 'l-h'dm*
Isa 29.10	*ky-nsk 'lykm yhwh rwḥ trdmh*

These suggest that the *trdmt yhwh* in the following text should be understood as an alternate way of expressing this agency:[16]

1 Sam 26.12 *ky klm yšnym ky trdmt yhwh nplh 'lyhm*

And the placement of Genesis 15.12, Job 4.13 and 33.15 in revelatory contexts suggests that the agent implied is divine. But in the seventh case the agent is sloth:

Prov 19.15 *'ṣlh tpyl trdmh*

The personification of sloth was noted by Duhm ([1922] 1968, 210); are we dealing here with not only a personification, but a divinization of sloth?

The second breakdown is by function. The *trdmh* causes sleep. In some texts this is explicit:

Gen 2.21	*wypl yhwh 'lhym trdmh 'l-h'dm wyyšn*
1 Sam 26.12	*ky klm yšnym ky trdmt yhwh nplh 'lyhm*

In Isaiah 29.10 the following clauses secure this interpretation: 'and has closed your eyes, the prophets, / and covered your heads, the seers'. Note here the heavy irony. In other texts the *trdmh* is involved in revelation. Here it precludes it.

The collocation of sloth and sleep elsewhere in Proverbs secures this interpretation for Proverbs 19.15, and in Job 33.15 the parallel line, *btnwmwt 'ly mškb*, brings the sleep-inducing sense of *trdmh* to the fore. But in two cases sleep is assumed, with primary focus on revelation:

Gen 15.12	*wtrdmh nplh 'l-'brm*
Job 4.13	*bś'pym mḥzynwt lylh bnpl trdmh 'l-'nšym*

c. *The Yšn group*

Table 2.7
Yšn group: prose/poetry

Word	Prose	Poetry
Yšn	16	20
Nwm		6
Rdm	8	5
Škb	42	18

To summarize: *Yšn* is the neutral, or unmarked term for sleep. *Nwm* is limited to poetry (table 2.7). Its use—four times the B-word for *šnh*, once in parallel with *yšn*, once in the phrase *btnwmwt* balancing *bnpl trdmh*—suggests that its appearances are dictated by poetic considerations only. *Rdm* is used for divinely influenced sleep. While there are no characteristic differences in the use of *rdm* and *trdmh*, there are a number of differences which cut across this division. First, in only some of the occurrences is revelation involved (table 2.8, col. 1). Even here, the picture is quite varied, for the contexts show that there is no uniform understanding of how revelation happens. In at least one case the appearance of the *trdmh* may represent a later theological judgment as to what was taking place (Gen 15.12, with Gunkel [1910] 1977, 181). And while in some cases the *trdmh* 'kicks off' the revelation (col. 2), in other cases *rdm* occurs in the context of the revelation (col. 3).

Second, the role of *Rdm* vis-à-vis sleep is variously pictured. In some cases it clearly induces sleep (col. 4). In other cases, *Rdm* is probably the cause of sleep, but this is not made explicit (col. 5). And in one of these cases (1 Sam 26.12), the emphasis is more on the *trdmh* as the cause of *continuing* sleep. Finally, in Job, the interest in the *trdmh* is in its relationship to revelation, not in its relationship to sleep (col. 6).

Table 2.8
Rdm patterns

Word	Text	1	2	3	4	5	6
rdm	Judg 4.21					x	
	Jonah 1.5	?				?	
	Jonah 1.6	?				?	
	Prov 10.5						
	Dan 8.18	x		x	x		
	Dan 10.19	x		x	x		
trdmh	Gen 2.21				x		
	Gen 15.12	x	?	?		x	?
	1 Sam 26.12					x	
	Isa 29.10	?			x	x	
	Job 4.13	x	x				x
	Job 33.15	x	x				x
	Prov 19.15				x		

This diversity (not to mention the number of question marks in the table!) goes a long way towards explaining why the Septuagint employs such a wide range of words in translating *rdm* and *trdmh*.

d. *The Yšn group across activity fields*

The purpose of this section is to indicate the degree to which the generalizations arrived at in the preceding section hold good once we move into other activity fields.

i. *Yšn*

Table 2.9
Yšn: prose/poetry, all fields

Activity Field	Word	
	yšn	*šnh*
Divine sleep	1/3	
Human sleep	8/7	8/13
Death	1/5	1/3

As indicated above, *Yšn* functions as the general (neutral, unmarked) term for sleep. And no particular shadings appear when other activity fields are included in the discussion. Two aspects of the resultant pattern should be noted. First, the number of activity fields is small. It is due to *škb*, not *Yšn* that a large number have been examined. Second, while the prose/poetry distribution is relatively equal for human sleep, it is heavily weighted towards poetry in the other fields.

ii. *nwm*

Table 2.10
Nwm: all fields (all poetry)

Activity Field	Word		
	nwm	*nwmh*	*tnwmh*
Divine sleep	2		
Animal sleep	1		
Human sleep	1		5
Death	2		
Wine		1	

While the occurrences of *nwm* are spread over a variety of situations, from another perspective they converge: all occur in situations that might be termed military or policing:

'yn-'yp w'yn-kwšl bw l' ynwm wl' yyšn

None is weary, none stumbles,
none slumbers or sleeps (Isa 5.27).

hzym škbym 'hby lnwm

dreaming, lying down,
loving to slumber (Isa 56.10b).

nmw r'yk mlk 'šwr yšknw 'dyryk

Your shepherds are asleep,
King of Assyria;
your nobles slumber (Nah 3.18).[17]

'štwllw 'byry lb nmw šntm

The stouthearted were stripped of their spoil;
they sank into sleep (Ps 76.6a).

'l-ytn lmwṭ rglk 'l-ynwm šmrk
hnh l'-ynwm wl'-yyšn šwmr yśr'l

He will not let your foot be moved,
he who keeps you will not slumber.
Behold, he who keeps Israel
will neither slumber nor sleep (Ps 121.3-4).

And the limitation of *nwm* to these situations suggests that it may have the specific force of 'dozing off'.

What of this applies to *tnwmh*? Three of its occurrences one would not identify as military or policing. But in two, in admonitions against sloth, we again have situations where one needs to be on guard (Prov 6.10-11; similarly 24.33-34):

m'ṭ šnwt m'ṭ tnwmwt m'ṭ ḥbq ydym lškb
wb'-kmhlk r'šk wmḥsrk k'yš mgn

A little sleep, a little slumber,
a little folding of the hands to rest,
and poverty will come upon you like a vagabond,
and want like an armed man.

The suspicion that the context here might be encouraging identifying 'dozing off' as the meaning of *tnwmwt* is bolstered not only by the picture being painted in Proverbs of someone making himself comfortable, but by both the grammatical number and the word ordering of the pairs.

In two cases *tnwmh* occurs in the singular, and in the B-position for *šnh*:

> *'m-'tn šnt l'yny l'p'py tnwmh* (Ps 132.4)
>
> *'l-ttn šnh l'ynyk wtnwmh l'p'pyk* (Prov 6.4)

In these cases there is no encouragement in the texts to look for some semantic difference between *šnh* and *tnwmh*. But in the two Proverbs texts cited above (Prov 6.10; 24.33), *tnwmh* appears in the plural and is in the A-position. Is the latter a sign that it has its own particular force and is not simply functioning as the poetic equivalent for *šnh*?[18]

The fifth case of *tnwmh* occurs in Elihu's dream description:

> *bḥlwm ḥzywn lylh bnpl trdmh 'l-'nšym btnwmwt 'ly mškb*
>
> In a dream, in a vision of the night,
> when deep sleep falls upon men,
> while they slumber on their beds (Job 33.15)

If the plural follows the use of the plural elsewhere, then 'doze off' should receive consideration, and the *trdmh* would be being pictured in its sleep-inducing capacity.

To summarize: the contexts in which *nwm* appears suggest that its force or meaning is not simply 'to sleep' but 'to doze off' or 'to fall asleep'. When *tnwmh* appears in the plural and in the A-position, it appears to maintain this distinctive force. When it appears in the singular and in the B-position, it appears to function simply as a synonym for *šnh*. In Job 33.15, where it is in the plural, but in the B-position, its semantic status is uncertain.

In drawing these conclusions, we may appear to be agreeing with Kennedy's judgment, viz. 'the idea of blameworthiness . . . seems essentially implied in all these words' (1898, 27). The position taken here is that blameworthiness is not a component in the meaning of *Nwm*. Rather, since *nwm* focuses on *falling* asleep, rather than simply sleeping, it is most likely to be employed in situations where falling asleep is an issue, i.e. in situations where one ought to stay awake.

Nwmh occurs only once:

ky-sb' wzwll ywrš wqr'ym tlbyš nwmh

for the drunkard and the glutton will come to poverty
and drowsiness will clothe a man with rags (Prov 23.21).

Since vv. 19-21 are an extended admonition against overindulgence, a translation for *nwmh* such as 'drunken stupor' (NEB) may be appropriate here.[19] A particular meaning such as this is also suggested by the fact that neither *nwm* nor *tnwmh* occurs in the drinking activity field. Thus the admittedly limited evidence here suggests that the use of *nwmh* is specialized, and while it has some semantic components in common with *nwm* and *tnwmh*, it has in its particulars gone its own way.

iii. *Rdm*

Table 2.11
Rdm: prose/poetry, all fields

Activity Field	Word	
	rdm	*trdmh*
Human sleep	5/1	3/4
Death	0/1	

The one occurrence of *rdm* in the death field is in Psalm 76.7:

mg'rtk 'lhy y'qb nrdm wrkb wsws

At thy rebuke, O God of Jacob,
both rider and horse lay stunned.

Gunkel's comment is suggestive ([1929] 1968, 311): 'gemeint ist hier eine im Tod endigende göttliche Betäubung: ursprünglich wohl eine zum Märchen gehörige Zaubervorstellung'. For while *Rdm*—unlike *Nwm*—is not clearly linked to military situations, it does appear in these a number of times: Judges 4.21; 1 Samuel 26.12; and here. In all three cases YHWH has used sleep as a weapon. It is, as indicated in table 2.8, possible to identify other subgroupings in the uses of *Rdm*. But only the function of marking divinely influenced sleep appears (save in Proverbs) to be common.

iv. *Škb*

Table 2.12
Škb: prose/poetry, all fields

Activity Field	*mškb*		*škb*		Total
	Prose	Poetry	Prose	Poetry	
Animal sleep				2	2
Sleep	1		41	18	60
Bedridden			5	1	6
Death			49	15	64
Intercourse	8	1	52	3	64
Mourning			3	1	4
Nocturnal activity			1		1
Wine				3	3
Unidentified			12	6	18
Total	9	1	163	49	222

For purposes of analysis, the occurrences of *mškb* have been split into two groups. In the larger group, it denotes a place of *škb*-ing, and is treated in the discussion of the *mškb* group (§2.e). That is, it is more like *'rś*, *mṭh*, etc. than like *šnh*, *tnwmh*, etc. In the smaller group, *mškb* is more like *šnh*, *tnwmh*, etc. and so is treated here as part of the *šnh* and *Yšn* groups.

The situation here is different than with *Yšn*, *Nwm*, and *Rdm*. These words appeared most frequently in the human sleep field with scattered occurrences in other fields. And while these other occurrences were of help in sketching out the precise contours of *Nwm*, they contributed little to the description of *Yšn* or *Rdm*. But in the case of *Škb*, three fields, human sleep, death, and intercourse share the bulk (85%) of its occurrences. The next step here would be a comparison of this distribution with the distribution of cognates in other semitic languages, a step beyond the boundaries of this topic.

v. *Summary*

There are three general patterns of distribution of roots across activity fields. Sleep and death are the two fields which use all four roots. This is true by definition of the sleep field, since roots not employed would not appear. This lexical pairing of sleep and death will be further discussed in subsequent chapters. The second pattern

Table 2.13
Yšn group: prose/poetry, all fields

Activity Field	*Yšn*		*Nwm*			*Rdm*		*Škb*	
	V	N	V	N	*nwmh*	V	N	V	N
				Prose					
Divine sleep	1								
Sleep	8	8				5	3	41	1
Bedridden								5	
Death	1	1						56	
Intercourse								52	8
Mourning								3	
Nocturnal Activity								1	
				Poetry					
Divine sleep	3		2						
Animal sleep			1						
Sleep	7	13	1	5		1	4	18	
Bedridden								1	
Death	5	3	2			1		8	
Intercourse								3	1
Mourning								1	
Wine					1				

Note: 'V' and 'N' indicate verb and noun forms.

takes in the Bedridden, Intercourse, Mourning, and Nocturnal Activity fields: only *Škb* (and twice more in the next two paragraphs) is employed. But for one occurrence of *nwmh*, Wine would also fall into this category. This is hardly surprising, and simply illustrates the range of situations in which one *škb*s. The third pattern covers the two fields defined by non-human sleepers. Divine sleep employs only *Yšn* and *Nwm*. Since we have argued here that *Rdm* is used for divinely influenced sleep, its non-use in this field is not surprising. On the other hand, if it meant 'deep sleep', one would have expected at least one psalmist to have employed it while calling on YHWH to wake up. The absence of *Škb* is probably not to be ascribed to avoidance of anthropomorphism; YHWH is said to *yšb*. Still, it may be part of a pattern of actions which are or are not assigned to YHWH. As for animal sleep, only *nwm* is used (once). A separate set of words seems to be employed for animal sleep.

The use of *Nwm* in poetry has already been noted. When *Yšn* moves from prose to poetry, the percentage of non-sleep uses rises (16% to 35%). The same sort of rise is not present with *Rdm*, and, again, this fits better with *Rdm* as marking divine influence on sleep, rather than quality of sleep. On the other hand, when *Škb* moves from prose to poetry, the percentage of uses for sleep rises (23% to 44%) while the percentage of uses for both death and intercourse drops (31% to 19% and 34% to 10% respectively).

5. *The mškb group*

This group is composed of the following words: *yṣw'*, *mṭh*, *msb*, *mṣ'*, *mškb*, *'rś*.[20] All of these words have been identified as belonging to the sleep activity field with the exception of *msb*, which is introduced into the group and discussion here for economy of presentation.

The problem this group poses is well expressed by Corswant: 'It may be possible to distinguish between beds meant for sleep, those used for rest during the day, and those on which people reclined at mealtimes, even though each type was undoubtedly used for other purposes' (1960, 48). But Corswant's article ('Bed') does not do this, though the author confesses 'the wealth of vocabulary is rather surprising'. How does the usage of these words differ? A number of suggestions relevant to this question have been made. Barrois (1939, 1.502) took both *mṭh* and *mškb* to be instrumental designations, rather than as referring to particular types of furniture. He took *'rś* as referring to a frame ('cadre'). This last would be in line with the suggestion in BDB (793a) that 'the common idea is apparently that of a *wooden structure, frame*', citing Nöldeke, who writes, 'Die semitische Grundbedeutung von *'rś*, [Syriac] *'arsā* . . . [Arabic] *'arš* ist "hölzernes Gestell". Ein primitives Gestell passt unter Umständen schon in einen sehr frühen Culturzustand als Bett' (1886, 737). Dalman ([1928-42] 1964, 7.185-86) took *mškb* as something to *škb* on, *'rś* as an elegant ('vornehm') bed, perhaps of Syrian origin (*'arsā*), and, like the *mṭh*, raised. Gese (1962, 427-32) in a study of Amos 3.12, assumes that *mṭh* and *'rś* can refer to the same object. Pope, in discussing *mṭh* in Canticles 3.7 notes (1977, 431) 'the term *miškāb* is commonly used when sexual activity is specifically mentioned'.

What can be said in regard to these suggestions? Barrois would appear to be correct in that when *mṭh* and *mškb* refer to items of furniture, they do not appear to refer to different items. In one case the same piece is referred to by both designations (2 Sam 4.7, 11). The suggestion that *'rś* properly refers to the frame has some support from other Semitic languages (Arabic, Aramaic, Ethiopic). But when construction material suitable for a frame is mentioned in the Old Testament, it is in conjunction with a *mṭh*.[21] Iron is mentioned for an *'rś* only in Deuteronomy 3.11, where 'sarcophagus' is perhaps a better translation (NEB, Craigie 1976, 120).[22] The use of *yṣ'* in the phrase *'rś yṣw'y* in Psalm 132.3 ('I will not enter my house / or go into my bed') argues further against taking *'rś* as 'bedframe' given the subjects (or objects, in the passive) of *yṣ'*: *wśq w'pr* (Esth 4.3), *rmh* (Isa 14.11). Dalman's suggestion that *'rś* is an elegant bed does not appear likely in that while *'rś* does occur in contexts in which one would expect an elegant bed,[23] the same can be said of *mṭh*[24] or *mškb*.[25] The suggestion of Syrian origin is now unnecessary in the light of Akkadian *eršu* and Ugaritic *'rš*. That either a *mṭh* or an *'rś* could be raised is implied by occasional collocation with *'lh*.[26] The possibility that *mṭh* and *'rś* can refer to the same object is suggested by both Amos 3.12 and Psalm 6.7. Pope's suggestion would appear correct (table 2.14), although part of this may be due to the fact that *mškb* is simply a higher-frequency word.

In summary, there has been little hard evidence on the patterns of usage in this group. The study undertaken here suggests that one reason for the previous shortage of reliable generalizations about different uses of words in the *mškb* group is the difficulty of making such generalizations. The material simply does not seem to be compatible with many generalizations. But this is not to say that nothing can be said, and in the following sections the results of this study are presented.

Table 2.14
mškb group: prose/poetry, all fields

Field	Words					
	yṣw'	*mṭh*	*msb*	*mṣ'*	*mškb*	*'rś*
	Prose					
Sleep		1			4	
Bedridden		10			3	
Death		4			1	2
Intercourse	1	1				
Nocturnal activity		1			1	

	yṣw'	*mṭh*	*msb*	*mṣ'*	*mškb*	*'rś*
Unidentified		7			10	
Total	1	24			19	2
		Poetry				
Sleep	1	2		1	2	2
Bedridden					2	1
Death	1				2	
Intercourse	1				5	2
Nocturnal activity	1	1			5	1
Wine		1	1			1
Unidentified		1			1	1
Total	4	5	1	1	17	8

There is a fairly clear breakdown between prose and poetry. The words *yṣw'*, *msb*, *mṣ'*, *'rś* (except in Deut 3.11) are poetic. And at this point the question may be raised of whether the anomalous prose usage of *'rś* in Deut 3.11 is not a signal that the word is here being used in a different sense. The word *mṭh* occurs primarily in prose; *mšbk* splits roughly evenly between prose and poetry.[27]

There are a number of clusterings, or distributions over situations, which appear to be significant: *mṭh* in the bedridden (63%) and death (40%) situations; and *mškb* in the sleep (46%), intercourse (50%), and nocturnal activity (60%) situations. But even here these situations are not the exclusive domain of these words.

These distributions can be thrown into somewhat sharper relief by comparison with those evidenced in other Semitic languages. It is, of course, far easier to establish patterns for some languages than others, and our ability to establish these patterns will always be limited by what is retrievable. For instance, *mškb*, well-attested in Phoenician, is attested only in funerary inscriptions.[28] Ugaritic has

Table 2.15
Ugaritic *mškb* group: prose/poetry, all fields

Activity Field	*mṭt*	*mškb*	*'rś*
Bedridden			0/6[a]
Intercourse			0/3[b]
Nocturnal activity	0/1[c]		
(Inventory)		3/0[d]	1/0[e]

a. 14.2.98,4.186; 16.6.35,36,51,52. b. 17.1.39; 2.41,42. c. 14.1.30. d. 1151.6; 1152.4; 2050.9-10. e. 1120.5

mṭt, *mškb*, and *'rš*, distributed over a variety of situations (using, for convenience, those developed for the Biblical Hebrew material; table 2.15). While all of the uses are exampled in the Old Testament, none of the clusterings are parallel.

In chart 2.1, only *mškb* had a place among the non-unique collocations of the sleep field. While other activity fields were not explored on their own terms, it was possible to test for collocations of words which were also members of the sleep field. This procedure yielded chart 2.6 and table 2.16.

Chart 2.6
Non-sleep field collocations

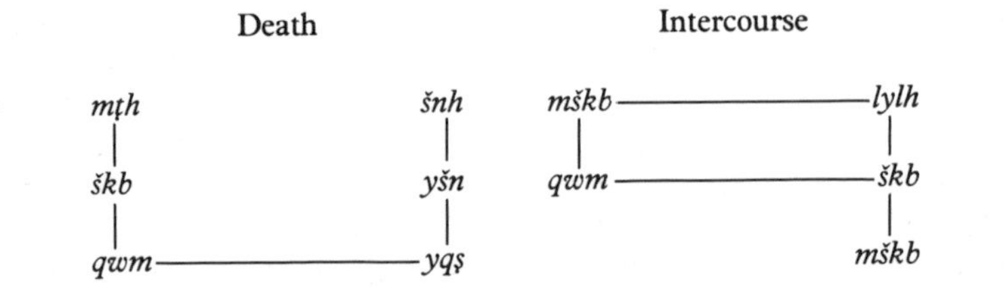

Note: *mškb* occurs twice in the right-hand chart, in the top line as a member of the *mškb* group, in the bottom line as a member of the *Yšn* group.

Thus, to pick up the discussion of the distribution of the *mškb* group over activity fields (table 2.14), not only does *mškb* appear most characteristically in situations of sleep and intercourse, but there it also shows characteristic collocations (table 2.16). Likewise, *mṭh* in the situation of death. The value of this information is, however, limited by at least two factors. First, the number of texts available to establish these collocations is relatively small, as the number of collocations and the number of examples of any particular collocation indicate. Second, only collocations between words which were part of the sleep field were examined. To do otherwise would be to swell massively the research involved in this section without any certainty of gain. But it does mean that in theory such a study could establish collocations with words in the *mškb* group not identified in this more restricted survey.

To summarize the results of this section: no clear difference in reference could be established between *mṭh*, *mškb*, and *'rś*. However, certain patterns could be observed. Both *mṭh* and *mškb* appear in

Table 2.16
mškb group: collocations in all fields

Activity Field	Word	Collocate	Frequency
Death	*mṭh*	*škb*	3
Sleep	*mškb*	*ḥzywm*	2
		ḥlwm	2
Intercourse		*lylh*	2
		qwm	2

Note: Texts in appendices A, C.

both prose and poetry, while *'rś* in the sense of 'bed' is limited to poetry. In situations of infirmity and death, *mṭh* is likely to occur, and it collocates with *škb* in the death field. In situations of sleep, intercourse, and nocturnal activity *mškb* is likely to occur, and it has characteristic collocations in both the sleep and intercourse fields. *'rś* shows no characteristic distribution over activity fields or collocations. Comparisons of distributions over activity fields between different languages can be usefully made, as illustrated by the Ugaritic cognates to the *mškb* group.

But the possibility remains that the difference between *mṭh* and *mškb* is dialectal, the former being a Northern word and the latter a Southern. Thus the stories of the monarchy through the death of Ishbosheth, the Elijah-Elisha cycles, and Amos use only *mṭh*. Isaiah, Micah and Ezekiel use only *mškb*. But *mṭh* appears in Gen 47.31 and Exod 7.28 (J), and in an account of Abner's death in Hebron which—if it has a slant—is in its present form pro-David (2 Sam 3), and *mškb* appears in Exodus 21.18 (E) and Hosea.[29] In short, the evidence is suggestive of a dialectal split in distribution, but not conclusive.[30]

6. *Conclusions*

In section 3, a method was presented which allowed the description of the associative fields of a number of words simultaneously. Because it is based on observed collocations in a particular set of texts, it minimizes, though it does not exclude, the effects of the observer's preunderstanding of the shape of these fields. Because collocation frequency is incorporated, it is possible to produce a mapping for whatever collocation frequency or range of frequencies is desired (charts 2.1, 2).

The lexical, rather than semantic, basis of the mapping produces holes where, for example, there are collocations on the semantic but not the lexical level. Thus in the study of *'yp*, while the fatigue/sleep collocation may occur more than twice, there are no corresponding characteristic lexical collocations, and thus *'yp* does not appear in the mapping.

Such mappings can be used to evaluate prior descriptions of associative fields. For instance, that of Strack (1929) proves, on inspection, to be seriously misleading. Thus in the section 'Ruhe, Bewegung, Arbeit' *yšn*, *nwm*, and a number of other words appear, but neither *škb* nor *yqṣ* appears. Likewise in the section 'Hausgerät' both *'rś* and *mṭh* appear, but *mškb* does not appear, and *yṣ'* and its derivatives appear in neither (43).

Such mappings can be an important comparative tool, as illustrated by an informal comparison between the Hebrew and Ugaritic collocations.

The study in section 4 confirmed the normal English translation of *nwm* ('be drowsy, slumber' in BDB) by identifying its occurrences as limited to military/policing situations. *Tnwmh* was found to have a similar meaning when in the plural and in the A-word position, but to function as a synonym for *šnh* when in the singular and in the B-word position. Whether the number or the position is operative for this distinction was not determined. But the behavior of *tnwmh* and the particular semantic weight of *nwmh* illustrate the methodological problem of combining all expressions of the same root (*nwm*, *nwmh*, *tnwmh*) at the start of the analysis.

Study of the occurrences of *Rdm* suggested that it was generally limited to divinely influenced sleep (the exceptions being in Proverbs). This, rather than quality of sleep (deep, etc.) appeared to be the operative distinction. The variety of ways in which it is associated with divine activity suggested a range of understandings on the part of the authors regarding this function, and this is in turn reflected in the varying Septuagint translations.

The most interesting studies of lexical groups (Coseriu and Geckeler 1974, Lutzeier 1982) defined these by means of substitution in a string ('Victoria was pleased about her __________.'). While this method could not be employed owing to the small size of the corpus, it was responsible for the inclusion of *škb*, which often appears in contexts ostensibly similar to those in which *yšn* appears. Means for predicting the occurrence of either *yšn* or *škb* were sought, but the most that could be given was a description of the contexts in which *škb* occurred. It was suggested that solution of this problem might be in a stylistic rather than lexical study.

The study in section 6 indicated the general inadequacy of past accounts of the difference between *mṭh*, *mškb*, *‘rś*, and related words. And in fact there is no textual evidence that different referents are in question. But attention to the prose/poetry distribution and to distribution over situations suggested that *mṭh* and *mškb* could be distinguished on the basis of the situations in which they characteristically appear and characteristic collocations therein, and that *‘rś*, appearing only in poetry (Deut 3.11 excluded), could be characterized by its lack of association with any particular situations. An informal comparison with a corresponding Ugaritic group illustrated the possibilities of comparison based on analysis of situation distributions.

Chapter 3

CULTURAL PATTERNS

Here we will be asking a set of spatial and temporal questions related to Israelite sleeping patterns. Of the spatial questions, while some have received passing attention (where did people sleep? on what? when?), others have received even less (in what positions? with what company?). The general procedure will be to start with the Old Testament and the relevant archaeological data from the Israelite levels. This will establish where evidence is still needed, and discussion will move to comparative material: literary, archaeological, and anthropological, although each of these will not necessarily appear at each stage. Finally, there will be a summary discussion of the combined evidence.

Bible encyclopedia articles provides a good indication of the changing sources of information employed in describing the cultural patterns in Israel during the Iron Age (that portion of the Old Testament period which will be the primary focus of attention in this chapter). Huré's *Dictionnaire universal de l'Ecriture Sainte* (1715, 2 vols.) treats 'bed' (*cubile*) only from the standpoint of the biblical text, and Calmet's *Dictionnaire historique critique . . . de la Bible* does not contain an entry. In Taylor's first edition of *Calmet's Great Dictionary of the Holy Bible* (1797-1801, 3 vols.), the third volume, added by Taylor, is entitled 'Fragments: being illustrations of the manners, incidents, and phraseology, of the Holy Scripture: principally selected from the most esteemed and authentic voyages and travels into the east . . . '. Two articles are of interest: 'On the mode of sitting in the east' and 'Beds of the east'. Braus's *Biblisches universal Lexicon* (1806, 2 vols.; 1.118) also uses travelers' reports.

By the mid-nineteenth century archaeological data begins to appear. While 'Bett' in Schenkel's *Bibel-lexikon* (1869, 5 vols.) does not use this data (1869, 1.422-23), it was already employed in Winer's *Biblisches Realwörterbuch* (1847, 2 vols.; 1.178-79), and the corresponding article in Kitto's *The Cyclopaedia of Biblical Literature* (1857, 2 vols.; 1.311-13) is illustrated with an Egyptian palm-stick bedstead (from mural paintings), and an Egyptian bed (with headrest and stool)—as well as illustrations of a Greek couch and a modern oriental bed. *Fairbairn's Imperial Standard Bible* (1891, 6 vols.; 1.271-72) includes an Assyrian bed. The article in Cheyne and Black's *Encyclopaedia Biblica* (1899-1903, 4 vols.; 1.509-11) employs information from the Amarna tablets and the list of Hezekiah's tribute. More importantly, it registers an awareness of the gap between the contemporary luxurious oriental houses and the Israelite houses, for we meet references to the 'poor construction of the houses in ancient Palestine' (1.509-11). After this, there is little that is new, although Weippert's introduction of bed models into the discussion deserves notice (in the second edition of the *Biblisches Reallexikon*; 1977, 228-32). In all of these treatments attention has been confined to the spatial—rather than temporal—dimensions.

1. *Sleeping Sites*

a. *Old Testament*

When sleeping in cities or towns, the one choice of sleeping site of which a point is made is the choice between sleeping in the streets and sleeping in someone's home. Only scattered references mention the various options within a home, and it is a safe assumption that not all the options are covered in the Old Testament.

In fact, the distribution of references to people sleeping might appear quite lop-sided. With the exception of Ishbosheth's siesta in his bedchamber (2 Sam 4), the roof is the place identified as the sleeping site, whether for David's siesta (2 Sam 11), or the spies at Jericho (Josh 2).[1]

These texts suggest different grades of roofs. In addition to these examples of sleeping in the open, there is one example of an enclosed roof space. After Elisha has become a regular guest of the wealthy woman of Shunem, she suggests to her husband (2 Kgs 4.9-10):

> *hnh-n' yd'ty ky 'yš 'lhym qdwš hw' 'br 'lynw tmyd n'śh-n' 'lyt-qyr qṭnh ynśym lw šm mṭh wšlḥn wks' wmnwrh whyh bb'w 'lynw yswr šmh*

> Behold now, I perceive that this is a holy man of God, who is continually passing our way. Let us make a small roof chamber with walls, and put there for him a bed, a table, a chair, and a lamp, so that whenever he comes to us, he can go in there.

The phrase *ḥdr mškb* appears only in court contexts: Pharaoh (Exod 7); the king of Syria (2 Kgs 6); 'Solomon' (Eccl 10.20). The references to the *ḥdr* in the following texts probably also are references to bedchambers: 2 Samuel 13; 1 Kings 1. As is obvious from the contexts, the bedchamber was not simply the place one slept, but a place where business was conducted.[2] The phrase *ḥdr hmṭwt* occurs in 2 Kings 11.2 and 2 Chronicles 22.11.[3]

b. *Israel*

The possible locations for sleeping are governed by the lay-out of the house, and so the Israelite house plan is an appropriate starting place.[4] Characteristic of the Israelite settlements, both walled and unwalled, is the four-room house, whose defining feature is 'a back room the width of the building, with three long rooms stemming forward from it' (Shiloh 1970, 180). Aharoni (1982, 163) sets his discussion of this type in the context of a description of the second stratum of Tel Masos, an unfortified village in the Negeb having three Iron I strata.

> There was discovered house after house, most of them pillared houses of the typical 'four-room' plan... The entry was to a central courtyard with rooms on three sides, usually with two rows of columns delineating the two side units from the courtyard. This type of house did not change, in fact, during the entire Israelite period, except for the addition of a second story. At Tel Masos, no staircases were found, such as were commonly used in the 'four-room' houses of the monarchical period (Aharoni 1982, 163).

The 'four-room' house is, however, a type, and the sort of variation possible within this type can be seen by comparing the floor plans from Tel Masos, Beer-sheba, Atar ha-Ro'eh, and Tell el-Far'ah (North) (Aharoni 1982, 164, 168, 171).

More difficult is the problem of specifying how various rooms were used, although here, too, there has been some progress. In discussing houses excavated at Tell Beit Mirsim, Albright draws a contrast between stratum B (Iron I) and stratum A (Iron II):

> In Stratum B, just as in contemporary levels at Bethel, Beth-

> shemesh and elsewhere, space within the limits of a town was not so crowded and people lived principally on the ground-floor. Some kind of paving became necessary under such conditions, and appears ... In Stratum A, on the other hand, where people slept and relaxed almost exclusively in the upper story, there is very little attempt at paving the floors of the first story, which consisted simply of trampled earth (1941-43, 52).

Thus 'probably every house was provided with an upper story, generally consisting of only one or two small rooms (Heb. *'ăliyyah*), in which the master of the house and his family slept' (1941-43, 51). More recently, Yeivin has suggested that the bottom rooms would be used for storage and the living areas would be characteristically upstairs (1954, 219).

c. *Modern Parallels*

As noted above, nineteenth-century Bible encyclopedias made extensive use of contemporary parallels. An excerpt from the McClintock and Strong 'bedchamber' entry is representative:

> Bedrooms in the East consist of an apartment furnished with a divan, or daïs, which is a slightly elevated platform at the upper end, and often along the sides of the room. On this are laid the mattresses on which the Western Asiatics sit crosslegged in the daytime, with large cushions against the wall to support the back. At night the light bedding is usually laid out upon this divan, and thus beds for many persons are easily formed ... This is a sort of general sleeping-room for the males of the family and for guests, none but the master having access to the inner parts of the house, where alone there are proper and distinct bedchambers. In these the bedding is either laid on the carpeted floor, or placed on a low frame or bedstead (1894-96, 1.716).

This divan appeared already in Taylor's revision of Calmet, and—to digress momentarily—was used to explain Amos 3.12 ('Thus says the Lord: "As the shepherd rescues from the mouth of the lion two legs, or a piece of an ear, so shall the people of Israel who dwell in Samaria be rescued, with the corner of a couch and part of a bed."'). The corner of the couch was the corner of the divan, 'which is the place of honor, the most easy, voluptuous, indulging station', and the problematic *wbdmšq* (RSV 'part') was derived from **dmh* 'level, smooth' and thence taken to refer to 'the broad smooth part of the divan'. Therefore the verse was understood to threaten 'those who sit, and those who are sat upon; those who oppress, and those who are oppressed' (1797-1801, 3.26). While this interpretation is questionable at many points, it is the same methodological move as that made by Gese (for which see below): to take the most recent archaeological or ethnological information and use it in a very direct way to interpret a problematic verse.

While Kitto had already noted that one could not assume that the divan was employed in the Old Testament (1857, 2.312), and Cheyne and Black had stressed the gap between the Israelite houses and the modern upper-class oriental houses, the divan continued to appear (Hastings 1903, 1.262; Eager 1915, 421-22 [*International Standard Bible Encyclopedia*]; and McCullough 1962, 1.373 [*Interpreter's Dictionary of the Bible*]).[5] As such divans have been encountered neither in the excavation reports of a number of major sites (Tell Beit Mirsim, Tell el-Far'ah (North), Tell en-Nasbeh, Beth-Shemesh) nor in current descriptions of the Israelite house (see beginning this subsection), it seems most likely that we have here an artifact of nineteenth-century ethnography rather than of Iron Age Palestine.[6]

Relevant to the question of sleeping sites are Dalman's observations, which, as more recent primary data, are quoted extensively.

> Sehr oft dient es [the roof] im Sommer als luftiger Schlafplatz, der in *inḥil* als *maṣīf* 'Sommerplatz' mit einer viereckigen, an den Ecken verzierten Einfassung aus Lehm versehen war ([1928-42] 1964, 7.58).

> Auf dem Dach haben wohlhabende Bauern öfters einen Söller . . . das heisst einen darauf gebauten kleineren Raum mit Tür und Fenster, der als 'Sommerhaus' (bēt ṣēfi) im Sommer Schlafstätte sein kann und stets gern Gästen als Schlafraum zugewiesen wird, weil ihre Anwesenheit im einräumigen Haupthaus nachts nicht angenehm wäre. Ein volles Obergeschoss eines Bauernhauses beobachtete ich in *geba'* . . . Sonst kommt es auch vor, dass das Untergeschoss des Hauses als Stall, das Obergeschoss als Wohnraum dient . . . Da der Söller eine der Hausfrau wichtige Ergänzung des Wohnraums ist, sagt man . . . 'Die Frau des Baumeisters begehrt einen Söller' ([1928-42] 1964, 7.59).

> Vor dem Hause rechts neben der Tür gibt es öfters als Sommerschlafplatz eine kleine Terrasse (*masṭabe*) mit einer Laube (*'arīše*) deren aus belaubten Zweigen über Stangen hergestellte Bedachung oft auf vier senkrechten Stangen ruht ([1928-42] 1964, 7.60).

> Für die Nachtruhe gibt es eine besondere Herrichtung des Wohnraums. Die hölzerne oder eiserne Bettstelle (*taht*) ist etwas Europäisches, wenn sie einmal vorkommt. Freilich würde nur ein sehr armer Bauer sich mit der Matte als Schlafunterlage begnügen, obwohl dies öfters nötig ist, wie Sprichwörter voraussetzen. Ein heiratsfähiges Mädchen klagt: 'Der Mann mit dem Schlafpolster kommt nicht, den Mann mit der Matte mag ich nicht'. Das Schlafpolster (*farše*, Pl. *frāš*) oder wenigstens ein kleineres Kissen (*ṭarrāḥ*^{a}) ist bei den Bauern die normale weiche und wärmende Unterlage . . . In jedem Fall sind sie nicht so fest gestopft und dick wie unsere Matratzen, so dass sie leicht weggenommen und gefaltet werden können ([1928-42] 1964, 7.178-79).

Dalman thus describes a variety of arrangements, depending on the means of the householders. During summer sleeping on the roof or in the verandah seems to be preferred. For other seasons the family sleeps inside (downstairs), and it is desirable to have at least part of the roof area enclosed for guests to sleep in. On the other hand, the downstairs can be used as a stable, with a (full) upstairs used as living quarters. The governing concerns appear to be the climate and the desire for family privacy. Dalman does not record a concern for privacy expressed in terms of different sleeping locations within the family.

Watson reported on a number of villages in western Iran. Part of her report on the village of Ain Ali is relevant:

> The living-room serves as a sleeping room at night . . . In the evening the family bedding will be unrolled and spread out on the rugs. Basically this bedding consists of a mattress (a cotton-filled pad), a bolster for a pillow, and one or more blankets. All are or folded neatly away in the daytime and stored at one end of the room (Watson 1979, 282).

Horne's report of field work in Baghestan (500 km east of Tehran) contains a number of observations relevant to the question of sleeping sites. First, a room can be used in a variety of ways during its history: 'little or no effort is required to alter a room's function—to downgrade it from a living room to a storeroom, or from a storeroom to an animal room' (1983, 19). Thus here it cannot be assumed that a room having the gross design characteristics of a living room is in fact being used as a living room. It is the living room, not incidentally, which is used for sleeping, the bedding moved off to the side or used for other purposes during the day.

The anthropological material suggests a variety of uses for the place where people slept, as well as day uses for the bedding. And this, incidentally, is noted by Galling for the Old Testament as well: 'Am Tage diente das B[ett] als Kline beim Essen (1. Sam 28.23; Hes 23.41; Est 1.6)' (1937, 110).

In summary, the Old Testament texts characteristically specify the roof as the place of sleeping, whether for guests (Josh 2; 2 Kgs 4) or residents (2 Sam 11). This is in line with the emerging picture of the patterns of use of the characteristic Israelite four-room house (Albright 1941-43, 52; Yeivin 1954, 219). This pattern would appear to be in line with some of the patterns described by Dalman, but differ from the nineteenth-century ethnography (represented in the Bible dictionaries) as well as current field work in Iran (Horne, Watson). Of course, once the houses become more elaborate, more options would be expected to develop.

2. *Beds*

The evidence available for beds and bedding is quite uneven.[7] While there are a good number of references to beds and bedding in the Old Testament, no beds have been preserved (the two beds found in Palestine are from the Bronze Age and the Persian period),[8] although some models of beds are preserved. On the other hand, the evidence for beds in both Egypt and Mesopotamia is comparatively rich. From here discussion moves to Palestinian burials: in what ways is the sleep/death equation reflected in burial practices, and what can be learned about bed size or sleeping positions?

a. *Old Testament*

Again, entries covering beds in Bible encyclopedias provide a useful point of departure. These contain, besides more or less complete summaries of biblical references, a number of useful suggestions. Thus Galling notes: 'Jacob, dying in Egypt, rests on a bed ('B[ett]-Statt') (Gen 47.31; cf. Exod 7.28) while in the same situation with Abraham and his servant (Gen 24.1ff) mention of a bed is remarkably absent' (1937, 109; tm). And this is used as a piece of evidence for the later use of beds in Israel relative to Egypt.[9] Thus Fohrer may be correct in his summary:

> Previously one slept on the ground under one's mantle (Exod 22.27; Deut 24.13) or a rug (Judg 4.18). Rugs or mattresses could

> serve as pads (Isa 28.20; Lev 11.7). As a piece of furniture the bed comes from Egypt, where it was used since the Old Kingdom in the court and since the New Kingdom in wider circles (Gen 47.31). In Palestine it was known first in the court (1 Sam 19.15; 2 Sam 4.7; 11.2; 13.5; 1 Kgs 1.47), however soon also among all the well-to-do (2 Kgs 4.10) (Fohrer 1962, 235; tm).

One means of access to our subject is provided by the following table, which displays the occurrences of references to beds or couches in the Old Testament.[10] As will be seen, 'bed' should be understood quite broadly.

Table 3.1
mškb group: distribution over texts and uses

Text	Bed/Couch				Owner	Use
	mṭh	*mškb*	*'rś*	other		
Gen 47, 48	x				Jacob	bedridden
49		x		*yṣw'*	..	intercourse
49	x				..	bedridden
Exod 7	x				Egypt	sleep?
Exod 21		x				bedridden
Lev 15		x			zâb	..
1 Sam 19	x				David	..
1 Sam 28	x				witch	sitting
2 Sam 3	x					bier
2 Sam 4	x	x			Ishb.	sleeping
2 Sam 11		x			David,	..
					Uriah	..
2 Sam 13		x			Amnon	bedridden
2 Sam 17		x			Shobi, etc.	sleeping?
1 Kgs 1		x			David	bedridden
1 Kgs 17	x				Elijah	sleeping?
1 Kgs 21	x				Ahab	pouting
2 Kgs 1	x				Ahaziah	bedridden
2 Kgs 4	x				Elisha	sleeping?
Isa 28				*mṣ'*	n.n.	..
57		x			..	death
		x			..	intercourse
Ezek 23		x			..	..
32		x			..	death
Hos 7		x			..	?
Amos 3, 6	x		x		..	feasting

	mṭh	*mškb*	*'rś*	other	Owner	Use
Mic 2		x			n.n.	thinking
Ps 4		x			..	..
6	x		x		..	weeping
36		x			..	thinking
41		x			..	bedridden
132			x	*yṣw'*	..	sleeping
149		x			..	rejoicing
Job 7		x	x		..	sleeping
17				*yṣw'*	..	death
33		x			..	bedridden
Prov 7		x	x		..	intercourse
22		x			..	sleeping?
26	x				..	sleeping
Cant 1, 3	x	x	x		..	intercourse
Esth 1, 7	x				var.	feasting
1 Chr 5				*yṣw'*	Jacob	intercourse
2 Chr 16		x				bier
24	x				Joash	bedridden

In general, beds are mentioned during Israel's stay in Egypt, but not again until the monarchy. For the reigns of Saul and David, at least some of the time *mškb* probably denotes simply bedding (e.g. 2 Sam 11.13 and 17.28). This, together with the mention of beds (*mškb*) in Exodus 21 and Leviticus 15, suggests that the lack of references to beds for the pre-monarchial period is mostly accidental. In the monarchial period and subsequently, beds appear with roughly equal frequency in royal and non-royal situations.

There is little textual evidence regarding the construction or design of beds. Beds whose composition is noted are restricted to the court (Samaria [Amos], Susa [Esth]).[11] One possible piece of evidence for design is the use of the pair *'lh / yrd* 'go up' / 'go down' in reference to beds. This has been taken as evidence for beds being somewhat elevated, but the non-textual material (see below) available at present does not resolve this issue.

Amos 3.12 has been the locus of discussion of beds in the Old Testament, if only for the court:

kh 'mr yhwh
k'šr yṣyl hr'h mpy h'ry šty kr'ym 'w bdl-'zn
kn ynṣlw bny yśr'l hyšbym bšmrwn bp't mṭh ûbidmešeq 'rś

Thus says the Lord:
'As the shepherd rescues from the mouth of the lion

two legs, or a piece of an ear,
so shall the people of Israel who dwell in Samaria be rescued,
with the corner of a couch and part of a bed'.[12]

This would appear to be a self-contained unit, with *kh 'mr yhwh* marking the beginning and *šm'w* in v. 13 marking the beginning of the next unit (as in 3.1; 4.1; 5.1; 8.4).[13] The primary lexical problem has been *ûbidmešeq*.[14] As pointed, it has usually been translated 'damask' or 'silk', with appeal made to Arabic *dimaqs*, the etymology of which is uncertain at best (BDB).[15] Thus, despite its relative congruence with the general context, this reading has, properly, tended to be abandoned for a reading parallel either to *bšmrwn* or to *bp't*. The versions take the former track, reading (or interpreting) *dmšq* as *dmśq* 'Damascus'. But this adds further complications to the verse, unless (so the Vulgate) Damascus is taken as modifying the bed, in which case the reverse word order would be expected (with Gese [1962, 429 n. 1]). The later track involves the attempt to recover from *dmšq*, and often from *p't*, some bed-related word.

Of the attempts along this line, one of the more persuasive is Gese's emendation *b'mšt*.[16] Gese's argument (1962, 427-32), though straightforward, involves a number of points. The Akkadian words *pūtu* and *amar(t)u* are used for the foot and the head of the Assyrian bed. In new and late Babylonian the latter appears as *amaštu*. The general picture painted by Amos, and 3.12, 6.1, 4 in particular, suggest that Assyrian beds could have been imported. Along with them would have come the technical vocabulary, and while the Israelites would have simply used their (cognate) *p'h* for Akkadian *pūtu*, they would have taken over *amaštu*. Thus Gese translates (1962, 431):

so werden die Israeliten gerettet,
die sich kauern in Samaria
an das Fussende des Lagers,
an den Kopfaufbau des Bettes.

With the passing of the Assyrian bed this terminology was no longer understood, and because of the similarity of the Aramaic cursive characters involved—and the proximity of *bšmrwn*—the word was eventually written as *wbdmšq*.

Mittmann (1976) critiques Gese and offers his own proposal. Against Gese, 'heisst *pūtu* 'Stirn-, Frontseite' und kann von daher nur auf die Kopfseite des Bettes bezogen sein' (1976, 158; so *AHw*

2.884).[17] Further, the examples of *amaštu* are all Seleucid—and only from Uruk. Not only does Gese have the problem of explaining why the Babylonian dialectal form would have been adopted for the Assyrian bed, but this form itself is badly attested (a problem Wolff acknowledges [1977, 196]). Mittmann in turn revives the proposal *wbdbšt*, suggesting that *dbšt*, used for a camel's hump (Isa 30.6), would be a natural word for a raised end on a bed. *p'h*—no longer being interpreted in terms of Akkadian *pūtu*—would function as a more general term, and thus Mittmann translates (1976, 150):

> so werden die Israeliten gerettet,
> die in Samaria sitzen
> an der Lehne des Lagers
> und am Stützpolster des Bettes.

Mittmann appears to have the better of the argument regarding the meaning of *amar(t)u* and *pūtu*. Thus Salonen cites *pūutu ša erši* as 'Stirnwand des Bettes' (1963, 151) and *amar(t)u* as 'Seitenwand des Bettes' (1963, 148), and there is *emartu* 'side' (*CAD*). However, a shift in the designations of these terms alone would not seriously undermine Gese's argument. The lack of attestation of *amaštu* before the Seleucid period (examples cited in Deller 1964) is a more serious problem. But at one critical point Mittmann's proposal is weaker than Gese's. If the presumptive original for *wbdmšk* is an indigenous term, it is more difficult to explain its corruption. Mittmann's contribution, besides putting pressure on Gese's lexical proposals, is perhaps more in his proposed identification of an indigenous Syro-Palestinian style bed, and this will be taken up below in the discussion of the archaeological evidence.

b. *Israel*

In the course of his discussion of Amos 3.12, Mittmann suggests

> By all appearances Syro-Palestinian culture had produced its own type of bed, which distinguished itself from the Egyptian and Mesopotamian types particularly in that both ends were equipped with a support (1976, 161-62; tm).

The evidence Mittmann offers consists of a steatite pyxis picturing two people in a bed (eighth [?] century),[18] some of the 'Bettlehne' (measuring 84 cm wide) also discovered at Nimrud, and a model bed from Lachish.

On the other hand, Weippert has suggested that the Assyrian bed made its way into Palestine, citing the same Lachish model, as well as models from Beer-Sheba and Ashdod. In addition, Weippert notes that simpler models have been found at Ai, Khirbet el-Mešāš and Tell en-Nasbeh (1977, 230).

The models from Ai, numbers 1494 and 1961, are from Early Bronze strata (area H, room 133 and area V2, room 235 respectively). While number 1494 is fragmentary (pl. 65.6), number 1961, lacking only the legs, appears to have had neither head nor foot-board (Marquet-Kraus 1949, 191, 241). The Ashdod model, number D4125/1 (Iron 2; fig 63.6), listed as an 'offering table' is consistent with Weippert's thesis (Dothan 1971).

The evidence from Beer-Sheba (all from stratum 2, dated by Aharoni to the eighth century BC [1973, 107]) is mixed. The model cited by Weippert (pl. 71.2 = 27.3) is a model of approximately 9×6 cm, with a footboard(?) preserved and a headboard(?) broken away. However, there is another model (pl. 28.5) which apparently lacked a footboard, as well as another model (pl. 28.6) which lacked a footboard, but is less clearly a bed (Aharoni 1973). The broken character of the first two models make it difficult to assess Assyrian influence; on the third it would appear to be lacking.

The bed model from Khirbet el-Mešāš (in the Negev) is from an area (G) dated in a preliminary report to the seventh century (Fritz and Kempinski 1976, 101). It is badly broken, but possessed a (head-? foot-?)board. The excavators note that it was colored 'im edomitischen Stil'.

The Lachish bed model does support Mittmann's suggestion.[19] What would appear to be the headboard is at almost a ninety-degree angle from the bed proper; the 'footboard' is at about a forty-five-degree angle. The legs are round and squat, and the width would make it—by our standards—a single occupancy bed.

The model from Tell en-Nasbeh, number 938 (pl. 84.25), looks from the angle of the back more like a couch than a bed. It is from cave 193, used during the Early Bronze 1, Iron, and Persian(?) periods (the report does not place it more precisely; McCown 1947, 60, 73, 299).

The ivory panels from Fort Shalmaneser are rather weak evidence, because neither their function nor their provenance is known. The panels in question are fifteen fragments of screens found in room SW7. The screens consisted of ivory plaques mounted on the concave sides of (now disintegrated) wooden frames. The average size was 80-90 cm long, 60 cm high. On the south wall, the screens were found 50 cm above the floor, and were therefore probably attached to 'some sort of pedestal at least 50 cm high' (Oates 1959, 105). What they were used for was, and is, still a matter of discussion.[20] In an initial report Oates ventures the guess that they were 'the more valuable portions of larger pieces of furniture, perhaps the heads of beds or couches' (1959, 106). Mallowan takes the identification of some of these pieces as heads of couches or beds to be 'a probable conjecture, for associated with one of them there was a strip of ivory carved with animals in relief, part of a framework which would have been too long for a chair, but admirably suited to a long couch' (1966, 2.411). Unfortunately, the couches had been stacked, so the excavators were unable to reconstruct the lengths of the pieces.

As to provenance, Mallowan suggests that 'the larger panels form a homogeneous group with stylistic affinities in north-west Syria and south-east Anatolia' (1966, 2.514). They could, he continues, have been 'imports, tribute, or booty', but the discernible Assyrian influence also allows the possibility that they were carved on site (1966, 2.515). Thus their usability for reconstructing a Palestinian type is minimal.

In sum, the evidence for a Syro-Palestinian type (Mittmann) is sparse. The head/footboards from Fort Shalmaneser and the pyxis are consistent with Mittmann's thesis, while the Lachish bed is not. In other words, the thesis appears to have a better chance of sustaining itself in the Syrian rather than the Palestinian sphere. On the other hand, the Beer-Sheba model (pl. 71.2) may provide some support for Mittmann.

As for Weippert's suggestion, while the Ashdod and Lachish models and two of the Beer-Sheba models are compatible with it, the necessarily (?) rough character of the models makes it difficult to judge whether there is Assyrian influence or simply a local tradition in which a smaller or larger section of the head end is more or less raised.

But these bed models raise a number of broader questions. In regard to the chronology of the bed in Palestine, the Ai model (Early Bronze; together with the Jericho bed in the Middle Bronze tomb, for which see below) suggests a long history. And in the Israelite period, the discovery of bed models in Ashdod, Beer-Sheba, Lachish, Tell Masos, and Tell en-Nasbeh (?) raises the question of how far down the social ladder one could go and still find beds in use. If many more such items are discovered, it could have the effect of pushing the dividing line lower.

c. *Egypt*

We may move from Palestine to Egypt through Sinuhe's description of his homecoming:[21]

> We went through the great portals, and I was put in the house of a prince. In it were luxuries: a bathroom and mirrors. In it were riches from the treasury; clothes of royal linen, myrrh, and the choice perfume of the king and of his favorite courtiers were in every room. Every servant was at his task. Years were removed from my body. I was shaved; my hair was combed. Thus was my squalor returned to the foreign land, my dress to the Sand-farers. I was clothed in fine linen; I was anointed with fine oil. I slept on a bed. I had returned the sand to those who dwell in it, the tree-oil to those who grease themselves with it (lines 285-95).

Baker (1966) provides the most extensive discussion of Egyptian beds, citing examples from the Early Dynastic period and the Eighteenth Dynasty. In all periods the beds tend to be low to the ground ('rarely exceeding twelve inches' [1966, 21]). From the First Dynasty a number of simple wooden frames are preserved. Already some of the legs are carved as animal legs (bull, lion, etc), a characteristic of later periods.[22] Generally woven rush, but sometimes leather would be stretched across the frame. From the Third Dynasty on foot-boards are provided for the beds (1966, 37), and, rather than being level, the head of the bed may be higher than the foot. Low side-rails are also provided. From the Fourth Dynasty there is the bed of Queen Hetepheres, having legs shaped as lion's legs, and a solid board for the mattress.

From the Eighteenth Dynasty come a number of examples, in all of which the side pieces dip to a greater or lesser degree in the center. Three examples come from the tomb of Yuia and Thuiu, parents of the wife of Amenophis III. Baker describes the foot-board panels of the finest bed:

> They show again figures of the god Bes with his tambourine, and the hippopotamus goddess Thoeris, carved in gilded plaster... These figures appear on both sides of the foot-board, and in the centre panel on the back Bes is shown holding hieroglyphic signs which were believed to give protection to whoever might be the occupant of the bed (1966, 72).

Five beds were recovered from the Tutankhamun tomb, one of which also has a foot-board worth noting. Baker provides a description:

> The three panels, which are divided by the usual papyrus rods, each contain three carved and cut-out figures decorated with gold-leaf. The god Bes . . . crouches in the centre and is faced on each side by a standing lion with his forepaw resting on the hieroglyph signifying protection. On the ebony bands framing the foot-board at top and ends are inscriptions, filled with yellow paint, which repeat magic formulae on behalf of the king (1966, 103-4).

Also from the Eighteenth Dynasty are two beds from the tomb of Kha, whom Baker identifies as being 'upper-middle-class' (124). Both are well-made, constructed of wood which was subsequently painted. Moving further down the socio-economic scale, Baker suggests 'low benches of mud brick could in most cases serve the purpose of wooden furniture; spread with a woven mat, a bench of this kind also made a bed, raising the sleeping person above the floor' (1966, 110).

For an earlier period, a vivid sense of the variety of sleeping arrangements is conveyed by the 'Admonitions of Ipuwer' (12th dynasty). Among the many examples of reversal we find (Lichtheim 1973, 149-63):

> Lo, citizens are put to the grindstones,
> Wearers of fine linen are beaten with [sticks].
> Those who never saw daylight go out unhindered,
> Those who were on their husbands' beds,
> 'Let them lie on boards' [one repeats] (4.9-10).
>
> See, noble ladies are on boards,
> Princes in the workhouse,
> He who did not sleep on a box owns a bed (7.11).
>
> [See], those who owned beds are on the ground,
> He who lay in the dirt spreads a rug (9.1).

What were the physical dimensions of these beds? In terms of size and ratios, three types emerge. Referring to the examples by Baker's illustration references, numbers 6 and 7 (1st Dynasty) are short (just under 100 cm) and wide (approximately 1.4 : 1 length to width). Numbers 83 and 84 (18th Dynasty) are quite narrow (approximately 4.5 : 1 length to width; approximately 173 cm long). The remainder (1st to 18th Dynasties) have a length to width ratio of 2.2 : 1, with an

Table 3.2
Egyptian bed dimensions

Illus.	Provenance	Dyn	Height	Length	Width
6	unknown	1	37	95	72
7	Tarkhan	1	29	95	67
8	..	1		175	81
37	tomb Hetepheres	4		178	97
83	tomb of Yuia & Thuiu	18	76	177	76
84	..	18	58	174	39
85	..	18	56	171	38
132	tomb of Tutankhamun	18	69	160	
134	..	18	75	185	90
136	..	18	50	179	69
138	..	18	71	180	80
170	tomb of Kha	18	70	193	85
1	..	18	66	174	76
219	unknown	11	28	161	69
220	Kerma in the Sudan	12			66

Source: Baker (1966, 335-40)
Notes: The illustration numbers are Baker's. All measurements in centimeters, and rounded to nearest centimeter.

average and mean length of 176 cm. The first group is noticeably shorter than the other groups (below 37 cm vs over 50 cm—with the exception of no 219). While these figures will later be compared with other data, for purposes of comparison it is helpful to recall that a cot measures 183 by 61 cm (3 : 1 length/width), and modern mattresses show the following range of length, width, and length/width ratio (in cm): 191, 99, 1.9 : 1 (twin); 191, 137, 1.4 : 1 (full); 203, 193, 1.1 : 1 (king).

In addition to the beds preserved—and not all of those which Baker describes have been noted here—there are murals which provide some additional information, but which do not change the basic picture presented here. Fischer notes that some clay models of 'zweischläfrige' beds are known (1977, 767). There is also an entry in a list of gifts from Amenophis IV to the Babylonian king Burrabu(ra)riaš (Knudtzon 1910):

I iršu ḫurâṣu uḫḫuzu šêpē-šu lamassē
I iršu ḫurâṣu uḫḫuzu I ša ri-e-ši ḫurâṣu uḫḫuzu

> I Bettgestell, mit Gold überzogen,
> dessen Füsse Schutzgötter sind.
> I Bettgestell, mit Gold überzogen,
> I (Gestell) für das Haupt, mit Gold überzogen (VAB 2 14.2.19-20).

Mittmann makes the following suggestion:

> These *lamassu* feet are probably not simply the obligatory lion legs, which certainly the other beds possessed. Rather this unique example is probably a ceremonial bed, equipped also at least with lion heads, which one might also gather from the fact that the headrest, otherwise supplied with each bed, is not mentioned here (1976, 160; tm).

That Mittmann may be correct in suggesting that more than simply the normal theriomorphic legs are being described is suggested by an excerpt from a neo-Assyrian throne description: 'the feet (of the throne consist of) *l*.-representations, below the *l*.-representations are claws, there are eight *l*.-representations atop the two cross pieces of the long side' (*CAD*, *lamassu*). Alternately, Galling made the suggestion that the reference here was to one of the footboards carrying images of Bes or Thoeris (1937, 109). That the *lamassu* were not characteristically connected with protection during sleep may be seen from the entries in *CAD*, *lamassu*.

d. *Mesopotamia*

The Mesopotamian evidence presented by Baker is considerably thinner than the Egyptian. There were traces of a bed in one of the Ur tombs. There are clay and terracotta bed models from the Old Babylonian and Isin-Larsa periods respectively, showing unornamented legs, lack of either head- or foot-board, and a woven material stretched across the frame. Past these, Baker relies on inscriptional evidence and bas reliefs. Quite heavy beds with curved head-boards appear in Neo-Assyrian feasting scenes, but the same head-board style appears in a relief of booty being taken from a captured city, and another shows an officer using one in the field (1966, 178-205).

The material presented by Baker may be supplemented to some degree by Salonen. In reviewing the development of the bed, Salonen appeals to *ḫāmū* 'bed of litter' as evidence that many slept on the ground or mattresses. He surveys representative two- and three-dimensional evidence, including a bed model from the Early

Table 3.3
Mesopotamian bed dimensions

Illus.	Item	Prov.	Date	height	length	width
282	model	Ischali	O.B.	3.49	10	6.03
283	..	Ur	Isin-Larsa	3.17	11.43	6.98
319	panel	Nimrud	9-8 Cent.	59		80
320	..	..	..	66		84
321	..	..	..	66		84
322	..	..	..	66		84

Source: Baker (1966, 341-2)
Notes: The illustration numbers are Baker's. All measurements in centimeters, and—except for models—rounded to nearest centimeter.

Dynastic, a clay plaque from Ur III, a large number of clay models from the Larsa period, and a good number of representations in palace reliefs in the neo-Assyrian.

Eight model beds from the Isin-Larsa period (now in the British Museum) are published for the first time. Measurements are not provided, but the length-width ratio is approximately 1.5 : 1.[23] Two points are of interest. The bed appearing in figure 18, 1 has two people in it; perhaps they also slept in a bed of this size. The bed appearing in figure 19, 1 appears to have had a headboard(?) subsequently broken off, which would make it unique among the bed models Salonen cites for this period.

However, the bulk of Salonen's study is lexical. It confirms what the bed in figure 19, 1 suggested: more types were in use than are attested in models. Thus, for example, Salonen notes (1963, 116):

> [giš]*na2-aš-na2* = *dinnūtu*
> einschläfriges Bett, Diwan
>
> [giš]*na2-gu2-zi-ga* = *eršu ša rešāšā šaqā*
> Bett, dessen Stirn- und Fusswand hoch sind.

Occasionally theriomorphic legs are described, normally of oxen (1963, 112-18).

But often the trees tend to obscure the forest. For instance, at one point Bottéro is cited: '*eršu* pourrait être de "lit" proprement dit, pour le repos nocturne, et *majālu* le "divan", ou pendant le jour l'on s'étendait et l'on s'accroupissait "à l'arabe"' (1963, 124). It would be of considerable interest to know in what periods or regions—if any—

this lexical distinction was consistently maintained, particularly in light of the difficulty already described in giving an account of the use of the different Biblical Hebrew words for 'bed'. Salonen, however, does not pursue this question, although in the course of his discussion texts are cited where *majālu* denotes beds used for nocturnal sleeping (1963, 142; including Gil 1.5.12; 2.2.44; 7.6.8, 13, 190).

e. *Palestinian Burials*

The relative lack of evidence for Israelite beds[24] encourages exploration of burials in Palestine, starting—arbitrarily—with the Bronze Age, and ending—less arbitrarily—with the Persian period. Apart from the fragments of beds preserved in tombs it is not assumed that there is any direct relationship between Israelite sleeping practices and various aspects of burial practice. But a review of the relevant aspects of burial practice will at least make clear where sleeping patterns have perhaps influenced burial practice, whether the size of sleeping area, the use of pillows, or positions assumed during sleep.

(i) *Bronze Age*

Aharoni (1982, 51) identifies family burial caves as one of the new features of the Early Canaanite (Bronze) Age. Kenyon describes the Early Bronze tombs at Jericho, where multiple interments were the norm: 'Apparently the bodies were originally placed in the tombs complete. But when the available space became full many of the bones of the earlier burials were thrown out' (1970, 122). As a result there are few intact skeletons from which to draw conclusions about characteristic placement of the body. For instance, in tomb A 127, only the skeleton labeled 'T' is intact, and from the drawing it would appear to have been laid out on its back (Kenyon *et al.* 1960, 86).

In light of later practice, the use of platforms or enclosures in some multiple-burial sites is worthy of note. As Stiebing describes the practice, 'each platform or enclosure seems to have been designed to hold one or two bodies at most. The bodies were usually placed on the platform or within the enclosure intact, sometimes contracted and sometimes extended' (1970, 43). Since this practice does not seem to have lasted past the beginning of Early Bronze II (1970, 44), a connection with the mudbrick platforms in Middle Bronze Jericho does not appear likely.[25]

In Kenyon's EB-MB period, individual interment is the standard practice (Aharoni 1982, 83). At Jericho Kenyon identified five types, some with articulated, others with disarticulated burials. In the Dagger-type tomb, the skeleton is 'lying in a crouched position necessitated by the small size of the tomb chamber' (Kenyon 1970, 139). In the Square-Shaft and Outsize-type tombs the burials were also articulated. In the Pottery-type tombs 'the body was put in literally as a bag of bones, disarticulated and lying in disorder, apparently dumped in in some sort of textile or matting container' (Kenyon 1970, 139). The burials were also disarticulated in the Bead-type tombs. At other sites of this period there is only partial correlation with the Jericho typology. Thus the crouched position appears in rectangular shaft tombs at Tell Ajjul (Kenyon 1970, 145). But the evidence from Jericho for burial after the body was dismembered does appear to clarify the situation at Megiddo (Tomb 1101-1102B Lower, Shaft Tombs; Kenyon 1970, 148-50).

For the Middle Bronze I period at Jericho Kenyon describes 'a brick-built tomb and a grave . . . In it [the tomb] were the remains of about a dozen individuals, the earlier bodies being disarranged to make room for the later ones. The grave contained the bodies of two individuals, lying on their left sides in a flexed position' (1970, 169).

The evidence for Middle Bronze II Jericho is more extensive. Again, multiple burials are the rule, averaging about 20 persons.

> The tombs are cut into the soft rock of the lower slopes of the hills . . . Apparently the tomb shaft was filled after each burial and re-excavated for the next one. Each dead person was put in the tomb with food and equipment for the after-life . . . The body was placed on its back with limbs untidily disposed, and often with the knees raised. When the next burial was made, the body and offerings belonging to the earlier ones were pushed roughly towards the back and sides of the tomb chamber (Kenyon 1970, 189).

In a number of cases there were simultaneous burials which were not subsequently disturbed. Tomb H 18, which Kenyon described here, was particularly interesting:

> With the family groups was placed the family furniture, of which the important item was a long, narrow table . . . Most of the dead lay on rush mats, on which they probably slept and sat during life. Only one individual lay on a bed, probably a man of importance,

> for he occupied the centre of the tomb, and the members of his family were disposed round the edge (1970, 191).

As reconstructed and drawn (Kenyon *et al.* 1960, 495), the bed measures 161 by 45 cm. That is small, not only in comparison to a modern cot (183 by 61 cm), but also in comparison to the average height of Bronze Age males at Jericho (170 cm; Hughes 1965, 664-84). In addition to this bed, in three other tombs one or more bodies were placed on platforms made of mud brick. Generally one course of bricks was used, though in tomb P 21 three courses were used, producing a height of 50 cm (Kenyon *et al.* 1965, 428). The dimensions—measured from the report drawings—are given in table 3.4.

Table 3.4
Bed dimensions in Middle Bronze tombs

Tomb	Site	Length	Width	Page
H 18	Bed	1.61 m	0.45 m	495
H 6	Platform	1.69 m	0.76 m	454
J 14	Platform	1.61 m	0.92 m	313
P 21	Platform	1.44 m	0.40 m	429

Note: Tombs H 6 and H 18 are reported in Kenyon *et al.* 1960; tombs J 14 and P 21 are reported in Kenyon *et al.* 1965.

Thus these platforms appear to have been built to roughly the same dimensions as the one extant bed. And they appear to serve as a functional substitute for a bed. In tomb P 21 Kenyon reports 'fragments suggesting the frame of a bed lie round skeleton B, and there are also fragments of wood beneath C's torso' (Kenyon *et al.* 1965, 430). But the platform appears to have been the honored position, which Kenyon concludes in part because 'the fact that the body on the platform was the most completely disarranged [the tomb was robbed] would suggest that there were more valuable objects associated with it than with the others' (Kenyon *et al.* 1965, 430).

As to the arrangement of the bodies, Kenyon observes:

> The general position of the bodies is supine. They lie on the back, in strong contrast to the crouched position of the majority of the E.B.-M.B. bodies. But very little care was taken in disposing the bodies. The limbs straggle and are bent, and the impression is that the bodies were simply dumped down . . . There does however

> seem to have been almost a predilection for placing the bodies with the knees raised (Kenyon *et al.* 1965, 575).

Might one hazard a guess that the position of the knees reflected a sleeping practice, since the beds were made shorter than the people?

(ii) *Iron Age*

An overview of Iron Age burial practices is provided by Abercrombie (1979), although his dissertation is also evidence of how far we are from being able to account for the wide variation in burial practices. Abercrombie attempts to derive a number of burial types from the criteria of interment method,[26] burial context,[27] pottery pattern (five are identified), and non-ceramic grave goods. Five types are identified involving 159 examples, but then an additional 80 examples are identified as mixed pattern (1979, 177). One intriguing pattern Abercrombie identifies is regional variation in burial practice. Thus his type 1 occurs almost exclusively in the coastal plain, type 2 occurs only in Transjordan, and types 3 and 4[28] occur in the hill country between Tell en-Naṣbeh in the North and Lachish in the South (1979, 183-84).

Abercrombie provides a summary of the body position used in primary burials:

> Skeletons of adults, adolescents, and children lie in a supine position with limbs fully extended. The legs are seldom crossed or flexed . . . The arms are either fully extended or slightly flexed so that the hands lie in the pelvic region . . . The skull generally faces up in most primary burials (1979, 14).

Abercrombie also notes that pair burial, 'an adult male and female interred together' is a common practice (1979, 22-23).

Aharoni (1982, 238) provides a description of the Israelite (Iron Age) burial cave:

> The entry was through a vertical shaft with a few steps at the end leading though a small rectangular entrance (stomium) to a rectangular vestibule (atrium). This opened onto several burial chambers with benches or arcosolia along the sides, the number of which may vary from one to four, with additions being made as needed.

This description does not include, however, notice of provision for deposition of previous burials, such as that which Meyers (1970, 14-

15) describes for Tomb 5 from Tell en-Nasbeh:

> The ledges apparently were used for the primary burials and the chamber at the rear for collection of skeletal remains . . . The more standard Iron II repositories such as are found . . . at Lachish or in Beth Shemesh . . . clearly were designed to provide a compartment for storing earlier burials, though it is difficult to ascertain with certainty the place of primary burial.

Loffreda (1968) has developed a (primarily diachronic) typology of these rock-cut tombs. While suggestions for revision have already appeared (Abercrombie 1979, 49-52), his study is particularly useful in providing listings of a large number of such rock-cut tombs. Using these listings, it is possible to gain a clear picture of the dimensions of the ledges used in the primary burials. In the Iron I period the dimensions are quite irregular. The length may reach 4 m (Lachish 521; Tufnell 1953, pl. 126), but generally are shorter, and often the shapes are irregular. Reported ledge heights vary from 12 to 100 cm.[29]

In Iron II the characteristic design is a continuous ledge on three sides of the room, with the entrance on the fourth side. For a group of 15 tombs, the average side length is 3.15 m (range 2.2-4.1 m; median 3.2 m).[30] For virtually the same group, the length of the ledge at the back is somewhat shorter: 2.85 m (range 1.7-4 m; median 2.8 m).[31] For a group of 20 tombs, the average width is 0.995 m (range 0.6-2.2 m; median 0.95).[32] For a group of 13 tombs, the average height is 0.73 m (range 0.25-1.2 m; median 0.7 m).[33] Since the bench is continuous, where one resting place left off and the next began is unclear, and for purposes of discussion the areas common to two benches, i.e. the corners, will be allotted evenly to the sides and back, thus giving an effective length for the side of 2.65 m and 1.85 m for the back.

But of particular interest here for the potential light shed on sleeping practices are a number of groups of tombs around Jerusalem (cf. Rahmani 1981-2). Ussishkin has described a necropolis currently located in the village of Silwan. He reports three types of tombs there: tombs with a straight ceiling, monolithic above-ground tombs, and a group of seven tombs with gabled ceilings, all assigned by the author to a period between the ninth and mid-seventh centuries (1970, 44). The last group is the most elaborate:[34]

> All tombs are made for a single or a double burial, and only one tomb contains resting-places for three bodies . . . The resting-place

> is cut in the long wall of the chamber, to the left or to the right of the entrance. It has the shape of a rectangular trough, in which the dead person was placed on his back . . . At the bottom at one end of the trough, a 'pillow' was cut in the rock for the head of the dead person. A depression was cut in the pillow to support the head. It should be noted that all the pillows were cut at the end of the trough nearer to the entrance.
>
> Two tombs contain a double resting-place. The shape of the double burial trough is identical to those described above but its width is doubled. Here also a pillow was cut in the rock, containing two depressions for the two heads. It must be assumed that here a man and his wife were interred . . .
>
> A comparison between all of the resting-places in the tombs indicates that they have nearly the same measurements in such matters as the width and height of the trough, the width and height of the pillow, the width and height of the ledge. The only measurement which clearly differs is the length of the trough. While the longest one is 2.10 meters long (almost seven feet), the shortest one is only 1.75 meters (just under six feet). For various reasons it seems clear that the tombs were prepared by their owners while still alive, and thus we have to conclude that each tomb-owner ordered a tomb to fit the measurements of his own body (1970, 35-38).

As indicated, while the length of the trough varies, the width is constant, reported (via a diagram) at 110 cm (1970, 36). The resting-place information provided for the other two tomb groups is more cursory: the straight-ceiling group used either benches or a simpler troughs.

Barkey and Kloner (1976) provide a description of three burial caves now on the grounds of the Ecole Biblique (north of the Damascus Gate).[35] All three are multi-chambered, the first two having antechambers leading to the burial chambers. From the description of the first cave:

> The burial chambers are all of the same type, with burial benches along the walls opposite the entrance and on both sides. The benches at the sides of the entrance have small head-rests cut in the rock with a depression for the head, all at the end nearest the entrance. The benches opposite the entrance are longer than those at the sides and they have head-rests at both ends. In the easternmost burial chamber, entered through another chamber, deep resting-places resembling sarcophagi replace the benches. These resting-places are 0.50 m. wide and approximately the same

> in depth . . . It appears that the burials in the innermost chamber were the most respected ones, to judge from the difference in the arrangements there; compare the laying of King Asa's body in a 'bed' inside a sepulchre (2 Chron. 16.14) (1976, 56).

From the description of the second cave:

> All the burial chambers but the southeastern one are of the same pattern. They have three benches along the walls, and the benches have head-rests with depressions. A slightly elevated parapet around the benches retained the corpse and the burial goods in position (1976, 56).

Mazar (1976) published two tombs north of the Damascus Gate, discovered in 1937, but only in the light of more recent discoveries assignable to the First Temple period. Both have an antechamber leading to the burial chambers. The first has benches in most of the burial chambers (no dimensions given). Note Mazar's description of the rear chamber of the second cave:

> This room is symmetrical with benches along three sides. At the southern end of the east and west benches and the western end of the north bench are rock-cut horseshoe-shaped head-rests (1976, 5).

Tombs with benches are common in Iron Age Israel. But embellishments such as the 'pillows' are confined to the Jerusalem area. One exception to this pattern is the first of a series of caves at Khirbet el-Kôm, published by Dever (1969). It consists of an antechamber leading to three burial chambers, each containing three benches.

> Chambers 1 and 3 vere more elaborate than chamber 2; in each there was a repository under the end bench and on all three benches were shallow body recesses *ca.* 5-7 cm. deep, with carefully-fashioned niches at each end for the head and the feet. These niches are unique in the published tombs of the period (although the writer has seen identical niches in another robbed Iron Age tomb in the vicinity of Kh. el-Kôm) (1969, 142).

f. *Summary*

The first order of business is to draw together the quantitative data on bed sizes and ratios (table 3.5). How does the relationship between bed length and average (human) height compare then and now? For Bronze Age Jericho Hughes (1965) offers the following means: male, 170 cm, female, 154 cm.[36] Baker suggests that the average height of the early Egyptians was 'a few inches over five feet' (1966, 21), or approximately 157 cm. For the present, the 1985 projected means of 178 cm (male) and 163 (female) may be used (Webb Associates 1978), although these may be on the high side. The picture that emerges is that the Egyptian bed types 2 and 3 tended to be approximately 10% longer than the average male height. On the other hand, the Egyptian type 1 bed and the Jericho bed were somewhat shorter than that average. In the case of the Jericho bed and the Egyptian beds (note the range), it may be that the beds, like some of the Iron II tombs, were cut to fit.

Table 3.5
Comparative bed dimensions (averages)

Group	length	width	l/w
Egyptian beds-1	95 cm	70 cm	1.2 : 1
Egyptian beds-2	173 cm	39 cm	4.5 : 1
Egyptian beds-3	176 cm	80 cm	2.2 : 1
Mesopotamian models	—	—	1.6 : 1
Mesopotamian models	—	—	1.5 : 1
Palestinian MB bed	161 cm	45 cm	3.6 : 1
Iron II tombs—side	270 cm	100 cm	2.6 : 1
Iron II tombs—back	190 cm	100 cm	1.9 : 1
Modern cot	183 cm	61 cm	3.0 : 1
Modern twin	191 cm	99 cm	1.9 : 1
Modern full	191 cm	137 cm	1.4 : 1
Modern 'king'	203 cm	193 cm	1.1 : 1

The bed widths are more revealing. Egyptian types 1 and 3 fall between modern cot and twin widths. One could easily sleep in a variety of positions. But the narrow width of the Egyptian type 2 and the Palestinian Middle Bronze bed suggest a customary side position. Probably all of these were single-occupancy beds. Only with the Mesopotamian bed models is the length/width ratio suggestive of double occupancy.

As for positions assumed during sleep, the archaeological evidence is suggestive, but not decisive for Israelite practices. Articulated skeletons are found laid out on the back (Early Bronze, Jericho, tomb A 127), characteristically with knees raised in Middle Bronze II Jericho, but with limbs fully extended in the Iron Age, or the side

(Early Bronze, Ophel, tomb 2), sometimes in a crouched position (EB-MB, Jericho, Dagger-type; MB I, Jericho). For Egypt, evidence has not been encountered for the sleeping positions of those not using headrests. When a headrest was used, it placed strict limitations on the positions possible, although, as will be seen, precisely how it was used has been a matter of debate. On the literary side, a possible indication of sleeping position is provided in the Pyramid Texts (Faulkner 1969, 135):

> The Great One falls upon his side, He who is in Nedrt quivers, his head is lifted by Rēʿ . . . (Utterance 412).

This would correspond to the design of the type 2 beds: probably only the side position would be possible.

On the Mesopotamian side, various positions—along with other sorts of sleep-related behavior—were incorporated into omen texts, traceable back to the Old Babylonian period, and later incorporated into *Šumma ālu ina melê šakin* (Köcher and Oppenheim 1957, 67):

> The first omens refer to the position of the sleeper (right and left side, on his back, on his belly, contorted like a praying person, arms folded over the belly or above the head), the balance mostly of noises produced by the sleeping person (snoring, laughing, grinding his teeth, speaking, moaning, etc.), with the exception of the last omen: 'if saliva(?) (IM) constantly comes out of his mouth: he will have an evil demon'. The next four omens deal with pronouncing good or evil words in one's sleep, whereupon the text turns to the eyes and derives predictions from the fact that the eyes or one eye of the sleeping person remains open (1957, 68).

The following are examples of protases (1957, 64):

> i.33 [If a ma]n's bed throws him off repeatedly:
> i.39 [If a man] laughs in his sleep:
> i.41 [If a man] grinds his teeth in his sleep:
> i.43 [If a man] cries [in] his [sle]ep:
> ii.1 If a man speaks in his sleep (VAT 7525).

But by the nature of the evidence all possible positions, rather than characteristic positions arebeing recorded. And on the basis of later portions of this text the authors are able to argue for a reconstruction of *Šumma ālu* such that 'omens derived from sleeping habits, etc., are followed by those which base predictions upon happenings occurring when awakening, when leaving the house, and eventually upon encounters in the street' (1957, 69). The lack of omens concerned with the events between awakening and leaving the house are striking—if distant—confirmation of the impression gained from the Biblical Hebrew associative fields that the morning toilet was indeed unremarkable.

3. *Bedding*

The most familiar references to bedding occur in the pledge law preserved in Exodus 22.25-26 and Deuteronomy 24.12-13. The outer garment (*kswt*) pledged by the debtor is to be returned at nightfall.[37] The *kswt* is mentioned as something to sleep in also in Job 24.7, and perhaps also in 31.19. In both cases those involved are outside.

The *kswt* also appears in the unmotivated law in Deuteronomy 22.12: 'You shall make yourself tassels on the four corners of your cloak with which you cover yourself'. Von Rad takes the explanation offered for the law in Numbers 15.37-41 to be secondary, believing the practice to be originally a part of 'a magical apotropaic custom' (1966, 141), although he does not offer a guess as to what sort of practice was involved. While neither the noun (*kswt*) nor the verb (*ksh*) limit the context to sleep, and while the (re)interpretation of the practice in Numbers appears to move in a different direction, the use of *kswt* elsewhere in connection with sleep and the concern evident elsewhere with the *pḥd lylh* may be the proper context for interpreting this custom. On the other hand, Milgrom (1983) has suggested that the innovative element in the command was the inclusion of a cord of blue (Num 15.38), an exception to the general command not to wear mingled stuff (as did the priests), thus making the tassel a powerful reminder.

Michal, helping David escape from her father, 'took an image and laid it on the bed and put a pillow of goats' hair at its head, and covered it with the clothes' (1 Sam 19.13). Michal spreads a *bgd* over the image. The lack of a precisely corresponding English term makes translation difficult at this point. RSV's 'clothes' implies that she used something someone wore at other times; NAB's 'spread' implies that she used something which stayed with the bed. Elsewhere *bgd*—a quite common word—occurs where it might be construed as bedding only in 1 Kgs 1.1 ('Now King David was old and advanced in years; and although they covered him with clothes, he could not get warm'). The limitation of this use of *bgd* to the court suggests that 'spread'—together with its implications—may be the more appropriate translation.

More troublesome is the reference to the *kbyr h'zym* which occurs only here. While McCarter (1980, 326) is not necessarily correct in suggesting that here it 'probably serves as a wig, and may be a woven piece of material or simply an intertwined tangle of goats' hair', he is probably correct in thinking that its function is to obscure the head of the image and/or look like David's hair, rather than serving as a pillow underneath the image's head. Thus we do not have here an example of the use of a pillow. Others have taken *kbyr* to be a mosquito net; recently, Fohrer (1962, 236). Fischer (1977, 768) may be consulted for mosquito nets in Egypt.[38] However, that pillows were used is suggested by the Iron Age tombs reported by Dever (1969), Ussishkin (1970), Barkey and Kloner (1976), and Mazar (1976).

In sum, the evidence from the Old Testament on bedding is quite limited. Comparative materials have not been employed here, although two Egyptian items may be noted in passing. That the norm was to sleep with the head covered is suggested by references to the practice in 'The short hymn to the Aten' and 'The great hymn to the Aten' (Lichtheim 1976, 91, 97).

The classic Egyptian piece of bedding is the headrest. Because of its intrinsic interest and because it appears later in this study (§5.d), attention is given it here. The first example discussed by Baker comes from the bed of Queen Hetepheres (Fourth Dynasty):

> the Egyptians slept with their feet towards the bed panel, their heads resting on rigid head-rests set at the other end. It is easy to understand why women in countries like Japan might wish to protect their elaborate head-dresses by using head-rests, but it is difficult to understand why the Egyptians, who shaved their heads, should adopt such an apparently uncomfortable habit. Yet a head-rest, carefully cut to fit a particular head, might, in spite of the intractability of the material, offer more comfort on a hot, sticky night than a pillow of soft, clinging down. A head-rest might, furthermore, be cushioned in some way, like one in the Metropolitan Museum where the hard upper surface has been softened with linen bandages. The usual design of head-rests consisted of a curved upper section supported by a column, ordinarily plain, but occasionally fluted, and sometimes very elaborate, resting on a base. Although those in daily use were ordinarily made of wood, more formal ones were made of alabaster or other stone, and those made for royalty were even covered with precious metals, as was that found in the tomb of Queen Hetepheres (1966, 45).

A similar understanding is reflected in Fischer (1979). But precise details of the headrest's use are more difficult to specify, as exampled by the following two suggestions. In both cases, the assumption is being made that the use of the headrest was uniform.

> we find that a wooden head-rest was used as a pillow at all periods. This was pushed under the neck so that the head hung free over the cushions; the artificial wig of the sleeper thus remained uninjured, this being the sole *raison d'être* of this uncomfortable object (Erman 1894, 185).

Erman has a lengthy discussion of wigs used by both men and women (1894, 218-25). And the assumption is here that people would have slept with their wigs on, which is easier to imagine for midday sleep than for nocturnal sleep. On the other hand, Petrie:

> It is not to rest the neck upon, in order to leave the hair untouched; such a position would produce an impossible strain. It is entirely to take the weight of the head, being placed immediately above the ear, under the centre of gravity of the head. The edge of the top curve is always made thin, in order to pass between the top lobe of the ear and the head as the support is needed as near the ear as possible. This quite precludes the idea of any pillow or softening being placed over the support, nor is any such cover needed (Petrie 1927, 33).

4. *Proximity*

The anthropological parallels cited earlier would suggest that families slept in the same general area, particular sleeping areas being defined at most by mattresses or blankets. Callaway is probably correct: 'Privacy? Sooner or later everyone knew what everyone else did at night as well as by day' (1983, 45).

For those who could afford beds, the parallels from Egypt and Mesopotamia illustrate the possibilities of beds designed to sleep one or more people, respectively. The type 2 Egyptian beds with a 4.5 : 1 length/width ratio would only with difficulty accommodate two people, while the Mesopotamian models with their 1.5: 1 or 1.6 : 1 ratios closely approximate the modern full size ratio of 1.4 : 1.

The proverb in Ecclesiastes 4.11 assumes that two people might sleep together. The story of the two prostitutes implies that in at least some situations mothers slept with their babies (1 Kgs 3; cf. Lk 11.7, picturing father and children in bed). Moving to the court, the appearance of the *ḥdr mškb* implies separate sleeping quarters. And this is taken one step further: separate houses for Pharaoh's daughter and Ahasuerus's wives (1 Kgs 7.8 and Esth 2.9,11, cited in Dalman [1928-42] 1964, 7.79).[39]

5. *Time for Sleep*

Here the information on normal habits is quite scanty. The narratives in 2 Samuel 11 and 17 assume afternoon naps, which in the Mediterranean can be lengthy.[40] Proverbs commends the wife who rises before dawn (31.15), and Proverbs 27.14 is able to appeal to the common experience of having one's neighbor noisily about before oneself (which gives no information about absolute rising times). Nevertheless, the general picture from the constant exhortations against sloth in Proverbs suggests early rising as a value.

The evidence in the Old Testament becomes more plentiful when it is a question of breaking off or foregoing sleep for activity which is either explicitly cultic or which is drawn up into one's private devotions. All of this will be treated in the next section.

Here the comparative material appears to move along the same lines as the Old Testament, and until more information becomes available, may be used for provisionally filling out the picture. Montet summarizes the patterns in Egypt:

> The evenings did not last long, for, except for priests and guards on night duty, Egyptians rose with the sun and were early abed. In narrating the attempt at his assassination which taught him the ingratitude of mankind King Amenemmes I tells us that after eating *mesyt* or the evening meal he had relaxed for an hour after dark and had then gone to bed where, overcome with fatigue, he had quickly fallen asleep. We may conclude that after supper Egyptians spent an hour or more chatting over a smoky lamp and that silence reigned thereafter (1958, 91).

Kees (1933, 67) discusses the normal times for meals: breakfast at sunrise, a meal after noon, and an evening meal in twilight.

'The great hymn to the Aten' from El-Amarna gives a particularly clear picture of life lived by the rhythms of the sun (Lichtheim 1976, 97-99):

> Earth brightens when you dawn in lightland,
> When you shine as Aten of daytime;
> As you dispel the dark,

As you cast your rays,
The Two Lands are in festivity.
Awake they stand on their feet,
You have roused them;
. . .
<Those on> earth come from your hand as you made them,
When you have dawned they live,
When you set they die;
You yourself are lifetime, one lives by you.
All eyes are on <your> beauty until you set,
All labor ceases when you rest in the west;
When you rise you stir [everyone] for the King.

In rabbinic tradition appropriate times for sleep are ultimately governed by the set times for reciting the Shema. The subject is taken up by Rabbi Nathan (Goldin 1955, 97):

> Rabbi Dosa ben Harkinas says: *Morning sleep, midday wine, children's prattle, and sitting in the gathering places of the 'am ha'areṣ put a man out of the world.*
>
> Morning sleep: what is that? This teaches that a man should not plan to sleep until the time of reciting the Shema has passed. For when a man sleeps until the time for reciting the Shema has passed, he thereby neglects the study of Torah, as it is said, 'The sluggard saith: There is a lion in the way; yea, a lion is in the streets. The door is turning upon its hinges, and the sluggard is still upon his bed' (Prov 26.13f.) (*'Abot de Rabbi Nathan* 21.1).

An insight into evening activity patterns is provided by this citation (Goldin 1955, 26):

> When a man returns from his work, let him not say, I will eat a bit and drink a bit and nap awhile and afterward I shall recite the Shema; for he will sleep through the night and not recite the Shema. Instead, when a man returns from his work in the evening, let him go to the synagogue or to the study house. If he is accustomed to study Scripture, let him study Scripture; if he is accustomed to study Mishnah, let him study Mishnah; and if not, let him (at least) recite the Shema and pray (*'Abot de Rabbi Nathan* 2).

Turning to the classical world, Oepke writes: 'Both the Greeks and Romans were early risers. They went to sleep at sundown, but woke up with the first crow of the cock. In late autumn and winter this gave some hours to sunrise, 3 to 4 in Rome. These so-called lucubrations . . . are the main period of intellectual activity' (1965, 431). In short, both in the Old Testament and the comparative material surveyed, the picture is one of sleeping patterns closely connected to the sun's activity: one sleeps when it is too dark or too hot.

6. *Nocturnal Activity*

In Chapter 2, one of the activity fields identified was 'nocturnal activity', a somewhat heterogeneous collection of texts, some speaking of breaking off sleep to praise YHWH, others speaking of a variety of activities taking place in bed (meditating, planning, etc.). Here the question is what sort of information these give about cultural patterns related to sleep.

The petition psalms sometimes mention nocturnal activity:

> My soul yearns for thee in the night,
> my spirit within me earnestly seeks thee (Isa 26.9a).

> I am weary with my moaning;
> every night I flood my bed with tears;
> I drench my couch with my weeping.
> My eye wastes away because of grief,
> it grows weak because of all my foes (Ps 6.7-8).

> I think of God, and I moan;
> I meditate, and my spirit faints. Selah.
> Thou dost hold my eyelids from closing;
> I am so troubled that I cannot speak.
> I consider the days of old,
> I remember the years long ago.
> I commune with my heart in the night;
> I meditate and search my spirit (Ps 77.4-7).

What is the function of these references? Gunkel and Begrich still provide the most convincing answer:

> In the complaint what oppresses and torments the prayer's heart flows without restraint . . . What oppresses and torments him does not leave him alone. His sorrow pursues him in the night and in sleep and grants him no rest (1933, 215; tm).

The experience of worry or anxiety affecting one's sleep is per se hardly a pattern specific to Israelite culture. The treatment of the theme does, however, have a particular shape. It is not said explicitly that sleep is lost (contrast Jacob's explicit reference to loss of sleep in his argument with Laban). But the descriptions make clear that the problem facing the speaker has disrupted the normal pattern of waking and sleeping.

A form-critical observation is in order. In the previous examples, the description of disrupted sleep formed part of the complaint. But Psalm 77.6, 'I consider the days of old, / I remember the years long ago', indicates that the narration of events disrupting sleep could move in a different direction. And in fact this occurs in Psalm 63.6-8:

> My soul is feasted as with marrow and fat,
>   and my mouth praises thee with joyful lips,
> when I think of thee upon my bed,
>   and meditate on thee in the watches of the night;
> for thou hast been my help,
>   and in the shadow of thy wings I sing for joy.

Here the description of sleeplessness functions as part of the expression of trust, and this forms an appropriate transition to the next group.

A second group contains references to breaking off sleep for prayer. While the first example seems limited to rising before dawn (in anticipation of the morning offering?), the others speak of rising during the course of the night.

> My heart is steadfast, O God,
>   my heart is steadfast!
> I will sing and make melody!
>   Awake, my soul!
> Awake, O harp and lyre!
>   I will awake the dawn! (Ps 57.8-9 = 108.2-3).

> At midnight I rise to praise thee,
>   because of thy righteous ordinances (Ps 119.62).

> I will rise before dawn and cry for help;
>   I hope in thy words.
> My eyes are awake before the watches of the night,
>   that I may meditate upon thy promise (Ps 119.147-48).

> Arise, cry out in the night,
>   at the beginning of the watches!
> Pour out your heart like water
>   before the presence of the Lord! (Lam 2.19a).

Beyond this, evidence for night prayer (whatever its life setting) is sparse. Psalm 134 is explicitly a night psalm, and there are references to night prayer in conjunction with feasts in Isa 30.29, Josephus (*Contra Apion* 1.22), and the Mishnah (cited in the next chapter).[41]

A third group, composed of Hosea 7.14 and Psalm 149.5, is quite problematic:[42]

> They do not cry to me from the heart,
> but they wail upon their beds (*mškbwtm*);
> for grain and wine they gash themselves,
> they rebel against me.
>
> Let the faithful exult in glory;
> let them sing for joy on their couches (*mškbtwtm*).

In the first case the activity is probably being condemned.[43] The difficulty of specifying more precisely what is going on is a reflex of the general problem of describing Hosea's situation. One sort of solution is represented by Wolff (1974b, 128): 'they howl lustily . . . from their adulterous beds during their rites of fertility', and this fits well with the use of beds described in Isaiah 57.5-11.

Psalm 149.5 is more difficult. The references to the 'assembly of the faithful' (*qhl ḥsydym*) in v. 1 and to 'dancing' and 'making melody' (*bmḥwl btp mknwr yzmrw-lw*) suggest a public celebration. Thus it seems mistaken to take this verse as another example of the thesis that 'the bedroom was a proper place for the expression of emotions most deeply felt' (Dahood 1970, 357).[44] While there does not appear to be enough data to firmly establish the setting envisioned in the psalm (compare Kraus's discussion [1978, 1145-46]), the language is perhaps compatible with either a picture of a banquet or of a cultic gathering in Jerusalem.

Here a variety of groups of texts have been identified, which reflect different ways in which activities with a more or less explicit religious dimension took priority over sleep. In the case of the first group the experience of circumstances robbing sleep is familiar. In the case of the second group, rising for prayer, there are analogies in our culture, due largely to the continuing influence of texts such as these. But in the case of the third group, the particular practice or practices involved are considerably harder to pin down.

7. *Summary*

This chapter has been concerned to delineate with as much clarity as possible the particular spatial and temporal dimensions of sleeping patterns in Iron Age Israel. Beginning with the question of where people slept, the preponderance of Old Testament references to the roof was noted, and this correlated well with the limited evidence for the use of the 'four-room' house. The following picture appears probable, allowing for regional variation. The ground floor would be used for stalls, storage, and cooking. During summer sleeping on the roof, being desirable, would probably be widespread, although guests would complicate the picture somewhat. During winter the roof could also be desirable, particularly if partially enclosed. During particularly cold periods the area around the oven might also be utilized. Differences in needs, resources, and population density would all influence the actual practice.

The evidence for beds or bedding is quite limited. Lexically, no hard distinctions can be drawn between the use of *mṭh*, *mškb* and *'rś*. *mškb* shows a particularly wide range of denotation, from simply a place to sleep (2 Sam 11.13) to bedding (mattresses? blankets? 2 Sam 17.28) to a bed fit for a king (1 Kgs 1.47). The variation of denotation for *mṭh* and (even more so) *'rś* is perhaps narrower, increasingly concentrated on the upper end of the scale. In other words, for *mškb* and probably for *mṭh*, the functional nature of the etymology appears to be matched by a pragmatic approach: anything one could sleep on could be called a *mškb*. As one's sleeping place became more substantial, different words (particularly *'rś*?) might be used.

Bed models from a number of sites in Israel do not permit firm conclusions regarding the distribution of bed styles. Use of these models in addressing the question of how widespread the use of beds is hampered by, *inter alia*, lack of consensus on the use of these models.

Evidence from Egypt and Mesopotamia makes a number of contributions to our understanding of the Israelite material. The textual evidence cited for Egypt attests a correspondingly wide range of sleeping sites, and the beds from tombs give an indication of the workmanship and beauty which could be brought to this area of life. Further, the figures of protective gods and godesses stress in another way the dangers threatening also during sleep. On the Mesopotamian side, the failure of Salonen's study to suggest clear patterns in the use of different Akkadian terms for beds suggests that the problems encountered with the Hebrew material may not be specific to that language.

The contribution of the survey of Palestinian burial practices to the subject of beds per se is rather minimal. The variation in length in the ledges in the finer Iron II tombs, suggestive of measurement to fit, suggests that beds also may have been made to fit—at least lengthwise. On the other hand, the width of 100 cm, while normal for a bed by our standards (99 cm for a twin), is rather wider than the averages for the Egyptian bed types, and suggests that other factors may have been at work in determining this dimension.

Burial practices make a larger contribution to the question of sleeping positions, with numerous examples of bodies arranged on the back or side. Here too the ancient near eastern material is useful, the Mesopotamian material suggesting an extremely wide range of possibilities, the Egyptian material suggesting—in at least some cases—a regular side position.

Turning to bedding per se, a number of Old Testament references were noted. Here too the Iron II tombs make their contribution, for they suggest that pillows were normally used (at least in that stratum of society).

Regarding proximity of sleepers, one implication—and this is not a new observation—of the Israelite house discussion is that families probably slept in much closer proximity than is the practice in this culture. But again, the glimpses of court life in Samuel and Kings suggest that as wealth increased, so did the space between sleepers.

As for the temporal dimensions of sleep, the dominant picture—particularly from Egypt—is of a life governed by the movement of the sun. One rises with the sun, rests when the sun is at its strongest, and retires for the day with or soon after the sun's setting. But this pattern alone would consign too much of the day to sleep, and so modifications emerge. In the classical world these are attested in the form of lucubrations, the time after cockcrow, but before sunrise. In Israel, these are attested in the psalms which speak of rising during the night or early in the morning for prayer or meditation.

Chapter 4

ISRAELITE UNDERSTANDINGS OF SLEEP

Sleep is generally transparent, a part of experience to which little thought is given. But circumstances can bring it to our attention: sleep eludes us the night before an important meeting, we look with envy on those who get by on less sleep than we need, a friend tells us of a dream which oddly correlates with later events. Or we may notice that some animals have quite different sleep requirements and others do not appear to sleep in any recognizable sense, or notice that sleepwalking, hypnosis, and some drugs make it difficult to apply some tests for distinguishing sleeping and waking.

Sleep research is still in its early stages. The discovery that some sleep is characterized by rapid movement of the eyes (REM) was only made in 1953.[1] This was a useful discovery, because other phenomena could be correlated with the presence or absence of rapid eye movement. Dreams were only reported during REM periods, while sleeptalking and sleepwalking occurred only during non-REM (NREM) periods. In addition to these behavioral correlates, different brain wave readings were recorded on an electroencephalograph during REM and NREM sleep. Thus sleep contains periods of REM and NREM sleep, periods which in fact alternate or cycle a number of times during the night. This description can be considerably elaborated, for by use of electroencephalograph readings four different NREM states can be distinguished. Further, the shape of the cycles changes during the course of sleep, and is markedly different depending on the age of the sleeper.

But enough questions remain unanswered for there to be but a slim basis for giving definite answers to the questions of the causes or functions of sleep. Widely different proposals are made as to the causes of sleep, and while some argue for particular functions for both REM and NREM sleep, others think of sleep as the default state, so to speak, and thus functionless.[2]

What were the Israelite understandings of sleep? Most of the evidence relevant to this question appears in the various contexts in which sleep becomes a topic. However, this evidence is often of a rather fragile kind, and can be easily overlooked. As an entry into the various aspects of the Israelite understandings of sleep, we will survey a number of contexts: ancient near eastern, rabbinic, and classical. Because both primary and secondary materials have been employed in these surveys, the goal has been for them to be representative rather than complete. Thus they can be used not simply to indicate the presence or absence of parallel material, but to indicate different sorts of responses to the same area of experience. Morenz (1973) has been particularly valuable for the Egyptian material. Jacobsen (1976) has been one entry into the Mesopotamian material, which in addition has been accessed lexically. The rabbinic traditions have been accessed in two ways: first, through the subject indices in Epstein (1948) and Freedman and Simon (1939),[3] second, through Preuss's *Biblisch-talmudische Medizin*. The latter is a gold mine of information, but Preuss in general does not attempt to distinguish between the real and the fool's gold. Some of the classical material has been treated by Ogle (1933), and Balz (1972) and Oepke (1965) have also been of help.

The classical literature is, of course, unique in that only here among the literatures surveyed is sleep spoken of as a god (cf. Jolles 1916). And both in classical literature and the New Testament 'sleep' is used for phenomena outside its range in the other literatures surveyed (e.g. the hymn in Eph 5.14).[4] Further, its use in situations of death in the New Testament would appear to be far more theologically conditioned than any uses in this situation in the Old Testament.

But classical literature and the New Testament are not alone in having their unique uses for 'sleep'. Thus in the 'Instruction of Amenemope' 'sleep' is used of wise silence (Lichtheim 1976, 150, 159):

> Don't start a quarrel with a hot-mouthed man,
> Nor needle him with words.
> Pause before a foe, bend before an attacker,
> Sleep (on it) before speaking (ch. 3).

Do not provoke your adversary,
So as to <make> him tell you his thoughts;
Do not leap to come before him,
When you do not see his doings.
First gain insight from his answer,
Then keep still and you'll succeed.
Leave it to him to empty his belly,
Know how to sleep, he'll be found out (ch. 22).

1. *Varieties of Sleep*

Here two topics are of interest: the quality of sleep, and gradations between light and heavy sleep.

a. *Egyptian literature*

Perhaps relevant here is an admonition from the 'Instruction of Amen-em-opet' (*ANET* 423):

If thou findest a large debt against a poor man,
Make it into three parts,
Forgive two, and let one stand.
Thou wilt find it like the ways of life;
Thou wilt lie down and sleep (soundly);
in the morning Thou wilt find it (again) like good news (ch. 13; 16.5-10).

That is, good sleep follows appropriate activity.

The effects of old age on sleep are registered in different ways. In the 'Instruction of Ptahhotep', there is the description (Lichtheim 1973, 62-3):

O king, my lord!
Age is here, old age arrived,
Feebleness came, weakness grows,
Childlike one sleeps all day.

On the other hand, in the tale 'The Magician Djedi', there is the description (Lichtheim 1973, 218):

Your condition is like that of one who lives above age—for old age is the time for death, enwrapping, and burial—one who sleeps till daytime free of illness, without a hacking cough.

b. *Mesopotamian literature*

There are a number of examples from Sumerian literature. Thus in the interpretation of Gudea's dream (Price 1927, 9):

> The large vessel that stood before thee,
> (on which was engraved) the *tibu* bird
> which shone brilliantly day and night;
> —(it means that) during the (re-)building of thy house to thee no good sound sleep shall come (Gudea Cyl A 6 9-11).

And one also speaks of a god having good sleep (Price 1927, 46-47):

> that to the couch of lapis lazuli, in his throne
> room, for a good sleep, he (Ningirsu) might
> go; that in the house of repose, his house of
> comfort, he might enter his chamber (Gudea Cyl B 9 8-11).

Gilgamesh complains (transliteration [hereafter 'translit.'] Thompson 1930; translation [hereafter 'trans.'] *ANET* 92):

> [*š*]*it-ta ṭa-ab-ta ul iš-bu-u pa-nu-u-a*
> [*e*]*-te-ziq ra-ma-ni ina da-la-bu: ši-ir-a-ni-ia nissâti um-tal-li*

> My face was not sated with sweet sleep,
> I fretted myself with wakefulness;
> I filled my joints with misery (Gil 10.5.28-29).

From the bilingual incantation series *Ti'u* comes the following chilling description (Thompson 1904, 86-87):[5]

> [*ṭi-'*]*-u ul-tu e-kur it-ta-ṣa-*[*a*]
> [*ul*]*-tu bît* ^{d}*Bêli it-ta-ṣa-a*
> *la-bar-tum pa-rit-tum:*
> *ul u-ša-aṣ-lal šit-ta ul uš-ṭa-a-bi*
> *mu-ru-uṣ mu-ši u ur-ra šu-u*:

> Headache from the underworld hath gone forth,
> issuing from the abode of Bel.
> A rushing hag-demon,
> granting no rest, nor giving kindly sleep.
> It is the sickness of night and day (*CT* 17 25.1-8).

When proper precautions are taken against evil spirits sweet sleep is possible (Thompson 1903, 196-97):[6]

> *ina mu-ši ma-šal ina šit-ti ṭa-ab-ti ina ma-a-a-lu*
> *ina ri-eš a-me-lu mut-tal-li-ka lu-u-ka-a-a-an.*

[By night (it is) a highway, a path,
And at dawn let him hold it in his hand.]
At midnight in a gentle sleep in bed
At the head of the wanderer let it stand (*CT* 16 45.152-54).

In all the examples cited the various descriptions of sleep have served as (attributive) adjectives rather than as predicates. In a number of cases there would appear to be no particular contrast established between good sleep and some other sort of sleep. Gilgamesh, for instance, is probably simply stating that he has not had enough sleep. To continue the question of contrast, no examples of adjectives used to indicate undesirable sleep were encountered, although the vocabulary to describe sleeplessness is not lacking (Speiser 1951 on *dalāpu*). In sum, while references to sweet or good sleep undoubtedly trade on the common experience of particularly good nights of sleep, in most of the cases the references appear to be largely formulaic, and may be appropriately compared to Homer's use of similar formulae (see below).

However, in an entry for the second day of the second month of a cultic calendar, 'good sleep' appears to be used euphemistically (Unger 1931, 268):

ina maialtum mûši ṭâbi ittanaialu šitta [*ṭâbta*]

[Nabû wird mit der Brautschaft bekleidet
mit dem Kleid der Anuschaft.
Aus Ezida tritt er hinaus zur Nachtzeit wie die Mondsichel,
wie der Mondgott Sin bei seinem Aufleuchten
erhellt er die Finsternis.
In Eḫuršaba geht er hinein, indem er leuchtend dahinzieht.
Er geht hinein vor die 'Herrin';
alles ist hergerichtet für die Brautschaft.
In Eḫuršaba macht er Helligkeit wie der Tag.]
Im Schlafraum der guten Nacht schlafen sie einen guten Schlaf (VAT 662.1.14-20).

c. *Rabbinic literature*

In some situations it was necessary to distinguish between different types of sleep. In the first example, there is a three-fold contrast between casual (*šynt 'r'y*), regular (*šynt qb'*), and deep (*rdm*) sleep:

Our Rabbis taught, Casual eating is permitted outside the *Sukkah*, but not casual sleeping. What is the reason?—R. Ashi said, We fear

> lest the person fall into a deep slumber. Abaye said to him, With reference, however, to that which has been taught, 'A man may indulge in casual sleep while wearing his *tefillin*, but not in regular sleep', why do we not fear lest he fall into a deep slumber?—R. Joseph the son of R. Ila'i said, [The latter refers to where] the person entrusts others [with the task of waking him from his] sleep (*b. Sukka* 26a).

There are, predictably, a variety of opinions recorded on the permissibility of the juxtaposition of *tefillin* and the various sorts of sleep. And this discussion in turn leads to the question of the definition of casual sleep: 'Rami b. Ezekiel taught, [Sleeping during the time] it takes to walk one hundred cubits'.

But the terminology for these different sorts of sleep is not fixed, as illustrated in the second example, which contrasts sleep (*yšn*) and dozing (*nwm*).

> It was taught: R. Joshua b. Ḥanania stated, When we used to rejoice at the place of the Water-Drawing, our eyes saw no sleep? . . . But it cannot be so! For did not R. Joḥanan rule, He who says, 'I take an oath not to sleep (*'yšn*) for three days' is to be flogged and he may sleep forthwith?—The fact is that what was meant was this: 'We did not enjoy a proper sleep', because they dozed on one another's shoulder (*l' ṭ'mnw ṭ'm šynh dhww mnmnmy 'ktp' dhddy*) (*b. Sukka* 53a).

And the question of defining more precisely this state is taken up in the following saying:

> *hyky dmy mtnmnm 'mr rb 'šy nym wl' nym tyr wl' tyr dqrw lyh w'ny wl' yd' 'ḥdwry sbr' wky mdkry lyh mdkr*
>
> What constitutes dozing?—R. Ashi replied: A sleep which is no sleep, a wakefulness which is no wakefulness, he answers when he is called, but cannot remember an argument; when, however, he is reminded of something he remembers it (*b. Taanit* 12a-b).

The characteristic concern is with different types of sleep, and this for the purpose of deciding cases of law. Thus all the examples are from the Talmud rather than the midrash. References to sweet sleep were not encountered.

d. *Classical literature*

Balz (1972, 545-46) notes the use of epithets like *glykos*, *nēdymos*, *hēdymos* for sleep in Homeric texts, thus

> You yourself must see to the cover and nimbly fasten
> a knot, so none may break in, while on your journey
> you rest in a pleasant sleep
> as you go your ways in the black ship (*Odyssey* 8.443-45).

'Sweet' appears to be simply a standard description of sleep, rather than a sort of sleep which occurs only under a certain set of conditions (e.g. ethical). Thus Athene gives sweet sleep both to Penelope (*Odyssey* 1.363-65; etc.) and to the suitors (*Odyssey* 2.395). As for the distinction between light and heavy sleep, Balz notes that it was used in the diagnosis of sickness (1972, 547).

e. *Old Testament*

The distinctions attested in the Talmud are of interest because of the discussion in Chapter 2 regarding the difference between *yšn* and *rdm*. There it was argued the the difference was not one of intensity, but that *rdm* was used for divinely caused sleep. The fact that in some of these cases the sleep induced was deep may well have been a factor in the subsequent semantic development of *rdm* so that in the first example it does appear to mark a difference in intensity.

In a poignant fashion the following example laments the lighter sleep that comes with age:

> *wsgrw dltym bšwq bšpl qwl hṭḥnh wyqwm lqwl hṣpwr wyšḥw kl-bnwt hšyr*
>
> and the doors on the street are shut; when the sound of the grinding is low, and one rises up at the voice of a bird, and all the daughters of song are brought low (Eccl 12.4).

The awareness that how much one plans to sleep and how much one in fact sleeps are not always the same (the basis for the rabbinic discussion of dozing in the Sukkah or when wearing *tefillin*) is evident in the proverb:

> *m'ṭ šnwt m'ṭ tnwmwt m'ṭ ḥbq ydym lškb*
> *wb'-kmhlk r'šk wmḥsrk k'yš mgn*
>
> A little sleep, a little slumber,
> a little folding of the hands to rest,
> and poverty will come upon you like a vagabond,
> and want like an armed man (Prov 6.10-11).

There are three references to sweet sleep: Jeremiah 31.26, Proverbs 3.24 (*'rb*), and Ecclesiastes 5.11 (*mtwq*). What sweet sleep is is taken as a given. But each text presents a different set of circumstances which produce sweet sleep: a hope-filled revelation(?) (Jeremiah), a life governed by wisdom (Proverbs), the status of being a laborer (Ecclesiastes):[7]

> *ʿl-zʾt hqyṣty wʾrʾh wšnty ʿrbh ly*
>
> Thereupon I awoke and looked, and my sleep was pleasant to me.
>
> *ʾm-tškb lʾ-tpḥd wškbt wʿrbh šntk*
>
> If you sit down, you will not be afraid;
> when you lie down, your sleep will be sweet.[8]
>
> *mtwqh šnt hʿbd ʾm-mʿṭ wʾm-hrbh yʾkl*
> *whśbʿ lʿšyr ʾynnw mnyḥ lw lyšwn*
>
> Sweet is the sleep of a laborer, whether he eats little or much;
> but the surfeit of the rich will not let him sleep.

The effect of the comparative material is to bring the Old Testament texts into somewhat sharper focus. Both Ecclesiastes and the Egyptian wisdom tradition register the effect of aging on sleep, although the particular observations made are different. There is a certain connection between the Biblical and post-Biblical use of *Rdm*.

But the primary impression is one of contrast. The rabbis are asking a different set of questions than the Old Testament, and so different demands are made on the language. Specifically, for legal purposes it becomes desirable to distinguish between different sorts of sleep, and so they made distinctions. Sweet sleep is often met in both the classical and Mesopotamian literatures, but characteristically for the sake of style rather than to make a point. On the other hand, when the Old Testament speaks of sweet sleep, it has a point to make.[9] That the point is not always clear is another matter.

2. *Physiological or Psychological Aspects*

Here we are interested in physiological explanations of sleep (shading off into magic) as well as observations on psychological states conducive or detrimental to sleep.

a. *Mesopotamian literature*

The following incident is narrated in 'The Tale of the Poor Man of Nippur' (Gurney 1956, 154-55):

ḫazannu šá ma-⌜na⌝-aḫ-⌜te?-šu?⌝ ra-ḫi šit-⌜tu⌝

[Gimil-Ninurta talked beside the Mayor for one night watch, (till)] the Mayor because of his weariness fell asleep.

Of course people fall asleep from weariness in many cultures. But not everywhere will this be narrated in so many words.

Worry and sleep are inversely related, as illustrated in an excerpt from an Old Babylonian letter (*CAD* '*salālu*'):

ina niziqtika muši'ātim ul a-ṣa-la-al

for worrying about you I cannot sleep at night (TCL 18 152.33).

Likewise in the 'Lamentation over the destruction of Ur' Ningal complains (*ANET* 457):

Because of its [affliction] in my nightly sleeping place,
in my nightly sleeping place verily there is no *peace* for me;
Nor, verily, *because of its affliction*, has the quiet of my
sleeping place, the quiet of my sleeping place been allowed me
(100-101).

A 'Prayer to Marduk' includes sleeplessness in a description of diseases which Marduk is asked to cure. Thus (Lambert 1959-60, 58, 59):

elî-šu ir-te-eḫ-ḫu-ú im-ṭu-ú ta-ni-ḫu

[They have continually poured upon him disease, malaria (?) . . .]
Sleeplessness, shrivelling and exhaustion.
[Consternation (?), panic, fright, scares
Are released at him, and have taken away his will] (125-28).

a-ḫu-uz qát-su pu-ṭur a-ra-an-šú
šu-us-si ṭi-' ù di-lip-ta e-li-šú

Take him by the hand, absolve him from his guilt.
Banish from him malaria (?) and sleeplessness (151-52).

Apparently incubation on the part of the priest was a part of the ritual (lines 111-12; Lambert 1959-60, 57). And, as noted in the previous section, spirits could be blamed for sleeplessness.

b. *Rabbinic literature*

Physiological observations regarding sleep include the following:

'śrh dbrym mšmšyn 't hnpš . . .whqybh lšynh . . .

Ten things serve the soul . . . the maw for sleep . . . (*Lev. R.* 4.4).

This understanding appears in an expanded form in the Talmud:

> *qybh yšnh 'p n'wr n'wr hyšn yšn hn'wr nmwq whwlk lw tn' 'm šnyhm yšnym 'w šnyhm n'wrym myd mt*
>
> [Our Rabbis taught: The kidneys prompt, the heart discerns, . . .] the maw brings sleep and the nose awakens. If the awakener sleeps or the sleeper rouses, a man pines away. A Tanna taught: If both induce sleep or both awaken, a man dies forthwith (*b. Berakot* 61a-b).

Preuss ([1923] 1978, 107) has noted the resemblance of this account to Aristotle's, for which see below.

More reflective of a magical understanding is the following excerpt from a discussion concerning what could be carried on the Sabbath.

> *Gemara. One may go out with a hargol's egg,* which is carried for ear-ache; *and with a fox's tooth*, which is worn on account of sleep: a living [fox's] for one who sleeps [too much], a dead [fox's] for him who cannot sleep (*b. Shabbat* 67a).

And Preuss ([1923] 1978, 145) notes that *Shabbat* 6.8b in the Jerusalem Talmud prohibits putting a Bible or phylacteries on a child to induce sleep.

c. *Classical literature*

Balz (1972, 546-47) provides a convenient summary of various scientific accounts of sleep in the classical period, including relaxing of bodily energy (Anaxagoras), loss of warmth (Empedocles), withdrawing of blood into blood-vessels (Alcmaion).

In light of the rabbinic material, Aristotle's account in *On sleep and waking* is of particular interest. In general terms, it runs as follows (compare Wijsenbeek-Wijler 1978, 170-201). Sleeping and waking are identified as contraries, and thus are states of the same subject (in the sense that 'off' and 'on' might be considered two states of the same light switch). More precisely, waking is an actuality, and sleeping its potentiality. The waking state requires the union of soul and body. For Aristotle, the actuality/potentiality relationship between waking and sleeping requires that sleeping also require that same union of soul and body. Hence any accounts of sleeping which would involve the soul leaving the body are by definition excluded.

Since both sleeping and waking are identified by the presence or absence of sensation or perception, the subject involved is not any particular sense organ, but the common sense organ, the heart. When the heart is warm, the person is awake; when it is cool, one is asleep.

There are a variety of causes for cooling; Aristotle's paradigm case is a good meal, for the normal cycle of waking and sleeping is taken to be driven by the body's nutritional needs. As digestion begins, the digested matter, being warm, rises in the blood to the head. And thus the feeling of heavy-headedness is accurate. But since the brain is cool, the matter is cooled, descends, and lowers the temperature of the heart, thus bringing on sleep. But there is still undigested food, so the body goes to work on this until it is digested. 'Awakening occurs when digestion is complete; when the heat . . . prevails, and the more corporeal is separated from the pure blood' (*On sleep and waking* §458a).

d. *Old Testament*

Preuss notes a physiological interpretation of Job 30.17 ('The night racks my bones, / and the pain that gnaws me [*w'rqy*] takes no rest'):

> As Rashi remarks, according to Dunasch ibn Labrat, the Arabs interpret the word *irk* to mean 'artery' (to the physicians it nevertheless refers to 'vein'); therefore the same meaning is presumed to apply here: 'my arteries pulsate so strongly that I cannot sleep' ([1923] 1978, 103-104).

The verb *'rq* occurs only here and in v. 3, which raises the question of whether there is some sort of word play occurring.[10]

The physiological or psychological observations in the Old Testament move in a rather different direction. Most of them are concerned with the effect of worry or anxiety on sleep, although it should be noted that there is no covering term corresponding to 'worry'. The first example is of interest because of its inversion of the lex talionis.

> *ky l' yšnw 'm-l' yr'w wmgzlh šntm 'm-l' ykšwlw*
>
> For they cannot sleep unless they have done wrong;
> they are robbed of sleep
> unless they have made some one stumble (Prov 4.16).

Micah 2.1 is perhaps also relevant here:

> *hwy ḥšby-'wn wp'ly r' 'l-mškbwtm*
> *b'wr hbqr y'śwh ky yš-l'l ydm*

Woe to those who devise wickedness
    and work evil upon their beds!
When the morning dawns, they perform it,
    because it is in the power of their hand.

Wolff comments: 'That they are not able to sleep because of evil thoughts belongs to the wisdom picture of the wicked (Ps 36.5a). They do not dream; they calculate. The greedy are not sluggards, but they are restless' (1980, 47; tm); and Rudolph (1975, 53) reads the passage similarly. But this text and Proverbs 4.16 may well move in different directions. While lack of sleep is common to both, in Proverbs it is presented as involuntary, while in Micah (and Ps 36.5) it would appear to be quite voluntary, a further sign of perversity: not only do they do evil during the day, but they lose sleep at night planning it out! In attempting to account for the different ways sleep comes into play in evaluative statements, one might place them on a continuum: the beloved of YHWH who sleep and are provided for (Ps 127.2), those who deprive themselves of sleep for 'good reason' (Ps 127.1; Eccl), those who lose sleep because they have not been successfully evil (Prov 4.16), and those who voluntarily lose sleep in order to plan for evil (Mic 2.1; Ps 36.5). But this continuum, while compatible, and perhaps explanatory, goes considerably beyond the degree of systematization present in the texts.

The next example is of interest in light of the classical and rabbinic discussions. In perhaps an overly romantic fashion, the sweet sleep of the working man—however much his stomach has to work with—is contrasted with the sleeplessness of the rich (Hebrew text cited above): 'Sweet is the sleep of a laborer, whether he eats little or much; but the surfeit of the rich will not let him sleep' (Eccl 5.11).

In the next two examples, the mention of sleep serves to exhibit the severity of the problem: even sleep is no haven.

> What has a man from all the toil and strain with which he toils beneath the sun? For all his days are full of pain, and his work is a vexation; even in the night his mind does not rest (*gm-blylh l'-škb lbw*). This also is vanity (Eccl 2.22-23).

> When I applied my mind to know wisdom, and to see the business that is done on earth, how neither day nor night one's eyes see sleep (*gm bywm wblylh šnh b'ynyw 'ynnw r'h*); then I saw all the work of God, that man cannot find out the work that is done under the sun. However much man may toil in seeking, he will not find it out; even though a wise man claims to know, he cannot find it out (Eccl 8.16-17).

There is a clear link here between these texts and the petition psalms which mention sleeplessness in the description of the situation from which the supplicant wishes to be rescued.

As noted, the pairing of sleep with the stomach is attested in both rabbinic and classical sources. But there is a second pairing, that between sleep and the eyes. It is characteristic of the Old Testament: 'Thus I was; by day the heat consumed me, and the cold by night, and my sleep fled from my eyes' (Gen 31.40). Note also Psalm 132.4; Job 27.19; Proverbs 6.4; 20.13; and Ecclesiastes 8.16. This usage is also attested in Akkadian, with Bezold offering '*ml*'... voll sein (Augen *ēnā*, von Schlaf *šetta*)'.[11] Homer also could speak of sleep in connection with the eyes, as seen in Aphrodite's request to Hypnos:[12]

> Sleep,
> lord over all mortal men and all gods, if ever
> before now you listened to word of mine, so now also
> do as I ask; and all my days I shall know gratitude.
> Put to sleep the shining eyes of Zeus under his brows
> as soon as I have lain beside him in love (*Iliad* 14.232-37).

It is perhaps not accidental that the sleep-eyes pairings occur in poetry and the sleep-stomach pairings in prose. The experience of drowsiness after a heavy meal is certainly enough of an experiential base for the sleep-stomach pairing, but it does not make good poetry. On the other hand, when the heaviness of the eyes is seen as causing sleep, a different sort of causality is in question. This move has not been characteristic of the literatures surveyed, but may reflect *Hypnos*'s methods, as it does the Sandman's (cf. Jolles 1916, 323).

To summarize, the literatures surveyed show a variety of psychological or physiological approaches to sleep and sleeplessness. As indicated, the association of sleep with the eyes is widespread, and appears to be characteristic of poetic texts. The association with the stomach is found in rabbinic and classical texts, but not earlier. Also relevant here is the association of reduced quality of sleep with old age in the Egyptian and Old Testament literatures. Magical approaches are evidenced in the Mesopotamian and rabbinic literatures, and, with a more thorough search, could probably be located in the classical corpus as well. The pairing of sleeplessness with worry, characteristic of the Old Testament, is also evidenced in the Mesopotamian material.

3. *Sleep and the Soul*

This section is devoted to the question of the activity of the soul *qua* center of consciousness detachable from the body in relationship to sleep.[13] In some of the material, it is self-evident that some such soul is assumed; in other material, it is precisely the presence of this assumption and the likelihood of its employment in relationship to understandings of sleep that is in question. We are not dealing here with a completely fixed item, for as Lewis observes, 'in many cultures man is considered to possess not one but several souls' (1971, 46). And the issue here is not the use of *npš* or its cognates, but the nature of the assumptions or beliefs about some localization of personality separable from the body.

a. *Ancient Near Eastern literature*

While there is evidence that in some circumstances notions of such souls were employed, there is little evidence that these notions were employed in interpreting the experience of sleep in general or dreaming in particular. For instance, in the Egyptian 'Tale of Two Brothers' (second millennium), Bata places his heart on a pine blossom for safe keeping.[14] On the Mesopotamian side, Oppenheim (1964, 199) has suggested that the four protective spirits (*ilu, lamassu, ištaru, šēdu*) are in fact to be understood as external souls, and Saggs (1974) has employed the notion in interpreting the *Maqlû* incantation series.

An exception to this pattern occurs in one of the Egyptian hymns to the sun in the fourth Chester Beatty papyrus, dated by Gardiner to the 19-20 Dynasties (ca 1250–1100 BC). The relevant lines read (Gardiner 1935, 34):

> HOW BEAUTIFUL IS THY SHINING FORTH in the horizon! We are in renewal of life. We have entered <into> the Nūn, and it hath renovated (a man even) as when he first was young. [The one] has been stripped off, the other put on. We praise the beauty of thy face. Search out the way, and lead <us upon?> it, that we may count (?) [every?] day (Papyrus 4, recto 11.8-10).

Gardiner glosses: 'The idea seems to be that the fortunes of man follow those of the sun, who enters the Nūn at night-time and is born afresh as a vigorous child in the morning'. And this interpretation is further developed by de Buck:

> Nun is the primeval ocean, the waters of chaos . . . He is the infinite

world from which the cosmos sprang forth and which still surrounds and supports this creation, the other world, the *Jenseits*. Therefore the dead are sometimes called the dwellers in Nun . . . In the evening the sun returns to Nun, in the morning he rises from Nun as in the beginning. The waters of Nun create the light. This creative power of Nun is well brought out by its use in the cult: there it is sometimes pictorially represented as liquid life, a stream of hieroglyphs of life. According to the texts it gives birth to the king, who is purified with it, like Re every day.

Our passage is a new and somewhat unexpected application of these ideas. Not only the sun and the dead king enter Nun and are reborn from him; the same holds true of the sleeper. During his sleep he dwells in the *Jenseits* (1939, 28).

b. *Rabbinic literature*

The question of the activity of the *rwḥ* 'spirit' or *nšmh* 'soul' during sleep comes up in a variety of contexts (trans. Friedlander 1965, 253):[15]

wmh šynt hlylh 'dm šwkb wyšn wrwḥw šwṭṭt bkl h'rṣ wmgdt lw bḥlwm kl dbr šyhyh šn'mr

And just as in the sleep of the night a man lies down and sleeps, and his spirit wanders over all the earth, and tells him in a dream whatever happens, as it is said, ['In a dream, in a vision of the night . . . then he openeth the ears of men' (Job xxxiii.15,16), likewise (with) the dead] (*Pirqe Rabbi Eliezer* 34).

Genesis Rabbah 14.9 contains an extended discussion of Job 34.14-15:

'm-yśym 'lyw lbw rwḥw wnšmtw 'lyw y'sp
ygw' kl-bśr yḥd w'dm 'l-'pr yšwb

If he should take back his spirit to himself,
  and gather to himself his breath,
all flesh would perish together,
  and man would return to dust.

Three opinions are presented in the midrash. R. Joshua b. R. Nehemiah and 'the Rabbis' interpret the passage on the assumption that the function of the *nšmh* is to warm the body:

nšmh mḥmmt 't hgwp. šl' yṣṭnn wymwt.

the soul (*neshamah*) warms the body so that it should not waste and die.

R. Bisni, R. Aḥa, and R. Joḥanan in R. Meir's name offer a different interpretation of the function of the *nšmh*:

> *hnšmh hzw mml't 't kl hgwp. wbš'h š'dm yšn. hy' 'wlh wšw'bt lw ḥyym mlm'ln.*
>
> The neshamah (soul) fills the body, and when man sleeps it ascends and draws life for him from above.

A third interpretation moves the discussion away from sleep, asserting that the *nšmh* 'repeatedly ascends'.

An interpretation of 'then proclaim peace to it' (Deut 20.10) moves in the same direction as the understanding of R. Bisni *et al.*:

> Come and see how great is the power of peace. Come and see: If a man has an enemy he is ever seeking to do him some [injury]. What does he do? He goes and invites a man greater than himself to injure that enemy. But with God it is not so. All the nations of the world provoke Him to anger, yet when they fall asleep their souls go up to Him [for safe keeping] (*whn yšnym wkl hnpšwt 'wlwt 'ṣlw*). Whence this? For it is said, 'In whose hand is the soul of every living thing' (Job xii,10). And yet in the morning He restores to every one his soul. Whence this? For it is said, 'He that giveth breath unto the people upon it' (Isa. xlii,5) (*Deut. R.* 5.15).

A different approach to the activity of the soul during sleep is provided in a discussion of Ecclesiastes 10.20:[16]

> *wb'l knpym ygyd dbr. 'mr rb 'byn bš'h šh'dm hzh yšn hgwp 'wmr lnšmh whnšmh lnpš whnpš lml'k whml'k lkrwb whkrwb lb'l knpym wb'l knpym ygyd dbr lpny my š'mr whyh h'wlm.*
>
> 'And that which hath wings shall tell the matter.' R. Abin expounded: When a man is asleep his body tells his spirit, the spirit tells the soul, the soul tells the angel, the angel tells the cherub, and the cherub tells him that 'hath wings' and he that 'hath wings' tells the matter—to whom? To Him at whose word the world came into existence (*Lev. R.* 32.2).

c. *Classical literature*

Juxtaposition of Plato and Aristotle is sufficient to illustrate the range of understandings relevant to the external soul. Wijsenbeek-Wijler (1978, 205) argues that *Phaedo* 60e4-7,64a4-6, *Phaedrus* 243e9-257b7, *Symposium* 220c1-d5 'seem to suggest that for Plato sleep and trance-like states consist in a temporary release of soul from the body so that it may have access to supernatural revelations of divine wisdom'. On the other hand, as indicated above, it would have made no sense within Aristotle's framework to have entertained that idea.

On the popular level, Nilsson discusses the external soul as a folk-tale motif ([1952] 1964, 54-55). And Balz notes 'Legend has it that the souls of many remarkable men could leave their bodies during life' (1972, 549 n26), citing Hermotimus of Clazomenai, Aristeas, and Epimenides of Crete. Nor are the travels of the soul always voluntary. There is at least one case cited by Clearchus of Soli of a magician who 'takes the soul of a sleeper out of his body and causes it to rove abroad'.

d. *Old Testament*

> *'sprm mḥwl yrbwn hqyṣty w'wdy 'mk*
>
> If I would count them, they are more than the sand.
> When I awake, I am still with thee (Ps 139.18).

Thomson, while arguing that the Old Testament texts as a whole move in a very different direction, suggests that this text may employ the notion of an external soul. 'The psalmist seems to be speaking of sleep, and on waking from sleep he finds that he is still with God; implying, tacitly at least, that during sleep he has been in the presence of God' (1955, 424).

There are two interconnected questions here. First, is this the most probable reading of Psalm 139.18b? Second, does the evidence for belief in external souls make Thomson's suggestion more or less likely?

Much of the evidence for belief in external souls in the Old Testament has been discussed by Lys, and there is no need to cover the same ground.

> The idea of a double animating the body and separable from it hardly appears. We have noted the rare texts containing the idea of an exterior soul (Elijah, Elisha, Ezekiel, Samuel at Endor . . .); what is astonishing is not that there are such texts, but that there are so few! (Lys 1959, 198).

In fact, Lys has doubts about Samuel's appearance at Endor. As Lys reads the text, it is Samuel himself rather than a *npš* which appears (1959, 138). The texts in the Elijah and Elisha cycles are taken as solid examples (1 Kgs 17.21-22; 2 Kgs 4.29, 32-37; 5.26). As for Ezekiel's accusation of women who hunt souls (13.17-23), while Lys points to the difficulty of distinguishing popular belief from Ezekiel's own belief, that some belief involving exterior souls is involved is affirmed (1959, 161-62).

In fact, with the exception of 2 Kgs 5.26, all of these texts are shaky evidence for belief in external souls.[17] But in addition to these texts cited by Lys, there are vision accounts (including 1 Kgs 22.17-23 and Jer 1.11-19), which, Wilson (1980, 144) recognizes, 'might have involved soul migration'. Common to all of these texts is that if external souls are moving around, it is through the agency of intermediaries. And this localization of evidence suggests that while some accounts of the activities of some intermediaries may have involved the notion of external souls, one cannot assume that in a different area (the sleep of people not identified as intermediaries) that notion would have been ready-to-hand for explanatory purposes.

Discussion of Psalm 139.18 may begin with Gunkel. Gunkel, rejecting both the suggestion that the psalmist had been engaged in nocturnal reflection ('sehr unschön') and the suggestion that the waking involved was a waking from death (the thought 'liegt ganz fern'),[18] followed Halévy in emending *hqyṣwty* to *hqṣwty* (from *qṣṣ*). In support, Gunkel cites two texts from Sirach:

> To none has he given power to proclaim his works;
> and who can search out his mighty deeds?
>
> When a man has finished, he is just beginning,
> and when he stops, he will be at a loss (18.4, 7).
>
> Though we speak much we cannot reach the end,
> and the sum of our words is: 'He is the all' (43.27).

Given these, the sense of the emended text would be that even if the psalmist could complete his description, YHWH would still be with him, i.e. he would still be staring infinity in the face. So Gunkel: 'Und wäre er zu Ende mit seiner Kraft, er würde sie noch lange nicht erschöpft haben' ([1929] 1968, 589). And this emendation is adopted by *BHS*, Kraus (1978, 1100), and Weiser (1962, 800). Dahood (1970, 284) retains the Masoretic text with an eschatological sense.

On closer examination, the emendation is less attractive. Of the two Sirach texts, only the second is preserved in the manuscripts collated by Smend (1906): *'wd k'lh wl' nswp / wqṣ dbr hw' hkl*. Note that a different word is employed than (hiphil) *qṣṣ*. In fact, *qṣṣ* does not appear in the hiphil in the MT, and where the sense assumed by Halévy *et al.* is desired, *klh* is employed (cf., conveniently, Young

1970, 298c). Since both the stem and usage of the emendation would be anomalous, it is preferable to stay with the Masoretic text.

Nor is Dahood's suggestion compelling. Dahood takes Psalm 139 as a 'psalm of innocence' and sees a contrast between the requests of vv. 18b and 19a: 'May I rise and my continuance be with you! / Oh that you, O God, would slay the wicked!' (1970, 284). But if, as Dahood thinks, the issue is the psalmist's present vindication, the psalmist's eschatological prospects are beside the point, nor do they really contrast with his non-eschatological desires for his foes.

While it would be desirable at this point to be able to state how v. 18b should be interpreted, it will have to suffice to offer two observations which place it vis-à-vis the subject under discussion: Israelite understandings of sleep. On the one hand, in light of the previous verses (7-16) which describe the various situations in which the psalmist has or could be in, the force of v. 18b could partially be 'so how much more am I with you when I simply wake up' without exhausting other interpretive options. If so, this verse would not give us information about understandings of sleep. On the other hand, if the psalm is a reflection of an experience of a cultic juridical procedure (see next chapter), then Thomson's suggestion is clearly excluded. That is, the model of God trying the heart of the sleeper and the model of the sleeper (via, say, the soul) being with God during sleep are two different models.

In sum, the Old Testament would appear to line up with the ancient near eastern and Aristotelian traditions over against the rabbinic, Platonic, and popular (Greek) traditions, the latter generally understanding sleep to involve the departure and varied acitivities of the soul.

4. *Sleep and death*

The use of sleep as a metaphor for death is common in our culture, and thus when we meet it in the Old Testament we are tempted to think that we are on familiar ground. As the following discussion will show, this is only partially correct. In addition to the metaphorical use there are two logically distinct non-metaphorical uses of sleep in relation to death. The metaphorical use is familiar, and trades on a variety of similarities between death and sleep. The first non-metaphorical use involves taking death to be a sort of sleep. This can, of course, be reversed, in which case sleep is taken to be a sort of death. The second use appears in answer to the question of what the dead spend their time doing: they sleep. Often there is not enough data to specify precisely which use is involved, but when possible this question will be addressed, as well as the question of the relation between the uses. Again, we start with comparative material.[19]

a. *Egyptian literature*

Morenz has brought together a number of Egyptian texts from the New Kingdom (16th Century) and later which reveal that juxtaposed with the elaborate preparations for the dead was deep skepticism regarding the effectiveness of these preparations. Two of these texts are relevant to the question of the relation between sleep and death (1973, 188). The first, from the period of the 22–23 Dynasties (950–730 BC), comes from Nebneteru, priest of Amon:

> The end of life is sorrow, [it] means the inadequacy of that which was with thee formerly, and emptiness in thy possessions, [it] means sitting in the hall of unconsciousness . . . at the dawn of a morning which does not come . . . , [it] means not knowing, [it] means sleeping when the sun is in the east, [it] means being thirsty at the side of beer.[20]

The second, from the end of the Ptolemaic period, comes from Taimhotep, wife of a priest:

> The West [i.e. the realm of the dead], that is the land of slumber, a heavy darkness, the dwelling-place of those who are there [euphemism for 'the dead']. Sleeping is their occupation. They do not awaken to see their brothers. They cannot behold their fathers and their mothers. Their hearts are deprived of their wives and their children.[21]

In fact, Morenz reminds us, this language reflects an association of sleep and death already suggested by Neolithic burials (1973, 191). Thus Brunton and Caton-Thompson (cited by Morenz) report regarding the excavation near Badari: 'The commonest attitude was a loose contraction . . . It was noticeable how all the attitudes were those which might be adopted for a comfortable sleep; and this idea was enhanced by the position of the dead, which was often raised owing to its being laid on the sloping side of the grave. There were no attitudes which could be called other than perfectly normal' (1928, 18-19).[22]

And the usage of 'sleep' in speaking of death in the written tradition is widespread. In the Pyramid Texts (5th Dynasty) this usage is encountered, both for the king (utterance 462),[23] but also for Osiris (Faulkner 1969, 231):

> Osiris was laid low by his brother Seth, but He who is in Nedit moves, his head is raised by Rēʿ; he detests sleep and hates inertness, so the King will not putrefy, he will not rot, this King will not be cursed by your anger, you gods (utterance 576).

In sum, the Egyptian material evidences both the metaphorical use and—probably—the notion that the dead are engaged in sleeping (Taimhotep). Here the middle terms between sleep and death are either the lack of activity or the common position of repose. The picture in the hymn to the sun of sleepers following the sun through the realm of the dead (cited above) would be an (apparently uncharacteristic) example of taking sleep as a sort of death.

b. *Mesopotamian literature*

Likewise in Mesopotamian literature one speaks of death in terms of sleep. Thus Gilgamesh complains to Shamash:[24]

> *iš-tu e-li ṣi-ri-im a-ta-al*(?)*-lu*(?) *ki da-li-im*
> *i-na li-ib-bu ir-ṣi-tim kak-ka-di*(?) *um-ma-du-u*
> *at-ti-il-lam-ma ka-lu ša-na-tim*
>
> After marching (and) roving over the steppe,
> Must I lay my head in the heart of the earth
> That I may sleep through all the years? (Gil 10.1.10-12).

And in the underworld both rest and its opposite are possible, again Gilgamesh provides an example:[25]

> *ša mu-ti sur* . . .   . . . [*t*]*a-mur* [*a-ta-mar*]
> *ina ma-a-a-al muši ṣa-lil-ma mê*^{meš} *za-ku-ti i-šat-ti*
> *ša ina ta-ḫa-zi di-e-ku ta-mur a-ta-ma*[*r*]
> *abî-šu u ummi-šu qaqqad-su na-šu-u*
> *u aššat-šu ina muḫ-ḫi-š*[*u*] . . .
> *ša ša-lam-ta-šu ina ṣêri na-da-at ta-mur a-ta-m*[*ar*]
> *e-dim-ma-šu i-na irṣitim*(*tim*) *ul ṣa-lil*
>
> 'Him [who died] a sud[den] death hast thou seen?' '[I have seen]:
> He lies upon the night couch and drinks pure water.'
> 'Him who was killed in battle hast thou seen?' 'I have seen:
> His father and his mother raise up his head, And his wife [weeps] over him.'

> 'Him whose corpse was cast out upon the steppe hast thou seen?' 'I have seen:
> His spirit finds no rest in the nether world' (Gil 12.147-52).

In Mesopotamian literature, the relationship between sleep and death is explored preeminently in the eleventh tablet of Gilgamesh. Gilgamesh has come to Utnapishtim seeking immortality; one of Utnapishtim's responses is to set Gilgamesh the following challenge:

> *ba-la-ṭa ša tu-ba-'-u tu-ut-ta-a at-ta*
> *ga-na e ta-at-til* VI *ur-ri u* VII *mu-ša-a-ti*
> *ki-ma aš-bu-ma ina bi-rit pu-ri-di-šu*
> *šit-tu ki-ma im-ba-ri i-nap-pu-uš eli-šu*
> *^{m}Uta-napištim ana ša-ši-ma izakkar(ar) ana mar-ḫi-ti-šu*
> *am-ri amela danna ša i-ri-šu ba-la-ṭa*
> *šit-tu ki-ma im-ba-ri i-nap-pu-uš eli-šu*

> 'Up, lie not down to sleep
> For six days and seven nights.'
> As he sits there on his haunches,
> Sleep fans him like the whirlwind.
> Utnapishtim says to her, to his spouse:
> 'Behold this hero who seeks life!
> Sleep fans him like a mist' (11.198-204).

Utnapishtim has his wife bake bread daily to provide evidence for the length of Gilgamesh's sleep. It is necessary, for when Utnapishtim wakes him on the seventh day:

> *^{d}Gilgameš a-na ša-šu-ma izakkara(ra) a-na ^{m}Uta-napištim ru-u-qi*
> *an ni-šit(?) šit-tum ir-ḫu-u e-li-ia*
> *ḫa-an-ṭiš tal-tap-tan-ni-ma ta-ad-di-kan-ni at-ta*

> Gilgamesh says to him, to Utnapishtim the Faraway:
> 'Scarcely had sleep surged over me,
> When straightway thou dost touch and rouse me!' (11.219-21).

But the evidence is convincing, and Gilgamesh can only respond

> *[^{d}Gil]gamiš ana ša-šu-ma izakkara(ra) a-na ^{m}Uta-napištim ru-u-qi*
> *. . .i-tip-pu-uš ^{m}Utu-napištim a-a-ka-ni lul-lik*
> *[libbi]^{meš}-ia uṣ-ṣab-bi-tum ik-ki-mu*
> *[ina] bît ma-a-a-li-ia a-šib mu-u-tum*
> *u a-šar [uznâ^{II}-ia lu-u]š-kun šu-u mu-tum-ma*

> Gilgamesh says to him, to Utnapishtim the Faraway:
> '[What then] shall I do, Utnapishtim, Whither shall I go,
> [Now] that the Bereaver has laid hold on my [members]?

In my bedchamber lurks death,
And wherever I se[t my foot], there is death' (11.229-33).

Interpreting this passage, Jacobsen writes, 'Gilgamesh accepts the challenge—a contest, it would seem, with Death's younger brother Sleep' (1976, 206). But the precise issue is brought into a different perspective by Eliade: 'What we have here is, undoubtedly, the most difficult of initiatory ordeals: conquering sleep, remaining "awake", is equivalent to a transmutation of the human condition' (1978, 79). Jacobsen is, in part, construing the story along classical lines. But Eliade's suggestion points in a different direction: the middle term between sleep and death is the inexorable quality of both. And Gilgamesh, having failed to hold off sleep, cannot hope to hold off death.

In terms, then, of the questions posed at the beginning of this section, the initial Gilgamesh quotation evidences the metaphorical use of sleep for death. The second quotation speaks of rest and unrest in the grave, which is not very far from speaking about the dead sleeping or not sleeping, but it is worth noting that this language is not used. Finally, in Utnapishtim's brutal lesson, sleep is seen, like death, to be inexorable.

c. *Ugaritic literature*

The use of 'sleep' as a way of speaking of death is also attested in Ugaritic. After the death of his son Danel utters a series of imprecations, one of which containing the use in question (Thomson 1955, 423; trans. *ANET* 154):

knp . nšrm (149) *bʿl . yṯbr.*
bʿl . yṯbr . dʾiy (150) *hmt.*
hm . tʿpn . ʿl . qbr . bny
(151) *tšḥṭann . bšnth .*

The wings of the vultures may Baal break,
    May Baal break the pinions of them,
As they fly over the grave of my son,
    Rousing him from his sleep (*CTA* 19.148-51).

d. *Rabbinic literature*

Sleep and death are related in at least two ways in the rabbinic literature. On the one hand, the Old Testament usage of the language of sleep for death was continued, and in texts such as Canticles 7.10, their reading tended to move in the direction of picturing the dead as engaged in sleep.

> *And the roof of thy mouth like the best wine.* R. Joḥanan said: At that moment the Holy One, blessed be He, called to all the ministering angels and said to them: 'Go down and kiss the lips of the ancestors of these men. For just as they braved the fire for My sake, so their sons have braved the fire for My sake.' R. 'Azariah said in the name of R. Judah b. R. Simon: At that moment the Holy One, blessed be He, called to the ministering angels and said to them: 'Go down and kiss the lips of these men; for had not these accepted My law and My kingship (at Sinai), I should have been brought into conflict with those who sleep in the cave of Machpelah' (*šhm yšnym bm'rt hmkplh*). *Moving gently the lips of those that are asleep.* R. Joḥanan b. Torta said: Even when one is dead, his lips quiver in the grave (*'p 'l py šmt šptwtyw rwḥšwt 'lyw bkbr*). How do we know? Because it says, *Moving gently the lips of those that are asleep* (*Cant. R.* 7.10).

This picture of the dead as engaged in sleep coexisted with other pictures and practices. The practice of feeding the dead was known, and at least one rabbinic tradition judged it acceptable (trans. Higger 1969, 58):

> *mmšykyn lpny ḥtnym wlpny klwt ṣynwrwt šl yyn wṣynwrwt šl šmn, w'yn ḥwššyn mšwm drky h'mwry, w'yn ḥwššyn mšwm 'ybwd 'wklyn*
>
> Pipes may be made to flow with wine and with oil before brides and grooms, without fear that this smacks of heathen practice, or that it is a squandering of food (*Ṣemaḥot* 8.4).

Nor, according to this midrash on Psalm 149.5, were the dead cut off from praise:

> R. Ḥiyya bar Jose taught: There is no difference between the righteous which are alive and the righteous who are dead except that the living have the power of speech. The dead, nevertheless, are able to sing praise to the Holy One, blessed be He, for he binds their souls in the bundle of life, as Abigal said . . . (1 Sam 25.29). And so 'Let them sing aloud upon their beds' clearly denotes a song of praise (*Midr. Ps* 30.3).

And that the soul does not sleep is argued on the basis of its likeness with the Creator (*Pirqe Rabbi Eliezer* 34).

Moving to a related issue, sleep could be taken as a sort of death:

šynh 'ḥd mššym lmyth

[Five things are a sixtieth part of something else: namely, fire, honey, Sabbath, sleep and a dream . . .] Sleep is one-sixtieth part of death (*b. Berakot* 57b).

rb ḥnyn' br yṣḥq 'mr g' nwblwt hn. nwblt myth šynh. nwblt nbw'h ḥlwm. nwblt h'wlm hb' šbt.

R. Hanina [or Hinena] b. Isaac said: there are three incomplete phenomena: the incomplete experience of death is sleep; an incomplete form of prophecy is the dream; the incomplete form of the next world is the Sabbath (*Gen. R.* 17.7).

The middle term between sleep and death is not defined in these passages, but, in light of the earlier material presented on the activities of the soul during sleep, the absence of the soul from the body during sleep may be this middle term. This is suggested by the following interpretation of Lamentations 3.23 in a discussion of Genesis 32.27:

It is written 'They are new every morning; great is thy faithfulness' (Lam 3,23). R. Simeon b. Abba interpreted this: Because Thou renewest us every morning, we know that great is Thy faithfulness to redeem us. R. Alexandri interpreted it: From the fact that thou renewest us every morning, we know that great is Thy faithfulness to resurrect the dead (*Gen. R.* 78.1).

The editors comment, 'Sleep is regarded as a minor death: God, by suffering us to awaken thus gives an earnest of the Resurrection'. In this connection Thomson cites a morning prayer, 'Blessed art thou O God who restorest the souls unto the dead bodies', and notes a similar tradition in the *Pirqe Rabbi Eliezer*.[26]

e. *Classical literature*

A convenient starting point is the question of the relationship between sleep and death. Plato's Socrates knows, but rejects, the idea that death is a sort of sleep (Oepke 1965, 433):

Death is one of two things. Either it is annihilation, and the dead have no consciousness of anything, or, as we are told, it is really a change . . . Now if there is no consciousness but only a dreamless sleep, death must be a marvelous gain (*Apology* 40 d/e).

Thus when Balz (1972, 548) characterizes the Greek philosophic tradition as emphasizing the closeness of sleep and death, it is in the direction of taking sleep as a form of death—not vice versa. His citation of Aristotle's statement is representative: '*hypnos* is the mean between *tou zēn kai tou nē zēn*' (*On the generation of animals* 5.1, p. 778b, 29f.). A propos here would also be physiological accounts of sleep in which it is 'a transitional stage to death' (Balz 1972, 547).

But the middle term between sleep and death was not always physiological. Vermeule suggests that in at least some cases the middle term might be stupidity:

> The Greeks disliked being stupid . . . The most familiar Greek virtue, *sophrosyne*, began as that quality of mind which would keep you safe and draw you back from the stupidity of the sleeping and the dead . . . After death, at least, most settle in their graves asleep, hard to rouse and generally inattentive, or seem penned more distantly in the underworld, sometimes irritable as sleepers are, and possibly dim witted (1979, 24).

In support, Vermeule notes Homer's decision to portray a sleeping Penelope, who must be awakened by her nurse:

> 'Wake, Penelope, dear child, so that, with your own eyes,
> you can see what all your days you have been longing for.
> Odysseus is here, he is in the house, though late in his coming;
> and he has killed the haughty suitors, who were afflicting
> his house, and using force on his son, and eating his property'
> (*Odyssey* 23.5-9).

But sleep can also be a point of access to knowledge, and thus Aeschylus (*Eumenides*, from Vermeule 1979, 121):

> The sleeping mind grows brilliant in its eyes,
> but in daylight the destiny of mortals cannot be foreseen.

A survey by Marbury Ogle (1933) includes a number of pre-Christian texts. And these are suggestive of other middle terms: deep, or inexorable sleep.

> Think how Promachos sleeps among you, beaten down under
> my spear, so that punishment for my brother may not go
> long unpaid (*Iliad* 14.482-84).

> They bent to their rowing, and with their oars tossed up the sea
> spray, and upon the eyes of Odysseus there fell a sleep, gentle,
> the sweetest kind of sleep with no awakening, most like
> death (*Odyssey* 13.78-81).

In other Homeric texts, Sleep and Death are identified as brothers, and these Ogle takes as the basis for Hesiod's description of the home of Night, located in Tartarus where Zeus has driven the Titan gods:

> And there the children of dark Night have their dwellings, Sleep and Death, awful gods. The glowing sun never looks upon them with his beams, neither as he goes up into heaven, nor as he comes down from heaven. And the former of them roams peacefully over the earth and the sea's broad back and is kindly to men; but the other has a heart of iron, and his spirit within him is pitiless as bronze: whomsoever of men he has once seized he holds fast: and he is hateful even to the deathless gods (*Theogony* 759-66).

How widespread was the use of sleep as a way of speaking of death? Ogle argues:

> The comparatively few references in pre-Hellenistic Greek literature and in Roman literature of the Republic to the sleep of death suggest the conclusion that the conception of death as a sleep is not a reflection of popular ideas but represents rather, as is surely the case with the Hellenistic epigram, a literary convention (1933, 84).

Ogle attributes the popularization of the association to foreign influences after Alexander, and finds this confirmed by Greek sepulchral art. In the archaic and classical periods:

> the figures of the dead which it represents are represented either as idealized types of heroes or of gods or as human beings still engaged in the activities of life whether those of joy or sorrow. During the Hellenistic period, however, a new motive is introduced into sepulchral art, that of the human figure stretched out at full length upon the cover of a sarcophagus as if sunk in a calm and dreamless sleep (1933, 87).

While Ogle does not speculate on the reasons for the non-appearance of the sleep of death usage, Balz's suggestion (1972, 549) should be noted: 'The infrequent use of the metaphor of the sleep of death in the earlier period is perhaps connected with the mythological distinction between *Hypnos* and *Thanatos* in popular religion.'

But this judgment would need to be corrected by Vermeule, who would sees the understanding of death as a sort of sleep as being widespread at an earlier period:

> the houses, *oikias* of the dead, and the *thalamos* or bedroom of the grave were early clichés in Greek . . . the Mycenaean chamber-tomb might even have an architecturally dressed or painted facade

> like a house, and inside the rock-cut chamber the family might provide simple benches, stone pillows, even blankets and tables (although these are all rare) to make a more pleasant setting for the big sleep (1979, 48).

There are, then, a variety of ways in which sleep and death are related. Death can be considered a sort of sleep (Bronze Age chamber tombs, Hellenistic sarcophagi). More characteristic of the philosophic/scientific traditions, sleep can be considered as a sort of death. Mythologically, the relationship is expressed with Hypnos and thanatos as brothers. And a variety of middle terms are evident: inexorability, inactivity, stupidity.

f. *Old Testament*

As the studies in Chapter 2 indicate, there is a significant lexical relationship between sleep and death. Of the different activity fields identified as sharing a common vocabulary with the human sleep field, the death field has both the largest number of words in common (*yṣw'*, *yqṣ*, *yšn*, *mṭh*, *mškb*, *nwm*, *'rś*, *rdm*, *škb*, *šnh*) as well as the largest number of occurrences of these words (relative to the other activity fields). That is, one talks not simply of death in terms of sleep,[27] but also of spreading out one's bed in Sheol (Ezek 32.25; Ps 139.8; Job 17.13; and perhaps Isa 57.2), and of rising from death in terms of waking up (2 Kgs 4.31 and elsewhere—cf. Appendix A, *yqṣ*). And while in one case (*'rś*, Deut 3.11bis) there appears to be a specialized (prose) term for a bed for the dead, in general one of the common words for 'bed' or 'couch' is employed (*mṭh* 2 Sam 3.31).

Chart 4.1
Selected death field collocations

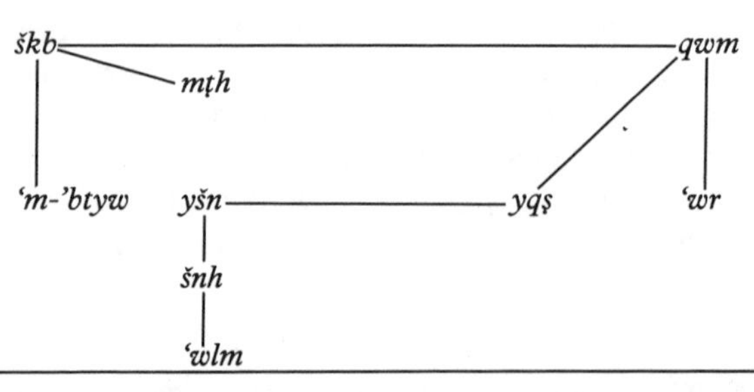

The lexical relationship between sleep and death extends to a similarity of collocational patterns. While there are fewer texts from which to derive these patterns, a mapping of the non-unique collocations of members of the human sleep field as used in the death field produces chart 4.1. For ease of presentation one phrase which does not appear in the human sleep field has been included: *'m-'btyw*. While most of the collocations are only minimally attested, that between *škb* and *'m-'btyw* is extensively used, although only in prose, and primarily in Kings and Chronicles.

The use of the expressions *škb 'm 'bwtyw* 'to sleep with the fathers' and *n'sp 'l-'myw* 'to be gathered to the fathers' has been well examined by Alfrink (1943, 1948).[28] Both are used quite selectively, and neither can be understood as referring to burial in a family tomb. Thus the former is used of Abraham, Moses, Aaron, David, and Manasseh (and Alfrink cites other examples as well) none of whom were buried in their family's tomb. What of Genesis 47.30? The RSV translates vv. 29b-30: 'and promise to deal loyally and truly with me. Do not bury me in Egypt, (30) but let me lie with my fathers; carry me out of Egypt and bury me in their burying place.' Alfrink objects to a similar French translation, and offers 'quand je serai couché avec mes pères (c.-à-d. quand je serai mort), vous me transporterez hors de l'Egypte' (1943, 107). But both translations assume an abnormal meaning for the *wāw*-consecutive (*wškbty*). Rather, 'and promise to deal loyally and truly with me: do not bury me in Egypt! I will lie with my fathers and you will carry me out of Egypt and bury me in their burying place.' Thus Alfrink's point, but not his translation, stands. As for *n'sp 'l-'myw* 'to be gathered to the fathers', it again is used for Abraham, Moses, and Aaron (1948, 129).

As Alfrink notes, Stade and many since have suggested a connection between these expressions and the family tombs known from excavations (1943, 106; 1948, 129-30). Eichrodt suggests this connection cautiously, not for the Old Testament, but for an earlier period:

> great importance is attached to being buried alongside the members of one's family . . . This, too, is the origin of the fairly common expressions 'to be gathered to one's fathers' and 'to go to or sleep with one's fathers' . . . To see one of the bench-type graves, which were the sort in most common use in ancient Israel, is to realize that such phrases are to be taken literally . . . the phraseology became generalized, and could be used in cases where there was no question of an ancestral grave, as with Abraham, Moses and Aaron (Eichrodt 1967, 2.213).

But, as Alfrink notes, this is simply to move into the realm of speculation.[29] What is worthy of note in regard to the expression *škb ʿm ʾbwtyw* in the Old Testament is not its prehistory but the particular restrictions governing its use. It is generally restricted to royal figures, and it is not used for kings who die a violent death. In other words, at the place where the lexical link between sleep and death is most prominent, that link is quite peripheral to the concerns governing the use of *škb ʿm ʾbwtyw*.

Turning to other collocations in chart 4.1, the most noticeable contrast between this chart and those previously generated for the sleep field is the relative balance here between the sleeping and waking sides (cf. charts 2.3, 2.4, 2.5). And this balance is suggestive both of a particular middle term between sleep and death, as well as the crucial difference. In the world we know, one awakes from sleep, but not from death. And thus the crucial difference is at the same time a peculiar sort of middle term, for the issue of waking can be raised for death as well as sleep. And thus when new, eschatological, possibilities are introduced, it is by a negation of this difference: the dead also will awaken. The following texts illustrate these relationships.

> *wtyšnhw ʿl-brkyh . . . wyqṣ mšntw wyʾmr ʾṣʾ kpʿm bpʿm wʾnʿr whwʾ lʾ ydʿ ky yhwh sr mʿlyw*
>
> She made him sleep upon her knees . . . And he awoke from his sleep, and said, 'I will go out as at other times, and shake myself free'. And he did not know that the Lord had left him (Judg 16.19-20).

> *ʾny škbty wʾyšnh hqyṣwty ky yhwh ysmkny*
>
> I lie down and sleep;
> I wake again, for the Lord sustains me (Ps 3.6).

> *whškrty śryh wḥkmyh pḥwtyh wsgnyh wgbwryh wyšnw šnt-ʿwlm wlʾ yqyṣw nʾm-hmlk yhwh ṣbʾwt šmw*
>
> I will make drunk her princes and her wise men,
> her governors, her commanders, and her warriors;
> they shall sleep a perpetual sleep and not wake,
> says the King, whose name is the Lord of Hosts (Jer 51.57).

> *wʾyš škb wlʾ-yqwm ʿd-blty šmym lʾ yqyṣw wlʾ-yʿrw mšntm*
>
> so man lies down and rises not again;

till the heavens are no more he will not awake,
or be roused out of his sleep (Job 14.12).

yḥyw mtyk nblty yqwmwn hqyṣw wrnnw škny ʿpr
ky ṭl ʾwrt ṭlk wʾrṣ rpʾym tpyl

Thy dead shall live, their bodies shall rise.
O dwellers in the dust, awake and sing for joy!
For thy dew is a dew of light,
and on the land of the shades thou wilt let it fall (Isa 26.19).

wrbym myšny ʾdmt-ʿpr yqyṣw
ʾlh lḥyy ʿwlm wʾlh lḥrpwt ldrʾwn ʿwlm

And many of those who sleep in the dust of the earth shall awake, some to everlasting life, and some to shame and everlasting contempt (Dan 12.2).

The relationship between beds and Sheol (e.g. *Yṣʿ* Isa 14.11; Job 17.13; *mškb* Isa 57.2; Ezek 32.25; 2 Chr 16.14; *škb* Job 21.26; cf. Holman 1970, 51, who also cites *UT* 51.8.7-9; Tromp 1969, 156-57), together with the Egyptian material raises the question of whether the dead were thought of as engaged in sleep. Murtonen makes this suggestion for the Old Testament:

> From Is xiv 9 sqq. we can, however, draw a conclusion concerning the normal condition among the dead. Since this parable describes the awakening of the dead as exceptional, the greater reason we have to suppose that normally they are thought to be in the state of unconsciousness or sleeping, as it usually is expressed (1958, 33).

Isaiah 38.18, Psalms 6.6, 88.11-13, and 115.17, all texts which deny that the dead praise YHWH, are cited as supporting evidence.

But taken alone, Isa 14.9-11 will not support this reading, although it is compatible with it. The particular verbs used, *rgz, ʿwr, qwm* communicate agitation in a general way.[30] The text would offer much stronger support for Murtonen's reading if *yqṣ* had been employed. The particular way in which the language of sleep and death interface in this text may be more clearly expressed in v. 11.[31]

hwrd šʾwl gʾwnk hmyt nblyk
tḥtyk yṣʿ rmh wmksyk twlʿh

Your pomp is brought down to Sheol,
the sound of your harps;

maggots are the bed beneath you,
and worms are your covering.

As for the other texts Murtonen cites, the lack of praise does not necessarily imply sleep, although it is compatible with it. Perhaps better candidates are a pair of texts from the book of Job. But even here we are probably well within the range of the metaphorical use:[32]

ky-ʿth škbty wʾšqwṭ yšnty ʾz ynwḥ ly

For then I should have lain down and been quiet;
I should have slept; then I should have been at rest (Job 3.13).

lʾ šlwty wlʾ šqṭty wlʾ-nḥty wybʾ rgz

I am not at ease, nor am I quiet;
I have no rest; but trouble comes (Job 3.26).

While there are thus certain continuities between speaking of death in terms of sleep and the grave, the discontinuities should not be overlooked. One has already been mentioned: Alfrink's demonstration that in the Old Testament the expressions *škb ʿm ʾbwtyw* 'to sleep with the fathers' and *nʾsp ʾl-ʿmyw* 'to be gathered to the fathers' are not directly employed of entombment. And a second one is equally significant: no evidence has been encountered that the variety of patterns of burial described by Abercrombie was related either to the beliefs about death or to the language used for it. Thus one could apparently talk about the dead as sleeping whether primary or secondary burials were involved, which brings to mind Dodds's observation that 'actual feeding-tubes are found even in cremation burials' (on the other side of the Mediterranean; 1951, 158 n8).

Before summarizing this section, a review of the comparative material is in order. The sleep/death juxtaposition is as much a symbol of differing ways in which sleep and death can be experienced as a symbol of their common elements. The inexorable quality of sleep which links it to death in Gilgamesh is quite foreign to the ways in which sleep and death interplay in the (Chester Beatty) hymn to the Sun. Again, the rabbinic speculation on the activity of the soul during sleep with its parallels to death and the Greek construal of sleep and death as states of stupidity further illustrate the many different experiences of sleep collected under an ostensively common metaphor. Again, differences were evident as to whether sleep was taken to be a sort of death (characteristic of the rabbinic literature) or vice versa (characteristic of later Greek sarcophagi). On the question of whether the dead could be thought of as engaged in sleep, while across the board there were examples of texts which could be interpreted in this way, perhaps the clearest case was the description of the underworld in the twelth tablet of Gilgamesh in which a contrast between the restful and the restless dead was drawn.

In the Old Testament there are two different sorts of ways in which sleep and death are related, and these, to some degree, run parallel to the choice between *yšn* and *škb*. Death could be spoken of in terms of sleep, a sleep from which one did not awake. And here the edge of the metaphor depended on the painful difference between the sleeping and the dead. But this usage in turn probably depended on a number of similarities (inactivity, body position) between sleep and death reflected lexically in the frequent use of *škb* for both. Thus the role of waking as a link and differentia between sleep and death is more pronounced here than in the other literatures surveyed. On the other hand, the similarities between sleep and death, perhaps most noticeably inertness and body position, reflected in *škb*, find parallels in these literatures. And this emerges not simply or even primarily on the literary level, but in the disposition of the dead in positions of sleep (Egypt, the Greek world, Palestine).

But this particular placement of death vis à vis sleep would not be expected to generate all the other ways of speaking of death in terms of sleep attested in the comparative material. Thus sleep is not spoken of as a sort of death. Nor, once the similarity of sleep and death are developed, is there any real push to explore the further question of whether the dead spent their time sleeping, although there are texts which were perhaps heard in this way.

5. *The Valuation of sleep*

> Even preschoolers may attend [afternoon cram schools]. 'Sleep four hours, pass', goes a plaintive Japanese saying. 'Sleep five hours, fail' (McGrath 1983, 66).

a. *Ancient Near East*

There is little material which has been identified as specifically relevant to this question. Nevertheless, the various Egyptian hymns to the Sun (in particular that from El Amarnah, cited above, ch. 3 §5), convey a strong sense of sleep as a natural part of the rhythms of life.

There is a fitting parallel to David's oath not to sleep (Ps 132.3-4) adduced by Bauer *et al.* in a lexical discussion of *dalāpu*: *lā addalipi* '(ich schwöre:) ich schlafe nicht, (um die Arbeit zu beenden)' (1933, 221).

b. *Rabbinic literature*

Given the importance of regular prayer (see ch. 3 §5), excessive sleep is condemned (text Schechter 1967, trans. Preuss [1923] 1978, 571):[33]

> *šynh šl šḥryt wyyn šl ṣhrym wšyḥt hyldym wyšybt bty knsywt šl 'my h'rṣ mwṣy'ym 't h'dm mn h'wlm*
>
> late morning sleep, wine at midday, chatting with children, and sitting in the meeting houses of the ignorant drive a man from this world (*'Abot de Rabbi Nathan* 21.1).

And in this vein sleep can be valued—strictly on utilitarian grounds:

> *'mr ršb'' whnh ṭwb m'd. whnh ṭwb hšynh. wky šynh ṭwbh m'd. 'tmh'. 'l kn tnynn yyn wšynh lrš'ym n'h lhm wn'h l'wlm. 'l' mtwk š'dm yšn qym''. hw' 'wmd wyg' btwrh hrbh.*
>
> R. Simeon b. Eleazar said: 'And, behold, it was very good' means, and, behold, sleep was good. Is there any sleep which is very good! Did we not learn thus: Wine and sleep when enjoyed by the *wicked* are beneficial to them and beneficial to the world! But [R. Simeon meant this:] a man sometimes sleeps a little and arises and toils much in the study of the Torah (*Gen. R.* 9.6).

The exegetical suggestion in the editors' notes commends itself: the sleep of the wicked is good because they are not hurting anyone. And the sleep of the Torah student is valued because it allows study when he is awake.

But in other texts the rabbinic tradition appears to move beyond a strictly utilitarian valuation of sleep (trans. Friedlander 1965, 86-87):

> *'mr lw hqdwš brwk hw' 'ny w't nzwn ṣ'nw šl 'dm wḥṣw šnyhm hlylh lhqb'h whywm l'rṣ mh 'śh hqdwš brwk hw' br' šynt ḥyym w'dm šwkb wyšn whw' mzwnw wrpw'tw wḥyym lw wmnwḥh lw šn'mr yšnty 'z ynwḥ ly*
>
> The Holy One, blessed be He, replied: I and thou [the earth] will (together) feed the multitude of mankind. They agreed to divide

> (the task) between themselves: the night was for the Holy One, blessed be He, and the day (was apportioned) to the earth. What did the Holy One, blessed be He, do? He created the sleep of life, so that man lies down and sleeps whilst He sustains him and heals him and (gives) him life and repose, as it is said, 'I should have slept: then had I been at rest' (Job 3.13) (*Pirqe Rabbi Eliezer* 12.7-8).

c. *Classical literature*

Oepke (1965, 431-32) describes a nuanced attitude towards sleep. It is a good which 'unravels care and gives refreshment' (Greek inscription honoring Hypnos, Vergil). Moderation is necessary, and Plato 'regards it as scandalous if the master or mistress of the house sleeps the whole night' (*Laws*). But sleep in the face of danger may be a sign of greatness (Plato, *Crito* 43b). Balz devotes an entire section to negative evaluations of sleep. His paraphrase of the Stoic judgment, 'It [sleep] robs man of half his life like a greedy creditor' (1972, 547) is a good example of the material available. Vermeule's summary is apropos:

> from the beginnings of Greek poetry, Sleep was a release . . . He is sweet, pleasure-giving, honey-hearted, soft, ambrosial like Night, warm . . . The sweet enervating aspects of Sleep did not always suit the army's charge of alertness; a soldier *malakō dedmēmenos hupnō* even with his weapons piled beside him might lose his life. Only children needed to sleep right through the night; a man could get bored with sleep and love-making; too much sleep without talk wasted time (1979, 147).

At the same time, this description should not be heard as underestimating the character of sleep as a transition:

> Once Sleep has settled on the eyelids anything may happen, travel, new experiences, dreams and visions, coma or love; it is transition, and though we know it has a normal cycle and should lift again (the little, not the big sleep) it may change events (Vermeule 1979, 152).

A different sort of valuation is present in the cult. Thus Jolles notes that Sleep was honored in a cult at Troizen in connection with the Muses. Sleep is also connected with Asklepios in dedication inscriptions (1916, 325-26).

d. *Old Testament*

Sleep is part of the created order, and thus may appear in descriptive celebrations of that order:

> Thou hast made the moon to mark the seasons;
> the sun knows its time for setting.
> Thou makest darkness, and it is night,
> when all the beasts of the forest creep forth.
> The young lions roar for their prey,
> seeking their food from God.
> When the sun rises, they get them away
> and lie down in their dens.
> Man goes forth to his work
> and to his labor until the evening (Ps 104.19-23).

This coordination of waking and sleeping with the activity of the sun is one of the themes common to this psalm and the El Amarnah 'Hymn to the Sun', treated above (ch. 3 §5). Thus perhaps both in Egypt and Israel the first affirmation is that sleep is a participation in the rhythms of the created order.

But more, alas, needs to be said. The days are often too short to complete one's labor. It is often not obvious that participation in this created rhythm is good: one must 'rise up early and go late to rest'. But—to continue the juxtapostion of Psalms 104 and 127—YHWH provides not only for the young lions at night, but also for his beloved (Ps 127.2). And thus participation in creation's rhythm becomes also an expression of trust in YHWH's continuing provision.[34] Thus the negative evaluations of sleep attested in the classical and rabbinic spheres are foreign to the Old Testament.

Protection, too, is needed. As noted (ch. 1 §1) sleep most characteristically comes into view as a situation of vulnerability. Sleep, then, is a good; but, like most goods, a vulnerable good.

It is, further, a relative good. Other goods may take precedence. Lexically this is reflected in the (partial) reservation of *Nwm* to situations of guarding. And one may break off sleep for prayer (ch. 3 §6). To treat sleep as other than a relative good is to join the slothful, the unwise (ch. 1 §1). And at this point the Old Testament appears to run in much the same direction as the rabbinic and classical traditions.

Sleep may be an occasion of encounter with the divine, most notably through dreams. But this dimension of sleep does not appear to have affected the general valuation of sleep. (Likewise, the various ways in which sleep language was used for death does not seem to have generated feedback affecting the perceptions of sleep.)

Finally, what of Vermeule's characterization of sleep as a state in which anything can happen? Are there parallels in the Old Testament? While the dominant concern in the Old Testament is with the dangerous things that can happen, to stress only these would be somewhat one-sided, and here the question posed by the shape of the classical tradition does push towards giving a more complete picture. Sleep is the occasion for dreams (ch. 1 §1). And on awakening from sleep one may encounter Eve (Gen 2), Ruth (Ruth 3), or Bathsheba (2 Sam 11).[35]

Chapter 5

SLEEP AND THE DIVINE

We have seen a variety of ways in which the human and divine intersect in the realm of sleep. The initial survey of contexts involving sleep identified as the largest groupings contexts concerned with vulnerability (ch. 1 §1.a), and contexts involving dreams (ch. 1 §1.b). One of the roots in Biblical Hebrew (*rdm*) is characteristically reserved for sleep brought on by divine agency (ch. 2 §4), and a cluster of words in the associative field of sleep (*yšn*) may be identified as connected with dreaming (ch. 2 §3). Again, moving from word to world, the two choices of sleeping site of which any point is consistently made are the choice between protected versus unprotected sites, and the choice of sites for receiving dreams. While Israelite beds are not preserved, Egyptian and perhaps Mesopotamian beds evidence desire for divine protection during sleep (ch. 3 §2).[1]

In this chapter the major concern is with the role of the divine vis-à-vis human vulnerability during sleep. But there are other issues. The first question is the relationship between falling asleep and divine activity, raised recently in Thomson's study. Is falling asleep normally the result of divine activity?

As indicated in the Introduction, while dreams occur during sleep, dreams involve a separate set of issues. On the one hand, the issues involved with dreaming are part of a larger set concerned with the divine-human interface. Sleep simply serves as an assumed pre-condition, and as noted (ch. 1 §1.b) is often not mentioned. On the other hand, the experience of dreaming did not affect the Old Testament account of sleeping (as it does, say, in the rabbinic tradition). That is, the relationship between sleep and dreaming was unproblematic, not needing explanation. Pedersen's attribution of the significance of dreams to their origin in 'the depths of the unconscious' (1926-40, 1.134), however valid on its own terms, is quite foreign to the understandings evidenced in the Old Testament. However, the relationship between sleep and divine communication becomes somewhat more intentional in a number of situations, and two of these are discussed here. First, one may choose to sleep at a particular place and after particular preparation in order to receive a dream, and the evidence for this practice in the Old Testament is examined. Second, there are a number of texts which are suggestive of an experience of divine communication during sleep. These are of interest because the experience has not yet been categorized, so to speak, as 'dream', 'vision' or the like. Here, if anywhere, there is perhaps an indigenous 'explanation' of dreams.

The remainder of the chapter is devoted to the twin themes of divine protecting and knowing during human sleep. These will be examined, as well as the various attempts to establish a life setting for some or all of them. A broader context will then be established through the Egyptian and Mesopotamian evidence, exploring means through which safety during sleep was sought. The elements of similarity and difference in the various approaches the different cultures take to the problem of safety during sleep will then be the object of reflection.

1. *Sent sleep*

What are we to make of Thomson's suggestion that the Old Testament understood sleep in general to be divinely sent (1955, 423)? When in the Old Testament or in surrounding cultures does one speak in this way?

a. *Egypt*

References to gods sending sleep have not been located. There is, however, a strong sense that the cycle of sleeping and waking is tied into the movement of the sun god. This has already been illustrated in the discussion of time for sleep (ch. 3 §5), and can be further demonstrated by a prayer addressing the sun for the king in El-Amarnah (Erman [1927] 1966, 292):

> Thou risest in the horizon of heaven to give life to all that thou hast made, to all men, (all beasts), all that flieth and fluttereth, and to all the reptiles that are in the earth. They live when they behold thee; they sleep when thou settest.

Particularly striking here is the contrast life/sleep.

A more distant parallel is encountered in the tale 'The Destruction of Mankind', which Lichtheim dates to the Middle Kingdom, in which Re saves mankind from the goddess by coloring a large quantity of beer with red ochre (1976, 199):

> The majesty of King Re rose early before dawn, to have this sleeping draught poured out. Then the fields were flooded three palms high with the liquid by the might of the majesty of this god. When the goddess came in the morning she found them flooded, and her gaze was pleased by it. She drank and it pleased her heart. She returned drunk without having perceived mankind. The majesty of Re said to the goddess: 'Welcome in peace, O gracious one!' Thus beautiful women came into being in the town of Imu.

b. *Mesopotamia*

Sleep can be sent in response to dream requests. This appears as a regular pattern in the fourth tablet of the Gilgamesh Epic as reconstructed by Landsberger:[2]

> (g) *ilîma Gilgameš ana (ina) muḫḫi* [*xxx*]
> (h) *maṣḫassu utta/eqqa ana* [*xx*]
> (i) *šadû bîla šutta/i amat* [*damiqti*]
>
> (n) *Gilgameš ina qin-ṣi-šu ú-tam-me-da zu-qat-su*
> (o) *šit-tum re-ḫat UN.MEŠ eli-šu im-qut*
>
> (g) Es stieg Gilgameš auf den Gipfel des Berges und . . .
> (h) libierte sein Räuchopfer dem [. . .]
> (i) O, Berg, bringe mir einen Traum, gute Botschaft!

For lines n-o, Landsberger notes Oppenheim's suggestion:

> it is said that Gilgamesh fell asleep in the rather unusual position of a person squatting on the ground, his chin touching his knees. This could mean that the sleep came upon him so suddenly and with such magic power and speed that he was caught in the described position before being able to lie down to sleep. But it could also mean that this position was required for the provocation of mantic dreams, and one might even venture to explain the position as imitating that of the so-called 'contracted' (or 'embryonal') burial position. All this is only guesswork (1956, 216).

In the Enûmu eliš, Apsu and probably Mummu are put to sleep by Ea's magic (cited below, ch. 6 §2).

c. *Old Testament*

To summarize the comparative material, examples have been found of gods sending sleep in particular situations (cf. also Athene sending [sweet] sleep, and Hypnos putting Zeus to sleep, both cited earlier). And one might say that Re brings on sleep on a regular basis by his setting. But this would be the closest approximation to Thomson's reading of the Old Testament.

In the Old Testament, the occurrences of divinely sent sleep are generally marked by *Rdm*. When sleep is divinely sent *Rdm* is used. When *Rdm* is used, divinely sent sleep is in question, with the exceptions of Jonah 1.5-6 and one (or perhaps two) texts in Proverbs (10.5; 19.15). Thus on the face of it, it is unwarranted to generalize that also when *Rdm* is absent the sleep is divinely sent.

2. *Sleep and divine communication*

As indicated, there are two particular questions here. First, what evidence is there in the Old Testament for incubation, the practice of soliciting dreams through particular procedures? Second, in addition to clear language about dreams or visions, is there also evidence for a less articulate, more generalized belief in divine communication during sleep?

a. *Incubation*

The practice of incubation first established its place in the discussion in the classical sphere. Based on Deubner's definition,[3] Ehrlich takes at least the following to be necessary conditions for incubation: (1) intention to elicit a divine revelation (2) to be received in sleep (3) in a holy place (4) after specific preparatory steps. And for this pattern numerous classical accounts can be cited. But in the Old Testament there were a number of factors 'durch die viel Material unter den Tisch gefallen ist' (1953, 18): the suppression of local cultic sites, the devaluation of dreams as a medium of revelation, the identification of incubation as a specifically heathen practice. As a result there is only one clear-cut case of incubation, although a number of other stories lie along the border.

That one account is Solomon's dream at the high place at Gibeon (1 Kgs 3.5-15 // 2 Chr 1.2-13). Solomon offers sacrifice and receives a dream (the connection is made more explicit in Chr than in Kgs); the intention is not narrated, but Ehrlich reflects a consensus in taking the pattern to establish it. Various factors militate against taking other stories as cases of incubation. The account of Jacob's dream at Bethel (Gen 28.10–29.1) narrates, at most, Jacob's discovery, rather than his use, of a holy place.[4] On the other hand, in the vision Jacob receives at Beer-sheba (Gen 46.1-5), the offerings, the holy place, and the night revelation are all suggestive of incubation. Only the use of *mr't hlylh* 'visions of the night' rather than *ḥlwm* 'dream' makes Ehrlich hesitate to identify this as an incubation account. The identification of the revelation to Abraham (Gen 15.1-6) as a case of incubation rests on a reconstruction of Hebron as the locale, and no offering is mentioned. Genesis 15.7-21 is perhaps a better candidate: both offering and sleep are present. But again, the locale is not certain, nor whether the events of vv. 18-21 were understood to occur during Abraham's sleep. The case of Samuel's call (1 Sam 3) is like Jacob's dream at Bethel: neither revelation was expected. In Psalms a number of elements are suggestive of incubation, but it cannot be established. Isaiah 65.4 is perhaps a polemic against pagan incubation (Ehrlich 1953, 19-55).

Ehrlich, choosing to err on the side of caution, has provided a useful survey: one case is clear (1 Kgs 3 // 2 Chr 1); others, in their present form, lack one or more elements. The overall impression is that what we have in the Old Testament is perhaps the tip of a much more extensive practice.

b. *Divine communication*

In previous sections (ch. 4 §§1.e, 3.d) two rather difficult verses have been encountered:

> Thereupon I awoke and looked, and my sleep was pleasant to me (Jer 31.26).

> If I would count them, they are more than the sand.
> When I awake, I am still with thee (Ps 139.18).

Common to these two texts is the statement that one has awakened in a context which has not established that the person was in fact sleeping. Past these common elements, the texts have common contexts only at a broad level of generalization, for the Jeremiah text occurs in a collection of prophetic oracles, and the Psalms text in a psalm which is probably to be identified as an individual petition.

When these two texts are placed together with Job 35.10-11 and

Psalm 16.7, a pattern begins to emerge:

> But none says, 'Where is God my Maker,
> who gives songs in the night,
> who teaches us more than the beasts of the earth,
> and makes us wiser than the birds of the air?' (Job 35.10-11).[5]

> I bless the Lord who gives me counsel;
> in the night also my heart instructs me (Ps 16.7).

These texts are suggestive of nocturnal intercourse between God and the speaker. The focus is on communication. But while these statements are the result of reflection, they do not appear to have been governed by a particular model or understanding of this intercourse, e.g. they are not categorized as dreams. Psalm 16.7 is particularly illustrative in this regard, precisely in its major interpretive problem: how to understand the ostensive contrast between divine (7a) and human (7b) activity. Lindblom solves the problem by collapsing the divine into the human:

> God examines the heart of the pious during the night, which means that the pious in the nocturnal hours examines his life before the mirror of the Torah, and allows himself to be judged by the Torah (1942, 8; tm).

Dahood (1965, 86-90) solves the problem by collapsing the human into the divine, appealing to Phoenician morphology and parsing the *y* of *klywty* as a third masculine singular, translating

> I will praise Yahweh who counsels me,
> and whose heart instructs me
> during the watches of the night.

That this may not be entirely misguided is suggested by Morenz's statement, 'There is ample evidence that the Egyptians felt that they received divine guidance from within their hearts' (1973, 63), which he illustrates—inter alia—from Sinuhe's account: 'my body quivered, my feet began to scurry, my heart directed me, the god who ordained this flight drew me away'. That is, to speak of the activities of the kidneys at night may be another way to talk about YHWH giving counsel.

Kraus (1978, 266) suggests a complementary relationship: 'from the context one may understand in v. 7b that "the interior" constantly reminds one of Yahweh's helpful revelation' (tm).

Likewise Wolff (1974a, 65): 'his kidneys chastise him in the night, that is to say his conscience reproves him'.

Of course, most of the time divine nocturnal communication was construed as dream or vision. But as 1 Samuel 3 shows, it was quite possible to narrate an experience in a way which cut across the canons of both dream and vision. And the point of this section has been to indicate, in part, why this was possible. Behind the specific categories of dream and vision there was a more fundamental belief that YHWH communicated—also at night. And this could be brought to articulation, as in the passages discussed, without recourse to the categories of 'dream' or 'vision'. To put it another way, this communication could relativize the categories of 'awake' and 'asleep'. And it is perhaps for this reason that the texts with which we began this discussion, Jeremiah 31.26 and Psalms 139.18, could employ *yqṣ* 'awake' without being concerned to set the preceding text in the context of sleep or identify the onset of sleep. It would be putting matters too strongly to say either that this communication occurred characteristically in the night or in a qualitatively different way at night. The study of 'test/heart' speaks against the former, and there is no evidence for the latter. It is simply that this was a part of experience registered and articulated.

If there is a common thread in the two issues examined in this section, incubation and common divine communication, it is perhaps the interface of divine freedom and human initiative. On the one hand, incubation, which threatens to encrouch on divine freedom with an assertion of human initiative, is downplayed in the Old Testament. On the other, divine freedom to communicate in a variety of ways, during the night, during sleep, is affirmed. In fact, the divine indifference to day and night ('even the darkness is not dark to thee, the night is bright as the day; for darkness is as light with thee' Ps 139.12) is perhaps a clue that the boundary between waking and sleeping is not going to be of great concern. But this freedom does not negate human initiative. Rather,

> I bless the Lord who gives me counsel;
> in the night also my heart instructs me (Ps 16.7).

3. *The Sleep of the accused*

Discussion conveniently starts with Schmidt, whose reading of a group of the individual petition psalms closely links divine protection, divine knowledge, and salvation in the morning—to sleep! In Schmidt's reconstruction the accused whose case is brought to the temple is protected by God during sleep, is known by God while sleeping, and receives vindication upon awakening. If Schmidt's thesis stands, it pulls together a number of seemingly disparate elements, and establishes the life-setting out of which grew the language about YHWH watching and knowing one during sleep.

Schmidt's *Das Gebet der Angeklagten im Alten Testament* attempts to correlate a variety of references to sacral judicial proceedings scattered throughout the Old Testament with the bulk of the individual complaints. Among the former (which also include Deut 17.8; Exod 22.6f.; Num 5.11f.; Deut 21.1-8) he cites part of Solomon's prayer, which occurs at the dedication of the temple:

> And hearken thou to the supplication of thy servant and of thy people Israel, when they pray toward this place; yea, hear thou in heaven thy dwelling place; and when thou hearest, forgive. If a man sins against his neighbor and is made to take an oath, and comes and swears his oath before thine altar in this house, then hear thou in heaven, and act, and judge thy servants, condemning the guilty by bringing his conduct upon his own head, and vindicating the righteous by rewarding him according to his righteousness (1 Kgs 8.30-32).

Schmidt notes that v. 30 is a general request to hear prayer and respond, and that the following verses describe a number of situations in which YHWH's action is desired, the first described in vv. 31-32. While these verses speak only of an oath, Schmidt takes the reference to prayer in v. 30 to mean that in the situation described in vv. 31-32 someone was also praying.[6] Who? On the basis of Psalms 107.13 and 118.5, Schmidt argues that the accused prayed. Do we know what the accused prayed? Yes, we have a number of examples of such prayers. Better, we can recover a number of examples of such prayers, for Schmidt's examples are arrived at by generous pruning. They are Psalms 4; 5; 7; 17; 26; 27.1-6, 7-14; 31.1-9; 57; 142. The discussion of these texts has more the character of making isolated points than of a sustained attempt to reconstruct a life setting for these psalms. That is, while numerous observations are made which indicate how these psalms could reflect a sacral juridical process (incarceration: Pss 107.13; 118.5; 142.8; hand-washing: 26.6), the question of how these psalms really fit into that process is not convincingly handled. Thus, while in one case an oath occurs within a prayer (7.4-6), the implications of the occurrence for the place of the prayers in the overall procedure is not dealt with. The result is that Schmidt is quite vulnerable to a critique from a form-critical perspective, and such a critique may be found in Gunkel and Begrich (1933, 252-54).

Nevertheless, Schmidt isolates some very interesting material relevant to sleep. This discussion begins with Psalm 17.3, 15:

> If thou triest my heart, if thou visitest me by night,
> if thou testest me, thou wilt find no wickedness in me;
> my mouth does not transgress.
> . . .
> As for me, I shall behold thy face in righteousness;
> when I awake, I shall be satisfied with beholding thy form.

Noting that 'when I awake' is sometimes emended, Schmidt argues that it corresponds to the mention of God's activity at night, and thus should be retained. And v. 3 is an important clue to the working of the juridical procedure:

> It is clearly stated that the divine examination, to which the accused submits himself through oath, happens *in the night*, i.e. involuntarily, during sleep. So it is quite natural that the conclusion of it all, the declaration of innocence, is shifted to *the moment of awakening* (1928, 21; tm).

Schmidt sees the following texts in terms of this understanding:

> I lie down and sleep; I wake again,
> for the Lord sustains me (3.6).
>
> In peace I will both lie down and sleep;
> for thou alone, O Lord, makest me dwell in safety (4.9).
>
> I lie in the midst of lions
> that greedily devour the sons of men;
> their teeth are spears and arrows,
> their tongues sharp swords.
> . . .
> Awake, my soul!
> Awake, O harp and lyre!
> I will awake the dawn! (57.5,9).
>
> If I would count them, they are more than the sand.
> When I awake, I am still with thee (139.17).[7]

To gain perspective on what is being proposed here, it is helpful to review some of the other possibilities for these psalms. Mowinckel (1921, 155-56) adduced a number of examples of incubation (Gen 26.24; 28.10f; 1 Kgs 3.5) and then suggested:

> It is also possible that those sick and seeking help sometimes employed this form of recourse to an oracle and after certain preparation and consecration spent a night in the temple, or rather in the sanctuary, in order to obtain a dream revelation concerning his sickness (1921, 155; tm).

Psalms 3.6, 4.9, and 17.15 might, Mowinckel thought, be examples of this. And this understanding of Psalm 17.15 he contrasted to seeing the waking as a waking from death (Jewish exegetes, Geier, Delitzsch, Hofmann, Kittel), a waking from a figurative dark night (Calvin, Baethgen, Hitzig), or a simple waking with Psalm 17 identified as an evening psalm (Ewald, Hengstenberg, Duhm). How a dream was to help the recipient vis-à-vis those accusing him is not a question Mowinckel addresses.

As noted, Schmidt is not attempting to reconstruct a life setting in detail, so the question of the relation between particular elements in the psalms (the reference to sleeping in the midst of one's enemies in 4.6 and 57.5 or the reference to shelter under wings in 27.5-6) and the actual practice is not addressed. But that the psalms do reflect a sacral juridical procedure which involves divine examination of the accused during sleep Schmidt affirms.

So the first group of psalms Schmidt treats. The second group, characterized by concern with sickness, Schmidt attempts to relate to the first group by arguing that the community in cases of sickness would interpret the sickness as divine punishment and so accuse the sick. While this dynamic is amply illustrated in Job, the connection is not as tight as Schmidt portrays, and thus his treatment of the second group has generally not been found convincing.

Beyerlin's *Die Rettung der Bedrängten* (1970) is essentially a refinement and development of Schmidt's position. He works with an expanded version of Schmidt's list.[8] Schmidt's suggestion that the accussed was imprisoned is explicitly dropped (1970, 43-44), and dropped without comment is Schmidt's interest in YHWH's nocturnal examination. On the other hand, Beyerlin follows the main lines of Schmidt's reconstruction of the process. A major modification is that while Schmidt focused on the defensive role of the ordeal (clearing the accused), Beyerlin highlights its double-edged character. Beyerlin also suggests that a theophany played a role in the announcement of the decision (1970, 108-10 [Ps 17]; 125-26 [Ps 27]).[9]

What was the function of these psalms? Beyerlin argues (contra Preuss 1933) that the divine decisions in the context of an ordeal were not conceived in a magical but in a personal way. The ordeal originally functioned in a magical way, but

> It can be easily recognized that this sort of divine judgment could have had no place in the Yahweh community. Even as the Yahwistic faith subjected the curse to the personal disposal of Yahweh, so the oath-curse connection of the ordeal must also have been subjected relatively early to the personal discretion of the God of Israel (1970, 59; tm).

And this personal cast to the proceedings opens the way for prayers:

> When that institutional legal aid depended on Yahweh's hearing, judging, and acting [1 Kgs 8.31-32], then correspondingly there must be room for an appeal on the human side with requests for hearing and legal help as well as with confessions of innocence and loyalty and accusing references to the conduct of the enemies (1970, 60; tm).

Beyerlin's readings of the psalms place them at different places in the proceedings. Thus Psalm 26 is taken to be used at an early stage (1970, 120) and Psalm 7 (where the oath is preserved in the text) is in fact the oath used in the proceeding (1970, 97). The close linkage of the psalms with different stages in the ordeal has form-critical implications, and a significant part of Beyerlin's agenda is the exploration of these implications. For example, in discussing Psalm 3:

> There is not, I believe, a form-critical designation which could comprehensively characterize the psalm in all its parts. The unity of Ps. 3 lies in that it accompanies a cultic divine court case through a particular phase (1970, 84; tm).

The ordeal model for interpreting these psalms has been criticized, and representative of this criticism is Gemser's analysis:

> These analogies and background of the *rîb*-terminology in the Hebrew Psalms, and its occurrence even where the distress of the psalmist clearly arises out of sickness..., prove that the *rîb*-pattern is often, if not mostly, used metaphorically... as a form of thinking and feeling, a category, a frame of mind... To interpret this class of Psalms as representing a real lawsuit and trial before a temple tribunal with decision by ordeal looks like a hermeneutic

> 'transsubstantiation' or substantializing of metaphor into reality. Undoubtedly the phraseology is often thoroughly judicial, but with this metaphor other comparisons vary (Gemser 1955, 127-28).

Beyerlin recognizes the difficulty, and appeals to consistency: where the language suggestive of an ordeal is mixed with other sorts of language, the psalm is probably not narrating salvation that occurred in a cultic context (1970, 18-19). And thus Beyerlin eliminates at the start a number of psalms from consideration.[10] But this still leaves eleven psalms (listed above) for which a case for linkage with cultically experienced salvation can be made.

But in the end, Beyerlin's account of the relationship of the psalms to the reconstructed ordeal fails to convince. There is certainly enough evidence in and outside the Psalms for such an ordeal, although most of the details remain unclear. (The following discussion will pursue the question of the possible role of nocturnal examination in such an ordeal.) But there are at least three major problems with Beyerlin's account. First, as Richards (1971) observes, it tends to be too static (institutional vs non-institutional settings), drawing too little on anthropological models. Second, and related, while it is reasonable to expect the conduct of the ordeal to be influenced by the fact that it was an ordeal before YHWH, the picture Beyerlin produces, with prayers possible at any number of points is a rather singular outcome. It looks as though the distinction between a personal and an impersonal procedure has been mixed with the distinction between a spare and an elaborated procedure. One might put the problem this way: if Preuss's account suggests a severe Roman style,[11] Beyerlin's suggests a verbose pentecostal style. Third, in Beyerlin's treatment the psalms become verbatim transcriptions of the events. Thus Psalm 3 is delivered in a situation where

> For his oppressors and for the many around him the unfolding saving intervention of God is still hidden (vv. 2-3 [EVV 1-2]): The hostility remains, and the dictum is unshaken: 'there is no help for him (the oppressed) in God' (1970, 81; tm).

And the break in tone between the two halves of v. 8 [EVV 7], *qwmh yhwh / hwšy'ny 'lhy* ('Arise, O Lord!/Deliver me, O my God!') and *ky-hkyt 't-kl-'yby lḥy / šny rš'ym šbrt* ('For thou dost smite all my enemies on the cheek, / thou dost break the teeth of the wicked'), is explained by the oracle coming at this point.[12]

Despite these difficulties, Kraus combines Schmidt and Beyerlin to produce the following reconstruction (1978, 58; tm):

1. 'To you I flee': 'I hide myself with you': The one in jeopardy, accused and pursued, seeks divine protection in the temple precincts.
2. Preliminary inquiry in the area of the temple entrance: Ps 5.6-8. The accused and pursued may enter in the temple—to worship.
3. He hides himself in the 'shadow of the wings' of Yahweh (Pss 17.8; 27.5; 57.2; etc.) . . .
4. Oath of purification and self curse as ritual acts, which the innocent accused performs (cf. 1 Kgs 8.31 and Ps 7.3ff . . .)
5. 'Judge me, Yahweh!' 'Execute justice for me!' The prayer aims at the granting of a divine judgment announcement, which is issued 'in the morning'. Previously the accused has exposed himself to examination and investigation by the *Deus praesens* through nocturnal incubation in the temple (Pss 17.3; 139ff.). With the offering in early morning and the final appeal the supplicant delivers himself up to the divine verdict.
6. It can happen that the enemies accusing and pursuing the supplicant do not acknowledge, not accept, the divine judgment (cf. Ps 4.2ff.). But the cultic process is only concluded when the enemies echo the divine judgment and with their discarded accusation 'are put to shame'.
7. If the saving acquittal occurs, then the one freed from jeopardy celebrates the *twdh* . . . in which often the event of defeated accusation and arrested pursuit is reviewed. In the feast of thanksgiving the *communio*-meal is prepared for the supplicant 'in the face of the enemies', who were and are present at the cultic site (Ps 23.5).

And where do the psalms involved—Kraus simply takes over Beyerlin's listing—fit in? Kraus does not address this question directly in a general way, but limits himself to observations on particular psalms. Thus regarding Psalm 4:

> It would be easy to assume an event in the temple as a 'Sitz im Leben' . . . So the explanation would be proposed that an innocent person, pursued and accused, received justice through a divine speech in the temple (1978, 167; tm).

But this does not explain all the elements present, which Kraus proceeds to explain by reconstructing a particular historical situation.

On the other hand, in his treatment of Psalm 3, he recognizes a much looser connection to that institutional setting (1978, 162), and in treating Psalm 139, takes that setting as the jumping-off point for reflection on the part of a religious officiary (1978, 1095). Thus one sees, for instance in the different treatments of the connection of Psalm 3 to the ordeal, the lack of unanimity among those working with this model.

To conclude this section, while Schmidt, Beyerlin, and Kraus have succeeded in gathering together texts which strongly suggest the existence of a cultic judicial procedure, and have shown that this is reflected in a number of psalms, they have not succeeded in establishing the role that these psalms played vis-à-vis that procedure.

The next task is to examine two of the themes encountered in the psalms and in the reconstructed life setting: divine knowledge and divine protection (for deliverance at dawn see Ziegler 1950). We will attempt to trace the history of these themes vis-à-vis sleep, and set them in a variety of comparative contexts.

4. *Divine knowledge*

The phrase of interest here occurs in the fifth point of Kraus's summary of the ordeal proceedings: the 'examination and investigation by the *Deus praesens* through nocturnal incubation in the temple'. How is this to be understood? Psalms 17 and 139 suggest that YHWH examines one during the night, and specifically (Ps 17.15) during sleep. Is this understanding of the divine nocturnal activity primary, so that the cultic activity grows out of it, or is the practice of sleeping in the temple primary, with the language about divine activity secondary? That is, is one particularly transparent to YHWH during sleep, so that sleeping before YHWH is incorporated into the judicial procedure, or does the reflection on transparency grow out of a situation of sleeping before YHWH that only accidentally involves sleep?

Kraus takes the former approach: 'The idea in play is probably that someone in nocturnal sleep no longer has the chance of hiding his thoughts' (1978, 275; tm). A similar approach is taken by Delitzsch:

> The result of the close scrutiny to which God has subjected him in the night, when the bottom of a man's heart is at once made

> manifest, whether it be in his thoughts when awake or in the dream and fancies of the sleeper, was and is this... ([1867] 1970, 1.234).

Delitzsch, note, is indifferent to the question of whether the person is awake or asleep, and the former option has received attention at least as far back as Calvin (whom Kraus notes):

> when a man is withdrawn from the presence of his fellow-creatures, he sees more clearly his sins, which otherwise would be hidden from his view; just as, on the contrary, the sight of men affects us with shame, and this is, as it were, a veil before our eyes, which prevents us from deliberately examining our faults (1949, 1.238).

That is, God is being invited to listen in, so to speak, at the time when people are most honest with themselves. Of course, in this reading, sleep has nothing to do with the matter.

On the other hand, the language of Psalm 139, which may well have grown out of a situation of incubation, would hardly suggest that YHWH is limited in his knowledge by one's location:

> Whither shall I go from thy Spirit?
> Or whither shall I flee from thy presence?
> If I ascend to heaven, thou art there!
> If I make my bed in Sheol, thou art there! (Ps 139.7-8).

So is there any other evidence for belief that sleep laid one open to YHWH's examination?

We may approach the problem lexically by noting that Psalm 17.3 contains the collocation 'try / heart / night'. Where else does this collocation appear? The collocation *bḥn / lb* occurs in the following texts (Jenni 1978b, 273):

> But thou, O Lord, knowest me;
> thou seest me, and triest my mind toward thee (Jer 12.3a).

> The crucible is for silver, and the furnace is for gold,
> and the Lord tries hearts (Prov 17.3).

> I know, my God, that thou triest the heart, and hast pleasure in uprightness; in the uprightness of my heart I have freely offered all these things, and now I have seen thy people, who are present here, offering freely and joyously to thee (1 Chr 29.17).

The collocation *bḥn/lb/klywt* occurs in these texts, tightly in the first two examples, somewhat more loosely in the rest:

But, O Lord of hosts, who judgest righteously,
who triest the heart and the mind (Jer 11.20a),

O let the evil of the wicked come to an end,
but establish thou the righteous,
thou who triest the minds and hearts,
thou righteous God (Ps 7.10).

The heart is deceitful above all things,
and desperately corrupt;
who can understand it?
'I the Lord search (*ḥqr*) the mind
and try the heart,
to give to every man according to his ways,
according to the fruit of his doings' (Jer 17.9-10).

O Lord of hosts, who triest the righteous,
who seest the heart and the mind,
let me see thy vengeance upon them,
for to thee have I committed my cause (Jer 20.12).

Prove me, O Lord, and try me (*wnsny*);
test (*ṣrwph*) my heart and my mind (Ps 26.2).

Scanning the texts cited, Jeremiah 11.20a, 12.3a, 17.9-10, 20.12, Psalms 7.10, 26.2, Proverbs 17.3, 1 Chronicles 29.17, the Psalms texts are not surprising, and are both treated by Schmidt and included by Beyerlin in his listing of psalms 'mit institutionsbezogenen Rettungsaussagen'. All but one of the Jeremiah texts occur in those passages which have been identified as 'confessions', and if Eissfeldt's listing is provisionally adopted (11.18-23; 12.1-6; 15.10-21; 17.12-18; 18.18-23; 20.7-18; [1965] 1972, 357), ostensively parallel material can be found in the remaining texts as well.

O Lord, thou knowest;
remember me and visit me,
and take vengeance for me on my persecutors (15.15a).

I have not pressed thee to send evil,
nor have I desired the day of disaster,
thou knowest;
that which came out of my lips
was before thy face (17.16).

Yet, thou, O Lord, knowest
all their plotting to slay me.
Forgive not their iniquity,
nor blot out their sin from thy sight (18.23a).

The simple answer to the question originally posed, of where else the cluster 'try / heart / night' appears, is that it only appears in Psalm 17.3. Thus the collocation of 'night' with 'try / heart' is not characteristic, and this suggests that YHWH's examination of the heart was not thought of as characteristically occurring at night. Certainly it would import something quite foreign into the Jeremiah texts to read them in this way.

But the Jeremiah texts do something more. Since Baumgartner (1917), the status of the 'confessions' as closely related to the individual complaint has been recognized. But neither Schmidt, Beyerlin, nor Kraus has incorporated them into the discussion regarding the life setting of their subgroup of these psalms. And this is important, because with Jeremiah we have both these complaints and some indication of some of the sacral legal situations Jeremiah found himself in. There are, of course, great difficulties in assessing the relationship between the prose accounts of Jeremiah's difficulties with the actual course of events. But it is at least significant that one recent attempt to reconstruct the events behind Jeremiah 26 (Hossfeld and Meyer 1974) approached the life setting Schmidt reconstructed in neither of its reconstructions. In other words, at the one point where it would have been reasonable to expect to find a correlation between psalms and life setting, we have drawn a blank. An argument from silence—nothing more, but also nothing less.

Support for an understanding of YHWH examining hearts of sleepers within the Old Testament has not been forthcoming, and in fact the clustering of texts in Jeremiah has tended to weigh against the notion that YHWH's nocturnal examination was an integral part of the understanding of the procedure. (Why is the theme of nocturnal examination lacking in psalms apparently reflective of ordeal? Perhaps the answer is that the relevant evidence was not to be found in the heart, but in the past disputed events to which YHWH had been a witness.)

The discussion up to this point has now cleared the way to the theme of divine protection, since it has been argued that sleep and examination of the heart appear to be only accidentally connected. And this impression is sustained by the comparative material. The Egyptians knew an examination of the heart, but located it after death, as illustrated in the Book of the Dead (Morenz 1973, 126). And there are numerous references to a variety of gods knowing the heart in Mesopotamian sources (cf. *CAD* '*barû*'), but these are not connected with sleep or the night.

5. *Divine protection*

Here the net could, with profit, be cast considerably further. Thus on the rabbinic side a midrash on Psalm 4.5:

> The verse means, we are taught, that a man reciting the Shema in the synagogue in the morning has done what he ought; but in the evening, [though he has recited the Shema in the synagogue,] he has not done what he ought unless he recites it again at home in his bed. Why? In order to drive demons away from the house (*Midr. Ps* 4.9)

A similar tradition is preserved in *b. Berakot* 5a. And in a midrash to Canticles 5.4:

> Before Solomon sinned he ruled over *sharim* and *sharoth*; as it says, 'I got me men-singers and women-singers, and the delights of the sons of men' (Eccl. ii.8), i.e. baths, *shidah* and *shidoth*, that is male and female demons, who used to heat them. But after he sinned, he appointed sixty mighty men of the mighty men of Israel to keep his couch, as it is written, 'Behold the litter . . . all men that handle the sword' (iii.8), because he was afraid of the spirits (*Cant. R.* 3.8).

Much closer to the Old Testament period is the amulet from Arslan Tash (text 27 in Donner and Röllig 1971 [hereafter *KAI*], to whose bibliography may be added Cross and Saley (1970), Caquot (1973), Tawil (1980), and Zevit (1977). The language is mostly Phoenician; the date is seventh (Cross and Saley, Caquot) or—possibly—sixth century (Gaster). The main incantation covers the obverse, reverse, and sides. In addition, figures of a winged sphinx, man-eating she-wolf (obverse) and ax-wielding god (reverse) appear, each with their own shorter incantation. The amulet, hung in a home (on the doorpost? [Cross and Saley]), probably protected against a number of demons, including, specifically, night demons.

The incantation on the winged sphinx reads as follows (Cross and Saley 1970, 46; the final *n* is read by Caquot and Du Mesnil, omitted in *KAI*):

> (1) *l'pt'. bḥdr. ḥšk* (2) *'br*
> *p'm. p'm llyn*
>
> O Fliers, from the dark room pass away!
> Now! Now! night demons!

The main incantation concerns three individuals or groups, the first being *l'ṭ'*.[13] Against these are set covenants with—minimally—Baal and Ḥoron. And the concern evidenced here corresponds well with that displayed in the rabbinic passages (above) as well as the Mesopotamian material (below).

a. *Egypt*

In the Old Kingdom 'Instruction of Ptahhotep' there are references to divine protection during sleep (Lichtheim 1973, 66):

> It is the god who makes him worthy
> And protects him while he sleeps (ch. 10).

From the Eleventh Dynasty there is a prayer preserved on a stela of King Wahankh Intef II (Lichtheim 1973, 94-95):

> Will you depart, father Re, before you commend me?
> Will sky conceal you before you commend me?
> Commend <me> to night and those dwelling in it,
> So as to find [me among your adorers], O Re,
> Who worship you at your risings,
> Who lament at your settings.
> May night embrace me, midnight shelter me
> By your command, O Re— —
> I am your deputy, you made me lord of life, undying.
> Commend <me> to night's early hours:
> May they place their guard upon me;
> Commend <me> to [early dawn]:
> May he put his guard about me;
> I am the nursling of early dawn,
> I am the nursling of night's early hours,
> Born at night, whose life is made [in darkness],
> Whose fear [besets] the herds with back-turned horns.
> With your eye's red glow as my protection
> You find me [hailing] your approach!

From the Ninth/Tenth Dynasty 'Instruction addressed to King Merikare' (Lichtheim 1973, 106):

> He made for them rulers in the egg,
> Leaders to raise the back of the weak.
> He made for them magic as weapons
> To ward off the blow of events,
> Guarding them by day and by night.

Examples of this divinely provided magic relevant to the present discussion would be the figures of Bes and Thoeris already noted as appearing on some beds (ch. 3 §2.a) and amulets.[14] For both the figures and the amulets a specialization of function to nighttime guarding is not evident. Rather, as one of the situations in which protection is needed, sleep falls under their domain. Thus Bonnet describes the function of the amulets: 'the amulets, which one carries during life, are, on the whole, created less for particular situations, but directed at the unknown dangers' (1952, 27; tm). And for a later period Kees characterizes the role of Bes and Thoeris: 'The cultured Egyptian of the New Kingdom decorates his bed area and the household effects of the sleeping room with the figures of particular protective spirits of family life, especially the dwarfish Bes or Thoeris, the thebean hippopotamus goddess of the Nile' (1933, 84; tm).

But specific precautions could be taken. Schott published a headrest bearing representations of Bes and what Schott took to be protective deities (who 'schützten vermutlich den Schlafenden gegen Geister, die nachts hinterrücks kommen'), together with the inscription (1958, 142):

> Gut schlafen, die Nase voller Freude,
> Wenn die Erde hell wird, Amon sehen,
> dem Webermeister *Knr*.

On the basis of a number of lines of evidence, including the protective deities, Schott took the headrest to be intended for use in this life. And thus on occasion specific steps could be taken to insure safety during sleep.

b. *Mesopotamia*

The sorts of supernatural dangers feared during sleep can be illustrated from two neo-Assyrian texts.[15] The first is a bilingual incantation text, listed by Falkenstein (1931, 12) as part of the eighth tablet in the series *Udug-hul-a-meš*. By Falkenstein's classification, this is an incantation used by the incantation priest for self-protection, and opens (as do some others of this type) with a poetic description of the demons to be warded off. Included in this description are the following lines.[16]

> MIN *ša ina ma-a-a-al mu-ši amêla ina šit-ti*
> *i-ri-iḫ-ḫu-ú at-ta*
> MIN *e-kim šit-ti ša amêla ana ta-ba-li iš-*[*at-ta*]

> (you are the evil *alû*-demon) who has sexual intercourse

with the man in his bed at night;
(you are the evil *alû*-demon who) takes away sleep,
who [seizes] the man to carry (him) off (*CT* 16 27.19, 21).

In another type of incantation identified by Falkenstein, the prophylactic type, the point is to keep the evil spirits away in the first place. Falkenstein quotes from a Sumerian incantation (1931, 40):

An den Menschen, den Sohn seines Gottes
sollst du deine schmutzign Hände nicht heranbringen,
deine Genossen nicht bei ihm schlafen lassen (UMBS 1, 2 128.3.13-15).

The second text occurs in the ritual series *bît rimki*. The ritual douching of the king was carried out in seven chambers; the text for the third chamber has been edited by Borger (1967).[17] In it, Shamash is addressed as the one who can give aid:

19 *ša nam-ta-ru iṣ-ba-tu-šú*
20 *ša a-sak-ku ik-mu-ú-šú*
21 *ša ú-tuk-ku lem-nu e-li-šú i-ši-ru*
22 *ša a-lu-ú lem-nu ina ma-a-a-li-šú ik-tu-mu-šú*
23 *ša e-ṭém-mu lem-nu ina mu-ši ir-mu-šú*

30 *ša ar-da-at li-li-i i-bi-ru-šú*
31 *eṭ-lu ša ar-da-at li-li-i ik-ri-mu-šú*

39 *^{d}Utu [bul]-luṭ-su-nu it-ti-ka ib-ba-áš-ši*

19 den ein *namtaru* erfasst hat
20 den ein *asakku* ergriffen hat
21 auf den ein böser *utukku* losgegangen ist,
22 den ein böser *alû* auf seinem Lager überwältigt hat,
23 den ein böser Totengeist in der Nacht niedergeworfen hat,

30 den das *lilû*-Mädchen zum Opfer erwählt hat,
31 der Mann, den das *lilû*-Mädchen umklammert hat,

39 es ist in deiner Hand, sie zu beleben, o Šamaš! (HGŠ 1).

Other examples may be found under *CAD* '*alû*', '*lilû*', '*majālu*', and '*ṣalālu*'.

And these texts are at the same time evidence for one of the major ways one sought to ward off these threats: incantations. But other means were available as well, and thus we meet the following instruction (*CAD* '*ṣalālu*'):

šapāla lamassāti u kāribāti lu ṣa-al-la

> they (the women) must sleep beneath the (statues of the) lamassu- and karibu genii (MDP 4.18 3.6)

c. *Old Testament*

References to divine protection during sleep occur in Psalms 3.6, 4.9, and 57.5 of the psalms treated above, and also in Psalm 91.1-6 and Job 11.18-9. The question here is how divine protection and sleep interrelate, particularly in light of the earlier discussion and the comparative material.

First, while it was argued earlier in this chapter that Schmidt, Beyerlin, and Kraus had not convincingly established a usage of their group of psalms in a cultic juridical procedure, their evidence for some such procedure is solid, and some of the psalms in question here may reflect to one degree or another such a procedure. To the degree that this is the case, the psalms would be affirming YHWH's protection in a particular cultic situation.

It is necessary at this point to distance this scenario from a somewhat similar suggestion. Taking a grouping of psalms rather similar to Schmidt's, Delekat (1967) attempted to argue that the basic theme was protection, and that they grew out of a generalized practice of asylum. It is one of the contributions of Beyerlin's study (1970) to have laid this suggestion to rest: while the judgment motif is present in all the psalms in Beyerlin's group, protection is only present in some. Even more basic, in Israel asylum was granted only for unintentional killing. None of the psalms in question speak of that, nor do they picture the sort of extended stay in the temple area which asylum would imply (Beyerlin 1970, 44-53). And, if Milgrom (1981) is correct, asylum privileges were early curtailed.

On the other hand, the most direct evidence for the hearing of these psalms moves in a different direction. The superscriptions to a number of these psalms set them not in a cultic but in a historical situation:

> A Psalm of David, when he fled from Absalom his son (Ps 3.1).

> To the choirmaster: according to Do Not Destroy. A Miktam of David, when he fled from Saul, in the cave (Ps 57.1).

Childs has suggested that such superscriptions are the product of late post-exilic midrashic activity, 'a process of scholarly study of the Psalms in relation to other Old Testament passages, in which historical inferences and logical combinations were made and which went beyond a simple reading of the text' (1971, 148). Thus for Psalm 3, in additional to general parallels in the situation, the specific reference to sleep (v. 6) may have recalled the events narrated in 2 Samuel 16.14-22. As for the motivation of this activity, Childs suggests:

> By placing a Psalm within the setting of a particular historical incident in the life of David, the reader suddenly was given access to previously unknown information. David's inner life was now unlocked to the reader, who was allowed to hear his intimate thoughts and reflections. It therefore seems most probable that the formation of the titles stemmed from a pietistic circle of Jews whose interest was particularly focused on the nurture of the spiritual life (1971, 149).

However, an additional factor at work is relevant here. A precondition for the ascription of these psalms to these situations was their perceived appropriateness for these situations. They were the sort of psalms one would be expected to use. And thus behind the particular historicizing moves described by Childs it is possible to discern a pattern of community use. These psalms were perceived as appropriate because they were already being used by the community in situations of danger. Therefore it was not inappropriate to associate them with particular situations of danger experienced by David. In other words, these psalms, however reflective originally of a cultic situation, were used in a broader context. Nor is this context otherwise unknown, for it is the context sketched out in the opening chapter. When sleep is mentioned, most often it is mentioned in connection with the issue of vulnerability. And thus it is not surprising that there be at least some indications that these psalms were heard against this larger background. On the other hand, the concern for protection against demons attested by the Arslan Tash plaque and the Mesopotamian material does not appear to be present in the Old Testament.

More hypothetically, Mittmann has suggested that the reference to the lion in Amos 3.12 was motivated by lion-shaped legs on his audience's beds. His stress on the motivation for such protection is more convincing than the reconstruction:

> Sleep was, like its perceived relative death, a situation greatly needing protection against outer and inner dangers. The image of the lion effectively guaranteed, one believed, this protection (1976, 165; tm).

One additional note is perhaps appropriate. In ch. 3 §6 the motif of disrupted sleep is used in the complaint/description part of psalms of petition. In Psalms 3.6, 4.9 and 57.5(?) the reverse motif occurs: sleeping in peace in situations not conducive to such sleep plays a part in the expression of trust.

6. *Summary*

The Old Testament, and primarily the book of Psalms, implies a wide range of divine activity related to human sleep. In this chapter we have been concerned to explore this range, assess the degree to which it is integrally related to sleep, and, in particular cases, set the activity within a larger context.

Treatment of this activity broke into three logical parts. The first is devoted to Thomson's suggestion—found unconvincing—that quotidian sleep was seen as the result of divine activity. The second part deals with divine communication; the third with the activities of knowing and protecting.

Two aspects of divine communication have been examined. On the one hand, Ehrlich's discussion of incubation in the Old Testament has been summarized. Only in one text (1 Kgs 3.5-19 // 2 Chr 1.2-13) is incubation clearly narrated, and even there it is not explicitly identified. But there are enough other texts containing one or more elements of the practice to suggest that its role in Israelite religion has been downplayed in the Old Testament. On the other, a variety of texts have been brought together which attest to an awareness of divine communication during sleep that has not yet been conceptualized as 'dream', 'vision' or the like. If these texts where sleep and divine communication interface have a common thread, it is the preservation of divine freedom by a limitation, but not denial, of human initiative.

In the third part, we started with Schmidt's hypothesis. This hypothesis, if correct, would draw together a number of apparently unrelated threads in the individual petition psalms: YHWH's knowledge of the psalmist and YHWH's protection of the psalmist. Further, it would establish a matrix out of which these psalms grew: accused persons would come to YHWH's sanctuary. There they would be protected, there—through a nocturnal examination—they would be examined, and there they would be vindicated.

We have argued that while these psalms, together with other

evidence from the Old Testament, make the existence of such an institution likely, the relationship of these psalms in question to this institution is far from resolved. If then, the situation of divine knowing and protecting has not been established for this sleep setting, are there other sleep settings in which these—individually or together—might be situated?

A negative verdict was returned for divine knowing. A survey of collocation patterns suggests no firm link between selected language about divine knowing and night—let alone sleep. In fact, even in a cultic juridical setting divine examination may have played no role in most cases, where the issue was not what was in the heart, but what had transpired in the past.

Divine protection is more closely related to sleep. In Egypt, Mesopotamia, and (Syro-)Palestine, sleep was perceived as a state needing divine protection, and a variety of measures could be taken. The perceived dangers differed. The Mesopotamian examples cited, together with the Arslan Tash tablet, reflect a concern with the supernatural. The Egyptian devices apparently guarded against both natural and supernatural dangers, although the examples cited are perhaps more reflective of the former. The Old Testament reflects concern with primarily natural dangers, although Psalm 91.5-6 and Canticles 3.7-8 are perhaps exceptions.

The psalms speaking of sleep can, then, be set in three contexts. The first is cultic, following Schmidt. There the danger is from those bringing the accusation. This is, however, at present a highly speculative context. The second context—only present in some cases—is that provided by the superscriptions. There the danger is danger to a particular individual, David, described elsewhere in the canon. The third context, more broadly, is the variety of dangers attested in the Old Testament and the surrounding cultures. It is in this context, we have suggested, that these psalms were heard, which lead to the creation—in particular cases—of the second context. However, for any divine protection to be effectual, the deity or deities must be awake. And to that problem we now turn.

Chapter 6

DIVINE SLEEP

Here we pursue a variety of topics. For the ancient Near East, the references to divine sleep are gathered, and some suggestions made regarding their function and significance in their settings. For the Old Testament: how are references to YHWH's sleep to be interpreted? Here it is necessary to clear out a few red herrings, such as the continued grouping—most recently by Kraus—of divine sleep and death. But this is part of the larger problem of find the proper context for these texts, and this is the primary question addressed.

1. *Egypt*

Introducing a hymn to the sun god from the Pyramid Texts, Erman writes:

> The gods in the temples were greeted in the morning with a hymn, consisting mainly of the constantly repeated summons 'Awake in peace,' followed each time by a different name of the divinity. Accordingly, it was assumed that the gods were also thus awakened in heaven, and, moreover, by goddesses, a circumstance which enables us to conjecture what this hymn originally was: the song with which the women in earliest Egypt awakened their sovereign in the morning ([1927] 1966, 12).

Morenz notes 'a complete cycle [of such hymns] was used in the cult of Sobek at Crocodilopolis in the Faiyum' (Morenz 1973, 91). An example is provided by this 'Morning Hymn to the Sun' from the Pyramid Texts (Faulkner 1969, 228):

> May you wake in peace, O Purified, in peace!
> May you wake in peace, O Horus of the East, in peace!

May you wake in peace, O Soul of the East, in peace!
May you wake in peace, O Ḥarakhti, in peace!
May you sleep in the Night-bark,
May you wake in the Day-bark,
For you are he who oversees the gods,
There is no god who oversees you! (Utterance 573)

And not only do the gods sleep at night, but they face the same problems people face trying to navigate at night: 'I detest travelling in darkness, for then I cannot see, but fall upside down' (Pyramid texts, utterance 260; Faulkner 1969, 69).

The case of the sun god is somewhat more complicated, for both nocturnal sleep and wakefulness are affirmed. Thus in the (Cairo) 'Hymn to Amon-Re' (*ANET* 365-66):

He who awakes in health, Min-Amon, (3.1)

Who spends the night wakeful, while all men are asleep,
Seeking benefit for his creatures. (7.1)

The sole king, like the *fluid* of the gods,
With many names, unknown in number,
Rising in the eastern horizon,
And going to rest in the western horizon;
Who overthrows his enemies,
(Re)born early every day (9.3-4).

In the case of Osiris, his death may be spoken of in terms of sleep. Thus from the Pyramid Texts (Faulkner 1969, 231):

Osiris was laid low by his brother Seth, but he who is in Nedit moves, his head is raised by Rēʿ; he detests sleep and hates inertness, so the King will not putrefy, he will not rot, this King will not be cursed by your anger, you gods (Utterance 576).

Examples of seasonal divine sleep or of sleep during a crisis have not been found. While the lack of the latter is perhaps in part explicable by the different sorts of relationships the gods were understood to have with people, there is perhaps a correlate to it in 'The Prophecies of Neferti' (Lichtheim 1973, 141-43):

The sundisk, covered, (25) shines not for people to see,
One cannot live when clouds conceal,
All are numb for lack of it

. . . .
Re will withdraw from mankind:

Though he will rise at his hour,
One will not know when noon has come;
No one will discern his shadow,
No face will be dazzled by seeing [him],
No eyes will moisten with water.

2. *Mesopotamia*

Discussion may begin with the hymns to the gods of the night,[1] for there the understanding of the great gods as being on a diurnal sleep cycle comes through most clearly. The beginning of one of them is particularly illuminating in this regard (translit. Dossin 1935, 180-81; trans. Oppenheim 1959, 295-96):

bu-ul-lu-lu e-bu-ú sí-ik-ka-t[*um*]
še-re-tum ta-ab-ka-[*a*(?)]
[*ḫa-ab-ra-tum ni-šu-ú ša-qú-um-ma-a*]
pi-tu-tum ud-du-lu ba-a-[*bu*]
i-lu ma-tim iš-ta-ra-a-at ma-tim
dAdad ù dÉ-a dŠamaš ù dIštar
i-te-ir-bu a-na ú-tu-ul ša-me-e
ú-ul i-di-in-nu di-nam
ú-ul i-pa-ar-ra-sú a-wa-a-tim
pu-uṣ-ṣú-ma-at mu-ši-tum
êkallum š-ḫ-ru-ù-ša ku_8*-um-mu at-rù*
a-li-ik ur-ḫi-im dNergal ú-si-e[*l*]-[*l*]i
ù ša di-ni-im uš-te-bi-ir-ri ši-it-ta
da-a-a-an ki-it-tim a-bi ki-it-tim
dŠamaš i-te-ru-ub a-na ku-um-mi-šu

The nobles are deep in sleep,
the bars (of the doors) are lowered, the bolts(?) are in place—
(also) the (ordinary) people do not utter a sound,
the(ir always) open doors are locked.
The gods and goddesses of the country—
Samaš, Sin, Adad and Ištar—
have gone home to heaven to sleep,
they will not give decisions or verdicts (tonight).
Night has put on her veil—
the palace is quiet, the countryside does not utter a sound—
(Only) the (lonely) traveler calls to the god (for protection)
(and even) the one for whom the (divine) decision (is sought) remains asleep—
Samaš, the just judge, the father of the underprivileged,
has (likewise) gone to his bedchamber (AO 6769.1-15).

Oppenheim glosses the text:

> People and cattle are lost in sleep, but there are gods on duty, not the gods that rule the world in the daytime but those who appear when the gates of heaven open, the stars. When beasts, men and the *dei superi* are asleep, the stars rule the world. Their grace and assistance have to be sought for all cultic activities that are to be performed at night (1959, 291).

While the major gods are thought to sleep at night, a morning ceremony corresponding to the Egyptian has not been identified.[2]

But again, the case of the sun god is more complicated. On the one hand, there are texts which imply that the sun god sleeps during the night (rather than traveling back to the east). So Wilcke (1969, 67-69, with examples), and Kramer (1972, 42; citing *HAV* 4.8-10 [Radau in the *Hiprecht Anniversary Volume*, 1909, pp. 374-457] and the tablet Kish 1932, 155):

> O Utu, shepherd of the land, father of the black-headed people,
> When thou liest down, the people, too, lie down,
> O hero Utu, when thou risest, the people, too, rise.
> Utu has gone forth with lifted head to the bosom of his mother Ningal.

On the other hand, in 'The Shamash Hymn' (Lambert 1960, 129) the picture is one of unceasing activity: 'In the underworld you care for the counsellors of Kusu, the Anunnaki, / Above, you direct all the affairs of men' (KB 6/2 18.31-32). And further:

> *[l]a ta-šu-uš* u_4*-me-šam-ma ul 'a-da-ru pa-r[u]-ka*
> *[tuš]-ta-bar-u ina mu-ši-im-ma tu-šaḫ-miṭ [x]-x*
> *⌜a⌝-na šid-di šá la i-di ni-su-ti u bi-ri la ma-n[u-ti]*
> *ᵈšamaš dal-pa-ta šá ur-ra tal-li-ka u mu-šá ta saḫ-r[a]*
> *ul i-ba-áš-ši ina gi-mir ᵈi-gi-gi šá šu-nu-ḫu ba-li-ka*
> *ina ilī*^{meš} *nap-ḫar kiš-šá-ti šá šu-tu-ra ki-ma ka-a-ta*

> You are not dejected during the day, nor is your *surface darkened*
> By night you continue to kindle[.]
> To unknown distant regions and for uncounted leagues
> You press on, Samaš, going by day and returning by night.
> Among all the Igigi there is none who toils but you,
> None who is supreme like you in the whole pantheon of gods (41-46).

During the day one praises Shamash, and speaks of his activities during the night. But his nocturnal activities are of no help to those who need his aid during the night. He might as well be asleep, and is described as such. Then one turns to the gods of the night.

But beyond this nightly sleep, the gods apparently need—or enjoy—large amounts of sleep (Pettinato 1966, 194). And this appears in the literary texts in a variety of ways. In one of the accounts of the creation of humankind, Enki's sleep renders him oblivious to the problems of the other gods (Kramer 1972, 70). In Adapa, we find the line (*CAD* '*majālu*'):

> [*MAŠ*].*SUD Ea ina ma-a-a-li ina šá-da-di*
>
> when wise Ea lies in his bed (*BRM* 4 3.17).

From the context this might equally well be taken as simply rest while others (Adapa) do the work.

On the other hand, with other gods the problem is that they do not sleep enough. Thus the following lines occur in a hymn to Nergal (Liagre-Böhl 1949):

> [*šá ú-ni*]-*ḫa* ^{iṣ}*kakkam* (*u*) *haṭṭam*^{am}
> *šá ṣa-la-la sa-rat ṣa-al-la*
>
> [Der dann niederlegt] das Schwert und den Stecken,
> Doch nur trüglicher Ruhe sich hingeben kann.

Is the sense here that Nergal only appears to leave off his warfare? Various incantation series contain references to the activity of demons during (human) sleep (*CT* 16.27.19-20; 45.154; 17.25.6). Thus it is not surprising that we meet the characterization:[3]

> u_4*-mu ša ši!it-ta! la i-du-ú*
>
> demon that knows not sleep (*SBH* 82.5)

One wishes to cover all the possibilities (*CAD* '*ṣalālu*'):

> *lu êrēta la tallaka lu ṣal-la-a-ta la tetebbâ*
>
> you (evil god) should not come to me if you are awake, not get up if you lie asleep (Maqlu 6.13)

In a bilingual liturgical text performed for temple singers there are the following lines (translit. Thureau-Dagan 1921, 26; trans. Langdon 1913, xiv-xv):

> [*ša*] *ṣal-lu be-lum ša ṣal-lum a-di ma-ti ṣa-lil*
> *šadu-ú rabu-ú a-bu* ^{d}*Mullil ša ṣal-lum a-di mat*
> *ri-'-ú mu-šim ši-ma-a-ti ša ṣal-lum a-di mat*

He that sleeps, lord that sleeps [,] how long shall he sleep?
Great mountain father Enlil, that sleeps, how long?
Shepherd that fixes the fates, he that sleeps, how long? (IVR 23 1.27-31)

Langdon suggests that these lines are in fact taken from some other Enlil liturgy (1913, xv-xvi), a suggestion supported by material discussed below. If so, they could well be protesting not Enlil's (characteristic) love of sleep, but his 'sleep' at a point where his wakeful (benevolent) attention is needed.

Up to this point we have been concerned with customary patterns, either with diurnal sleep or with sleep (or rest) that is (enjoyably) excessive. Equally important are the cases in which these patterns are disrupted. And this happens in two characteristic ways. Mankind may disturb divine sleep, or the gods (Enlil in particular) may be found asleep when one would expect them to be awake. And the awkwardness of the last sentence reflects a major difference in these ways, for in the former case there is nothing in the texts which tell against a straightforward understanding of divine sleep, while in the latter case the texts themselves push 'sleep' to a figurative level.

It is in three different myths that divine sleeplessness becomes an issue (cf. Pettinato 1966). First, Atra-ḫasīs, whose most recent publication[4] is based on an Old Babylonian copy made during the reign of Ammiș aduqa (17th Century). Here, the noise of the newly created people prevents Enlil from sleeping. According to Lambert and Millard's reconstruction, the pattern of Enlil's disturbed sleep and his response is repeated three times.[5] While the nature of the noise in question has been the subject of extended discussion (summarized, conveniently, in Oden 1981, 205), its effect on Enlil's sleep—and temper—is clear, as evidenced in Enlil's complaint:

ik-ta-ab-ta ri-gi-im a-wi-lu-ti
i-na ḫu-bu-ri-ši-na ú-za-am-ma ši-it-ta

'The noise of mankind has become too intense for me,
With their uproar I am deprived of sleep.' (2.1.7-8)

In the Enûma eliš it is Apsû who cannot sleep. Apsû complains about the new gods to Ti'āmat (translit. Labat 1935; trans. Jacobsen 1976, 171-72).

im-ʳtarˡ-ṣa-am-ma al-kat-su-nu e-li-ia
ur-ri-iš la šu-up-šu-ḫa-ku mu-ši-iš la ṣa-al-la-ku
lu-uš-ḫal-liq-ma al-kat-su-nu lu-sa-ap-pi-iḫ
qu-lu liš-ša-kin-ma i ni-iṣ-lal ni-i-ni

Their ways have become noisome to me!
I am allowed no rest by day; by night no sleep.
Let me abolish, yea, let me smash to bits their ways
that peace may reign (again) and we may sleep (1.37-40).

Pettinato (1966, 196) correctly observes that the use of the day/night formula suggests that rest rather than sleep per se is the issue here. Nevertheless there is a certain poetic justice in Ea's use of sleep as a weapon against Apsû:

u-nak-kil-šu šu-tu-ru ta-a-šu el-lum
im-ni-šum-ma ina mê u-šab-ši
šit-tam ir-te-ḫi-šu ṣa-lil ṭu-ub-qit-tum
u-ša-aṣ-lil-ma apsâm(am) ri-ḫi šit-tam

He formed, yea, he fixed against him the configuration of the All,
 skillfully made his overpowering sacred spell.
He recited it so that he quieted down in the waters,
 poured slumber over him, so that he soundly slept (1.62-65).

The third example occurs in 'The Poem of Erra', in the midst of a number of arguments the Sibitti use to motivate Erra to take up arms (translit. Cagni 1969, 66; trans. Cagni 1977, 28-30):

a-na ^{d}*a-nun-na-ki ra-'i-im šaḫ-ra-ár-ti damiqti(ti) ep-šá*
^{d}*a-nun-na-ki ina ḫu-bur nišī*^{meš} *ul i-re-eḫ-ḫu-ú šit-tum*

To the Anunnaki, who love deathly silence, do something good:
Because of men's noise the Anunnaki cannot fall asleep (1.81-82).

Pettinato is concerned to argue that the noise in question is not noise in general, or, say, the noise of the younger gods partying downstairs and disturbing sleep, but noise portending revolt. Thus sleep per se is not the issue:

> I think it extremely unlikely that the Sumerian conception, according to which the gods need much sleep, is at work here. Likewise it is singular, that even Enhil complains about lack of sleep, of whom it is said that he is always awake and only appears to sleep (1966, 192; tm).

But this may well underestimate the creativity involved in these literary works. While Pettinato may well be correct that the noise involved (*ḫubūrum*) carries specific overtones, and that therefore the complaint over lack of sleep functions to stress the seriousness of the problem, another layer is added to the poems with the common knowledge that the gods like to sleep and will—like any powerful neighbor—react if that sleep is disturbed.

Pettinato's discussion does indicate that the interpretation of this divine sleep is not self-evident. And here we will simply indicate two different directions interpretation can go, both of which relativize the importance of the human noise. On the one hand, there is Eliade, commenting of the lines from the creation epic:

> We can read in these lines the nostalgia of matter (that is, of a mode of being corresponding to the inertia and unconsciousness of substance) for the primordial immobility, the resistance to all movement—the preliminary condition for the cosmogony (1978, 70).

There is no question of a cycle here, but simply of the state at which (some of) the gods wish to maintain themselves. And this direction could be pursued further by exploring the larger theme of rest, e.g. as a motivation for the creation of people.

On the other hand, in Machinist's reading of 'The Poem of Erra', a different dynamic is perceived, for he takes as fundamental the contrast between activity and inactivity—broadly defined—which exists within both Erra and Ishum. Thus at the beginning

> Erra, although we are told that he is supposed to be warlike (I 13-14, 19)—and he becomes so later—here appears slothful and unresponsive to the call for war. His weariness, in fact, is so great that he cannot even sleep properly (I 15); and he is so negligent in watching over his surroundings that . . . the land falls prey to depredation and disaster. Išum, on the other hand, although portions of the *inclusio* describe him as caring and peaceful (I 3, 21-22) . . . is largely pictured as bellicose, goading Erra and the Sibitti to war (I 4-14) (1983, 223).

And Machinist summarizes his thesis as follows:

> Where, the poem is saying, there is rest among the gods or on earth, there will also or soon be violence, the two revolving together in a ceaseless cycle. But the matter does not stop here. For rest and violence are only part of the larger tension between inactivity and activity in the universe . . . activity is necessary for the universe to function. But too much activity brings on violence and potential chaos. Likewise, a certain inactivity, if understood as peacefulness and calm, helps to insure a balanced and just order. But too much inactivity is the equivalent of paralysis and death, and invites violent activity to fill the void it has left (1983, 225).

Here rest and activity would be cyclical, although the time period involved would not be tightly defined. But both Eliade and Machinist are engaged in a somewhat more abstract reading than the texts would themselves dictate.

The other class of non-cyclical sleep is the divine 'sleep' during human calamity. This is, to anticipate, the sort of sleep closest to the Old Testament usage, and discussion may start with the Sumerian congregational lament 'O Angry Sea', edited by Kutscher (1975). Kutscher has found exemplars of the lament from the Old Babylonian to the Seleucid periods, and suggests that

> very early in its history it was adapted for use as a standard balag to be chanted at ceremonies marking the demolition and rebuilding of temples... It may well be that the first half, namely, the lament (stanzas i-xiii) was recited during the ceremonies marking the demolition of the old temple, while the hymn and prayer were recited during the ceremonies marking the laying of the foundation to the new temple (1975, 6-7).

In the early stanzas different requests are made of Enlil, using a set of epithets, one of which is 'The One Who Feigns Sleep'.[6] Kutscher suggests the following interpretation:

> The seventh epithet, *ù-lul-la ku-ku* 'Who Feigns Sleep' (lit. 'Who Sleeps a False Sleep') is translated *šá ṣa!-lal sar-ra-a-ti ṣal-lu* (*BL* 208.17f.). The origin of the concept may be such allusions to Enlil's 'sleep' as expressed in *a-ab-ba hu-luh-ha* *153ff. His eventual rise to save his people renders such sleep 'false' (1975, 49).

In any case, the picture of Enlil as sleeping is made quite explicit (1975, 148-49):

> The Wild Ox is asleep, when will he rise?
> Enlil is asleep, when will he arise? (10.153-54)
>
> The sleeping Wild Ox, let him arise!
> The sleeping Enlil, let him arise! (12.172-73)

But the non-literal sense in which this language is being used is also made clear, as in the following plea (1975, 148):

> The Warrior Who Feigns Sleep, restore (your) heart, restore! (10.134)

Regarding this usage, Kutscher suggests: 'The implication of this appeal is that when Enlil is angry his heart is not in its proper place and its restoration marks pacification' (1975, 101). That is, Enlil is being asked to wake up and cool off.

Likewise relevant here are the images from a number of *balag*-lamentations. Cohen provides a convenient summary of this genre:

> the *balag*-lamentation was originally composed to placate the wrath of the gods during the razing of sacred structures. As early as the Old Babylonian period the laments also became part of a fixed liturgy for certain days of the month, presumably to pacify the gods over unknowingly committed offenses that may have been totally unrelated to the demolishing of temple buildings. This dual usage of the *balag*-lamentation was maintained throughout the First Millennium BC when the *balag* was even used in rituals to avert portended evil (1974, 15).

'The Steer in his fold' (*SBH* I, II, and no. 26), addressed to Mullil (Enlil), contains the epithet 'he who sleeps a false sleep'. But the line in which it is contained suggests a purely figurative use (Cohen 1974, 20):

> He who sleeps a false sleep, he who gazes about (155)

In 'His Word (is) a Wail, a Wail' (*SBH* nos. 43, 44) more extensive use is made of this motif. Cohen summarizes the plot:

> Mullil, by his utterance, had unleashed destruction upon the land, all the while Mullil feigning sleep, allowing the devastation to continue. The goddess of Uruk, Inanna, determines to take action... In the last preserved lines Inanna... has gained admittance, sitting on Mullil's lap, trying to awaken him (1974, 20).

The following lines illustrate the use of this motif (Cohen 1974, 20-22):

1 His word (is) a wail, a wail; he is asleep, a wail!

25 Feigning, my father feigns lying down.
26 The great mountain, Mullil, feigns lying down.
27 The shepherd of the black-headed feigns lying down.
28 He who witnesses everything first-hand feigns lying down.
29 The steer who causes the troops to wander feigns lying down.
30 He who sleeps a false sleep, feigns lying down.

60 May I soothe his heart! May I pacify his liver!
61 May I direct (my) words to his heart and liver!
62 May I direct my words to his distressed heart!

70 . . . . she sits on the great knees.
71 His head covering . . . . she asks him:
72 'Oh sleeping one, how long will you sleep?'
73 'Great mountain, father Mullil, how long will you sleep?'
74 'You have killed with hunger those who even possess extensive cultivated lands.'

There are, then, a variety of ways in which the gods could be spoken of as sleeping, and these ways generally occur in different types of literature, although there is not here a strict correlation. The gods can be spoken of as sleeping on a diurnal cycle. This appears in the hymns to the gods of the night, and the opposite image of Shamash not sleeping likewise appears in a hymn (to Shamash!). Tammuz/ Dumuzi operated on a yearly cycle, and his 'death' was apparently occasionally spoken of as sleep.[7] The relevance of this usage to the Old Testament usage will be addressed in the next section. On the other hand, equal if not more attention is paid to non-cyclical sleep, whether the lost sleep of the gods in the myths which triggers the disasters, or the 'sleep' of Enlil, who, for reasons of his own, makes himself unavailable.[8]

3. *Old Testament*

The following texts clearly use the language of sleeping and waking in relationship to the divine:[9]

> And at noon Elijah mocked them, saying, 'Cry aloud, for he is a god; either he is musing, or he has gone aside, or he is on a journey, or perhaps he is asleep and must be awakened' (1 Kgs 18.27).

> Woe to him who says to a wooden thing, Awake;
> to a dumb stone, Arise!
> Can this give revelation?
> Behold, it is overlaid with gold and silver,
> and there is no breath at all in it (Hab 2.19).

> Thou hast seen, O Lord; be not silent!
> O Lord, be not far from me!
> Bestir thyself, and awake for my right,
> for my cause, my God and my Lord! (Ps 35.22-23).

> Rouse thyself! Why sleepest thou, O Lord?
> Awake! Do not cast us off for ever!
> Why dost thou hide thy face?
> Why dost thou forget our affliction and oppression? (Ps 44.24-25).

> Rouse thyself, come to my help, and see!
> Thou, Lord God of hosts, art God of Israel.
> Awake to punish all the nations;
> spare none of those who treacherously plot evil. Selah
> (Ps 59.5b-6).

> Then the Lord awoke as from sleep,
> like a strong man shouting because of wine (Ps 78.65).

> He will not let your foot be moved,
> he who keeps you will not slumber.
> Behold, he who keeps Israel
> will neither slumber nor sleep (Ps 121.3-4).

While the first two texts do not appear problematic, it is the latter texts, those speaking of sleep in relationship with YHWH, which call for discussion.

A major part of the exegetical and theological challenge posed by these texts is the question of their proper positioning vis-à-vis the comparative material. At least two different positionings have been proposed, and these will be examined prior to articulating another way of relating the Old Testament and comparative material.

Widengren (1955) has proposed that these texts be understood in terms of a dying and rising god pattern, citing both Mesopotamian and Ugaritic material, but laying particular stress on the former. Starting with Psalm 78.60-64, Widengren collects a number of petitions (Pss 74.3-7; 79.1-3; Lam 2.12; 4.4, 9), from which he derives a group of motifs which include:

> 1. God abandons his own people and his temple to his enemies;
> 2. The enemies plunder the city and sanctuary and destroy them;
> 3. The conflagration is mentioned in particular (Widengren 1955, 65; tm).

Nine motifs are identified, and Widengren identifies parallels for each in texts identified as Tammuz or Ishtar liturgies by Witzel (1935).

However, this approach needs to be seriously qualified, for the following reasons. First, Witzel used a very wide net in identifying Tammuz liturgies:

> Naturally the first texts to come into question in the gathering of material were those in which the god Tammuz was explicitly named. Subsequently those in which any deity played the same

> role as the god Tammuz... The same applied for texts in which the goddess standing in a particular relation to 'Tammuz' played the same role as Ishtar played in the poems proving to be Tammuz poems (Witzel 1935, vi; tm).

Thus in the laments over the temple listed by Witzel (1935, xi), Tammuz and his woes appear in only one (VAT 617 obv. 2.32f.; Witzel 1935, 34), and there, it would appear, as an apt parallel to the woes being lamented.[10] The power relationships in the various Dumuzi stories are sufficiently clear to allow the generalization that once Dumuzi is set upon by the powers of the underworld, his role is simply passive. His death can—apparently—be spoken of as sleep,[11] but he is hardly in a position to wake up, to ascend from the netherworld of his own choosing. That decision will be made by others, most notably Gestinanna.[12] And it is this difference in the logic of Dumuzi's and YHWH's 'sleep' that is fundamental.

As for the Ugaritic material, while there is a clear connection between Baal's death and drought (see, conveniently, *CTA* 5.5.4-11, and discussion in de Moor 1971, 187-89), Baal's death is not connected with political misfortunes.

In fact, there is only a partial match between the texts Widengren assembles and those which actually call for YHWH to wake up. Psalm 35 is an individual, not a group, petition. Psalm 44 complains of scattering, but not of drought. Psalm 59 speaks of enemies threatening, but nothing has happened yet. So in fact Psalm 78 is the only call on YHWH to awaken which fits Widengren's paradigm, which is to say that it is the only text in which that particular cluster of distressing circumstances is responded to with language implying that YHWH has been sleeping. Thus Widengren's proposal that the use of sleep field language of these psalms has been influenced by a dying and rising god pattern lacks evidence.

Nevertheless, Kraus accepts Widengren's argument that talk of God sleeping and waking is relevant to the search for a dying-rising god pattern in Israel, and continues:

> In Ugarit the dead Baal was described as the sleeping one, and the resurrected one as the awakening one ([1967] 1972, 14; tm).

Kraus does not supply text references for descriptions of the dead Baal as sleeping, and so it is difficult to guess what he is thinking of, since there are at present no published texts which would obviously be read in this way.[13]

A second positioning of the comparative material is to set it in a general way over against the Old Testament: the language of sleeping is being used differently in Israel.

> In contrast to the heathen gods who sleep, circumstances permitting (1 Kgs 18.27), the God of Israel does not sleep (Ps 121.4). In Psalms 44.24 and 78.65 the talk of God's sleep in poetic language is figurative (Frohmeyer 1959., 1175; tm).

> There are apparent exceptions at Ps.44.23 (43.23) and Ps.78(77).65. But here only the mode of expression, not the conception, is mythological. The same is true of Gn.2.2f., where the mythological basis is that of rest rather than sleep (Oepke 1965, 435).

> God does not sleep (Ps 121.4); his help-delaying sleep is only figurative (Ps 44.24; 78.65) (Schilling 1968, 1539; tm).

> 'Sleep' is therefore in these Psalms a picture for the behavior of the deus absconditus, the God, who is silent and does not intervene, who does not—not yet—show his life and power to the broken . . . The Baals sleep, they are subject to the rhythm of coming into being and passing away. The psalmist however acknowledges and teaches: . . . your Guardian does not sleep! (Kraus [1967] 1972, 16-17; tm).

The problem here is that it is a dubious exegetical move to construe simultaneously Psalm 121 as a (literal) statement about the range of Divine activities, and Psalm 44 *et al.* as (non-literal) statements about Divine activity. Further, this process of 'cleaning up' the text by identifying some parts as literal and others as figurative is not really carried through consistently. In Psalm 44.24-25 both God's sleeping and forgetting are anthropomorphic, but the same exegetical moves are not made with each. There is a very legitimate desire evidenced here to engage in theologically useful exegesis, but that desire is perhaps obscuring the precise points of concern in the texts. Finally, this approach obscures the different sorts of divine sleep spoken of among Israel's neighbors.

At this point a summary of the preceeding sections is in order. The texts cited from surrounding cultures establish that there are different sorts of divine sleep, distinguished by the length of the cycle. There is sleep on a twenty-four hour cycle. It was assumed that the gods, like people, needed sleep, and slept at night. In general, this divine sleep was unproblematic and does not seem to have been a source of concern.[14] The cultic correlates of this sleep cycle included the ceremonies for waking the gods (Egypt), and the prayers to the gods of the night (Mesopotamia). It would be difficult to establish that this sleep cycle was associated with YHWH in the Old Testament; the temple practice alluded to in the Mishnah would appear to be the first solid evidence for it.[15]

The second sleep cycle is an annual cycle, and involves construing the death of a fertility god as sleep. As indicated, hard evidence for this construal in the literature reviewed is limited, confined at present to Mesopotamia. However, given the frequent use of sleep language for death, there would be no reason for surprise if more examples were discovered. This cycle, whether spoken of in terms of death or sleep, is more traumatic than the daily cycle. Still, its ending is predictable, even if one's own survival until that end is problematic. This cycle appears in the Old Testament in connection with Tammuz (Ezek 8.14), and Hosea also makes use of it. However, again it is not a cycle by means of which YHWH's (in)activity was interpreted.

A third sleep cycle might be spoken of on the basis of references to Osiris's death as sleep. Here, though, it is less a question of a cycle than of an occurrence in which one may share and thereby secure resurrection (awakening). Again, there is no evidence that YHWH was thought to sleep in this sense.

However, there is a fourth type of divine sleep, untimely sleep, the sleep which leaves the god's people helpless. This type was encountered most clearly in 'O Angry Sea' and in the *balag*s, and it is this type which we encounter in the Old Testament references to YHWH's sleep.[16]

But the length of the cycle is not the only variable among these different ways of speaking of divine sleep. The different ways had different places in the ongoing life of the respective communities. 'Enlil is asleep' would mean quite different things in reciting a hymn to the gods of the night (what else would one expect him to be doing?) and reciting a lamentation (when will he wake up and help us!).[17] And, equally to the point, these different ways would imply different hermeneutics, different ways of understanding the language about divine sleep. As for diurnal divine sleep, since this language operates on a perceived similarity between divine and human patterns, there would be no reason to understand the language other than literally—until shifts in theology disallowed that sort of divine activity. As for annual divine sleep, in the Mesopotamian and Ugaritic material, the language of death (of Tammuz, Baal) appears to be primary, with the language of sleep entering in in the same sorts of ways it enters in when speaking about human death. Thus the language of sleep here would operate on the literal-metaphorical scale in the same sorts of ways the language of sleep in reference to human death does. As for untimely divine sleep, in the Mesopotamian texts, the metaphorical use is clear.

Thus the Old Testament is clearly selective, speaking of YHWH and sleep not in terms of the experience of regular human sleep (diurnal), of the seasons (annual), or of death (Osiris), but in terms of the experience of acute need. And thus the proper positioning of the texts in question is not in parallel with the dying god texts (Widengren) or over against the non-Israelite texts (Frohnmeyer, Oepke, *et al.*), but with one sort of language about divine sleep (untimely sleep, common to Israel, Mesopotamia, and Syria[?]), over against other sorts of language about divine sleep (diurnal, annual). Thus when the psalmists spoke of YHWH as sleeping, they were not necessarily developing a new way of speaking about YHWH, but may well have been making use of a way of speaking that had been developed centuries ago.

It is a fair question at this point whether the Mesopotamian material is relevant: is not the proposed parallel too distant? No. On the one hand, Gwaltney (1983) has argued for close parallels between the book of Lamentations and the *balag-eršemma*s. And while Gwaltney correctly noted that the Mesopotamian element of rousing the god from sleep is lacking in Lamentations (1983, 208), we can note that it did find its way into Israelite liturgy. But while Gwaltney looked to the exile to explain Israelite familiarity with the Mesopotamian traditions, here we would need to assume earlier points of contact (perhaps mediated through Syria). On the other hand, in the psalms themselves the same sorts of juxtapositions of different requests are found, *whose net effect is to shift the language from a literal to a metaphorical level*. Thus:

> Rouse thyself! Why sleepest thou, O Lord?
> Awake! Do not cast us off for ever!
> Why dost thou hide thy face?
> Why dost thou forget our affliction and oppression? (Ps 44.24–25).

Nevertheless, it can still be asked whether all of the Old Testament examples fit this Mesopotamian paradigm equally well. Here it is necessary to note an additional element in this paradigm: the problem is not simply that the god is 'sleeping', but that this unresponsiveness is intentional. And this is an important element, because it is this element which secures the non-literal character of the divine sleep. The god must 'wake up' and 'simmer down'.

The closest parallels are provided by Psalms 44 and 78, which, like their Mesopotamian counterparts, are responses to destructions of sanctuaries (table 6.1).[18] Thus Psalm 44 speaks of YHWH selling his people 'for a trifle' (v. 13), of YHWH hiding his face (v. 25). And Psalm 78 speaks of YHWH being provoked, moved to jealousy (v. 58) and being 'full of wrath' (v. 59). And it is perhaps not coincidental that these psalms employ the most explicit language about sleep.[19]

Table 6.1
Psalms speaking of divine sleep

Psalms	Text	Situation/Form
44.24	*'wrh lmh tyšn 'dny* *hqyṣh 'l-tznḥ lnṣḥ*	loss of Jerusalem
78.65	*wyqṣ kyšn 'dny* *kgbwr mtrwnn myyn*	loss of Shiloh
35.23	*h'yrh whqyṣh lmšpṭy* *'lhy w'dny lryby*	individual petition
59.5b-6	*'wrh lqr'ty wr'h* *w'th yhwh-'lhym ṣb'wt 'lhy yśr'l* *hqyṣh lpqd kl-hgwym* *'l-tḥn kl-bgdy 'wn slh*	individual petition
121.3b-4	*'l-ynwm šmrk* *hnh l'-ynwm wl' yyšn šwmr yśr'l*	(*šyr lm'lwt'*)

The remaining two petitions are compatible with this paradigm, but Psalm 121, which goes its own way, suggests another way of reading them. Besides its denial of divine sleep, Psalm 121 is unique in employing *nwm*. In ch. 2 §4.b I argued that *nwm* occurred in characteristically military or policing situations. This, coupled with the frequent use of *šmr* 'guard', suggests that sleep as an image is functioning very differently than in Psalm 44. There it pictured the divine making-oneself-unavailable. Here it trades on the common problem of guardians who fall asleep, and affirms that YHWH, a reliable guardian, will not fall asleep on the job. And it is possible (probable?) that Psalms 35 and 59 are basically functioning with this image as well: YHWH will need to wake up, to be alert to fulfill his role.

Here two parallels to this language may be cited, one Biblical, one extra-Biblical. Earlier a number of lines from 'O Angry Sea' were cited, as parallels to the sleep language in Psalms 44 and 78. But for the image as the wakeful guardian, perhaps the closest parallels are provided by the following lines (Kutscher 1975, 144):

> A shepherd who would not lie down he installed over the sheep . . .
> A shepherd who does not fall asleep he placed on guard . . . (*3.36-37).

On the Biblical side, the use of *šqd* 'be vigilant' may be noted:

> *wyhy dbr-yhwh 'ly l'mr mh-'th r'h yrmyhw w'mr mql šqd 'ny r'h wy'mr yhwh 'ly hyṭbt lr'wt ky-šqd 'ny 'l-dbry l'štw*
>
> And the word of the Lord came to me, saying, 'Jeremiah, what do you see?' And I said, 'I see a rod of almond'. Then the Lord said to me, 'You have seen well, for I am watching over my word to perform it' (Jer 1.11-12).

Do we have here an example of a text belonging to a larger divine sleep circle?

If we ask then on which level this language is functioning, perhaps the main point to be made is that it would run counter to the use of the language to attempt to derive any information about YHWH's sleeping patterns. YHWH, so Psalm 121, will not fall asleep on the job. As for Psalms 35 and 59, attempts to derive information about YHWH's sleeping patterns from them would be like attempts to derive information about sleeping patterns in contemporary offices by counting the number of occurrences of 'Wake up!'.

To put the point differently, to read these texts in terms of the later concern with anthropomorphic language would be to miss their particular point. Helpful here is Barr's 'Theophany and Anthropomorphism in the Old Testament'. Barr begins by distinguishing between language which implies a human form ('God's hands, feet, ears, nose, his speaking, smelling, walking in gardens, shutting doors, laughing, whistling, treading winepresses, rising early in the morning, rejoicing, being disgusted, changing his mind, being jealous' [1960, 31]) and theophanies, for 'it is in the theophanies where God lets himself be seen that there is a real attempt to grapple with the form of his appearance' (1960, 30-31). While occasionally there is a definite form (Gen 18), more often there are only traces of that form (Gen 18.2; 28.13; 1 Sam 3.10; Amos 7.7; 9.1) or attention rather to the message or the surroundings (Exod 24.9-11). Why? Probably because 'the recording of the appearance in detail was felt by writers often to be too serious and difficult to attempt except in special cases' (1960, 32). Rather, the problematics are different, whether the deadly effects of seeing the deity (1960, 34, citing Exod 33.20 and Judg 13.22), or the problem of sin, both in regard to the *kabod* (1960, 35), and in Exodus 33, where 'the problem which interests the writer is not that of anthropomorphism and transcendence but that of sin and atonement in relation to (a) the accompanying presence and (b) the vision or appearance of Yahweh' (1960, 36).[20]

There are, then, two different ways in which the language of untimely sleep is used of YHWH, one trading on the experience of authorities making themselves unavailable (Pss 44, 78), the other trading on the experience of guardians sleeping on the job (Pss 35, 59, 121). Thus there are two rather different theological problems being articulated. The first is a situation of distress whose source is perceived to be YHWH. YHWH must wake up, simmer down, and as long as the problem is posed in these terms there is nothing to do but take whatever action is believed to help cool YHWH's anger. The second is rather different. It is a situation of distress, and YHWH does not seem to be responding. With the problem posed in this way, there are two choices. One may wait until YHWH shows himself a trustworthy guardian, one who in fact has not been asleep on the job, or look for another guardian, one with a faster response time.

In sum, a variety of ways of speaking about divine sleep in the ancient Near East have been identified: diurnal, annual, untimely. Each has characteristic settings in which it is employed; each has a particular range of hermeneutical possibilities. In the Old Testament, two ways of speaking about sleep in relation to YHWH have been noted, both falling under the general category of untimely sleep. On the one hand, Psalms 44 and 78 appear to use the language of divine sleep in much the same way as the cited Mesopotamian laments: 'sleep' serves as a way of picturing the deity making himself unavailable to his needy people. On the other hand, Psalm 121 (and probably also 35 and 59) trades on the requirement of alertness in guardians, affirming that YHWH does not doze off when needed. Here the focus of the language is on YHWH's dependability, rather than his sleeping habits.

Chapter 7

CONCLUSION

Human and divine sleep have been approached in the preceeding chapters from a number of directions. Here we will summarize the particular gains of these approaches, bring a number of strands together, and indicate further lines of research.

The Introduction (Chapter 1), besides a survey of prior research and an indication of the particular course to be taken in this study, offered an analysis of the situations in which sleep was remarked on in the Old Testament. Most frequently sleep was mentioned either because it was a situation of vulnerability, or because it was a situation in which one dreamed. While other clusterings appeared as well (sleep while on the road, the precedence of other activities before sleep, etc.), it is these two, and the first in particular, which reappear throughout the study.

In 'Lexical studies' (Chapter 2), the general question was how was language connected with sleep organized in Biblical Hebrew? This question was explored primarily through examining a number of different lexical groupings, or fields. The broadest field identified was the sleep field, containing fifty-four words, some related very closely (*yšn* 'to sleep'), some related rather more loosely (*gg* 'roof') to the activity of sleeping (table 2.2). This field was gathered by identifying texts in which sleep played a role (table 2.1), and this procedure provided a check on its limits. One surprise at that point was that none of the vocabulary for resting appeared, and this confirmed the decision to restrict the study to sleep, rather than the broader categories of rest or inactivity.

Did these sleep-related words interact with each other, occur in particular patterns or groupings? Meaningful joint occurrences, or collocations, are often organized in terms of a particular word, and thus one speaks of the associative field of, say, *nwm* 'slumber'. One word is placed in the center, surrounded by all the words with which it collocates. In this study a different method was used. Collocations examined were limited to those which occurred more than once. Approximately half of the words appearing in the sleep field passed through this grid. The collocations were then charted simultaneously, indicating graphically the collocational relationships between the various words (chart 2.3). A number of uses were noted of such mappings, including study of narrative technique, 'holes' (words which would be expected to appear, but did not), and collocational patterns of cognates in other semitic languages. To expand on the first use, the collocations indicated reveal a much stronger narrative tradition for the process of going to bed than the process of waking up. Washing, eating, drinking, lying down—all these have a place. But for the morning, not only are corresponding clusters of words lacking, but collocations are even lacking between words at increasing levels of generality. That is, while for the evening the narrator can become more specific, stringing together 'spend the night' (*lyn*), 'lie down' (*škb*), 'sleep' (*yšn*), collocations between 'wake up' (*yqṣ*), 'rise' (*qwm*), 'rise early' (*škm*) are lacking.

From here, attention turned to two more restricted groups, the *Yšn* 'to sleep' group and the *mškb* 'bed' group. Here the primary question was how they differed in meaning, how they differed in usage. For the *Yšn* group, it was argued that *yšn* 'to sleep' and *šnh* 'sleep' functioned as the neutral or unmarked terms, carrying no particular weight. *Nwm* (traditionally) 'to slumber' appeared from its contexts to focus on the beginning of sleep, dozing off. The deverbal noun *tnwmh* appeared also to have this particular sense when in the A-position and in the plural, but to function simply as a synonym for *šnh* when in the B-position and in the singular. It was not determined whether the position or the number was the determining factor. The use of *rdm* 'sleep' and the deverbal noun *trdmh* suggested use when sleep was divinely initiated, as opposed to when sleep was deep. A number of texts can, however, be read either way. And the use of the root in Proverbs does not fit particularly well with either of these hypotheses. More puzzling was the use of *škb* 'lie down'. Here the difficulty is not in distinguishing its sense from that of *yšn*, but of accounting for the choice between the two in any given text. Some progress was made, but for most of the texts studied this problem remains.

For the second group studied, the *mškb* group, again the question was how to account for the different patterns of usage between *mṭh*, *mškb*, and *'rś* (all) 'bed'. Distribution suggested, but did not firmly establish, a dialectical pattern with *mṭh* northern and *mškb* southern. The distribution patterns also suggested, perhaps more clearly, that the situation being described affected the choice of words. Thus *mṭh* tended to occur more often in situations involving bedridden people or death, and *mškb* tended to occur more often in situations involving sleep, intercourse, or other nocturnal activity. With the exception of two occurrences in Deuteronomy 3, *'rś* appears only in poetry. It was suggested that the break in the distributional pattern in Deuteronomy was evidence that there Og's 'bed' was in fact being referred to as a sarcophagus. In one respect, as will be seen below, this lack of clear distinctions within the group is significant in itself.

It should be noted at this point that there is not a particularly good fit between the concerns identified in the first chapter (vulnerability, dreams, etc.) and the distinctions present within the *Yšn* and *mškb* groups. While the distinctions within the *Yšn* group are operative—the same cannot be claimed at present for the *mškb* group—they do not follow the main contours of concerns traced at the beginning.

'Cultural patterns' (Chapter 3) treated the spatial and temporal dimensions of sleep in Iron Age Israel. The roof (whether enclosed or not) appears to have been the most desirable place to sleep, although a variety of factors were noted which would affect this practice. Beds, as indicated both by the vocabulary and the bed models from various sites, were known. Certainly very elaborate beds were known. But the sorts of distinctions between various grades of beds which would have been important to the upper classes do not appear to have embedded themselves in the language, and whatever is still embedded in the soil awaits discovery.

A survey of Egyptian and Mesopotamian beds produced material useful in a number of respects. Particularly the Egyptian beds evidenced a concern with safety during sleep, and this dovetailed well with the Old Testament's interest in sleep as a time of vulnerability. In Mesopotamia this concern was also present, but the evidence is preserved in texts rather than furniture. The richness of particular beds, again, particularly Egyptian, indicated the beauty (and, to give Amos his due, money) that could be lavished on sleeping places.

Palestinian burials were surveyed for additional information about sleeping practices. Most usable were the finer Iron II rock-cut tombs.

In some cases the lengths of platforms on which the bodies were laid seemed to have been cut to fit. If stone was cut to fit, how much more one's bed? The platform widths, on the other hand, appeared rather too wide to reflect beds in use. But beyond questions of measurement, the burials were useful in suggesting a variety of sleeping positions.

As for the temporal dimension, what evidence there was suggested a pattern governed by the movement of the sun. One rises with the sun, rests when the sun is at its strongest, and retires for the day with or soon after the sun's setting. On the other hand, to retire is not to sleep, and references to prayer or meditation suggest that the bed, far more than in our culture, was the site of a wide range of activities.

'Israelite understandings of sleep' (Chapter 4) pursued a variety of questions, using comparative resources to get a closer fix on the particular moves or concerns expressed in the Old Testament. There are different types of sleep, and the different literatures surveyed expressed characteristic interests. Thus the rabbinic traditions evidenced interest in defining different sorts of sleep for the purpose of making rulings: when was it permitted to doze off? Homer and the Mesopotamian texts spoke often of sweet sleep, but generally without intending a contrast with simple sleep. The Old Testament too spoke of sweet sleep, but only with a real (if obscure) point to make.

Turning to physiological or psychological factors affecting sleep, the Old Testament tended to concentrate on the psychological, anxious care stealing away sleep. (But that physiological factors were also known was already noted in the introduction, where age, sickness, and cold were noted as detrimental to sleep.) The Mesopotamian material tended, on the other hand, to focus on sickness (often interpreted in terms of the demonic) as a threat to sleep. But the major divide would be between these approaches and those evidenced in the classical and rabbinic spheres which explored the stomach as a locus of sleep.

The rabbinic and selected classical traditions reveal a major 'hole' in the Old Testament understanding of sleep, as these speculate on the travels of a center of consciousness during sleep. However, this lacuna in the Old Testament is common to the ancient Near East. Even the counterexample of the Chester Beatty hymn to the sun does not suggest that one consciously participates in the travels of one's 'soul'.

The primary contribution of the comparative material to consideration of the relationship between sleep and death in the Old

Testament was to indicate how protean this equation was—and is! Behind the equation of sleep and death lie many different perceptions, many different experiences. Is sleep like death because it is inexorable, because it robs one of intelligence, because one is then with the divine, because one is motionless, or because the dead also sleep? The relative lack of interest in the physical similarities between the sleepers and the dead was evidenced in the Old Testament usage of the phrases 'sleep with the fathers' and 'be gathered to the fathers', although Israelite burial patterns in different ways acknowledged those similarities. Rather, the point and the flaw in the sleep–death equation was summed up in the prospect of awakening. Sleepers awake; the dead—except by the action of YHWH—do not. (Nor was this exception easily won!)

In the Old Testament and Egyptian literature, sleep is taken to be good, a part of the natural cycle. This appears unremarkable until contrasted with the rabbinic tradition, in which—most of the time—the instrumental character of sleep is stressed, or with the classical tradition, in which sleep can be spoken of as a thief. Pushed far enough, consideration of this topic would dovetail with the question of the valuation of quotidian human existence. In other words, explanation for the particular judgments expressed about sleep might be explained in terms of more generalized judgments about life in bodies which need food, shelter, and sleep.

'Sleep and the divine' (Chapter 5) continued the pursuit of Israelite understandings of sleep, examining sleep as a locus of different sorts of divine activity. Here negative results are as prominent as positive. Sleep in general was not understood as a result of divine activity, either in Israel or in the ancient Near East. In the Old Testament, when divine activity initiated sleep, generally that sleep was marked with *Rdm*. Nor is sleep understood as a time of transparency, a time in which one's heart is particularly open to the divine. Language about YHWH or particular Mesopotamian deities examining the heart is not lacking, but this examination does not characteristically occur at night.

Sleep is a time for divine communication. Through incubation one can attempt to elicit such communication; and the possibility of viewing this attempt as an instance of encroachment on divine freedom was perhaps one of the reasons behind the reticence the Old Testament demonstrates vis-à-vis the subject. How did this communication take place? There is no formal theory in the Old Testament comparable to the rabbinic speculation regarding the activities of the soul. On the other hand, a number of texts were identified which in a general way witnessed to such communication. Perhaps the more specific categories of dream and vision grow out of this undifferentiated communication.

The divine activity most desired during sleep was protection, both in and outside of Israel. In Israel, the first localization of this protection examined was the temple. The sacral-juridical procedure reconstructed by Schmidt was judged to be probable in its broad outlines, and this would then be one place where divine protection was sought. However, the treatment of the petition psalms by Schmidt, Beyerlin, and Kraus was judged unconvincing, and thus there is no certainty at this point that these psalms were at any time associated with this procedure. The evidence of the superscriptions points, rather, to a practice of individual usage in the face of a variety of temporal dangers.

The background to this concern with vulnerability during sleep is not simply the variety of Old Testament texts addressing this concern, but the ancient Near Eastern evidence. Whether the Egyptian beds with the figures of Bes and Thoeris, the Arslan Tash tablet, or the wealth of Mesopotamian incantations, the concern with this vulnerability comes through clearly, although the perceived threats differ. This background remains, however, extremely general, and further study would be necessary to place the individual petitions vis-à-vis these dangers more precisely or to describe the contexts in which they—or other wards—were employed.

'Divine sleep' (Chapter 6) critiqued two common ways of dealing with the language about YHWH sleeping in the Old Testament. On the one hand, the dying and rising gods do not form an illuminating parallel. On the other, one cannot simply set the Old Testament usage over against other usages, taking the former to be metaphorical and the latter to be literal. Rather, the language must be set against the variety of ways in which the gods were spoken of sleeping in the ancient Near East. Three major types of sleep (diurnal, annual, and untimely) were identified, and it was suggested that each had its own setting (often liturgical), and each its own hermeneutic. Against this backdrop, the Old Testament usage is selective and restrained. Selective: only untimely sleep is spoken of in relation to YHWH. Restrained: the language implies, but does not assert, YHWH's sleep (which does not, however, blunt the force of the implication). But even within untimely sleep there is variation. Some texts appear to use the larger ancient Near Eastern tradition of speaking of the divine making-oneself-unavailable in terms of sleep, a usage clearly marked as metaphorical. Others use the language of sleep to raise issues of YHWH's faithfulness or reliability. There the question of whether the language of sleep is to be understood literally or metaphorically is quite overshadowed by the more pressing concerns of faithfulness or reliability which the texts are concerned to raise.

In the introduction sleep was noted as one of the few lacunae in Pedersen's treatment of Israel. However, Pedersen makes an extremely suggestive comment about rest, and with a consideration of this we close.

> In every people rest must of course be an indispensable link in the economy of life. But there is a decisive difference between the two conceptions as to whether rest is considered a necessary means towards a higher aim, i.e. to gain strength for the effort, or whether it must in itself be considered the supreme state. And it cannot be denied that the mental development of Israel carried it far in the latter direction.
>
> This appears in the words of the Yahwist when he tells of primeval man, to whom work in the soil is assigned as a curse. Cursed is the ground for thy sake; in sorrow shalt thou eat of it all the days of thy life (Gen. 3,17). He would prefer to see everything shooting up without any effort on his part . . . The work, the strenuous effort is not the pleasure, but the misery of life. Rest is the same as happiness (Ruth 1,9) (1926, 326).

In this study rest as a topic was excluded. This decision was made both on lexical grounds (the activity fields of sleep and rest did not overlap) and on pragmatic grounds (sleep in itself was already a substantial topic). But material relevant to the topic and to Pedersen's suggestion was encountered—particularly in the picture of the Mesopotamian deities.

In discussing divine sleep in Mesopotamian mythology, it often appeared neither possible nor apropos to distinguish between the gods' desire for sleep and for rest. The gods like to stay in bed; what they do in bed is their own concern. (Therefore they do not like noise, because one has to get out of bed to do something about the noise.) Thus humankind is created to allow the gods more time in bed, and it is this idyllic situation which is pictured in the beginning of Adapa: Adapa doing the work, and wise (!) Ea on his couch.

It is not our purpose here to critique Pedersen's suggestion, but simply to note a number of questions it raises, questions which would also be logical extensions of this study. Whether humanity is in the image of the divine, or vice versa, Pedersen's account, if correct, would suggest Israelite man in image of Mesopotamian god. Both Eliade and Machinist have made suggestions regarding ways to interpret this divine inactivity, and it is not our intent that the typology of divine sleep developed here for the purpose of interpreting the Old Testament texts should cut off this discussion.

On the Israelite side, the evaluation of sleep, while positive, is not obviously supportive of Pedersen's suggestion. Pedersen's appeal to the Yahwist is provocative. But what does Genesis 2 mean now that it follows Genesis 1? Does Genesis 1 speak to the worth of the first six days, as well as the seventh? Certainly YHWH appreciates rest, to which the continuing Jewish observation and celebration of the Sabbath attest. But Genesis opens with YHWH putting in a full week's work, which does at least suggest a different set of priorities than those of his Mesopotamian counterparts. The Creator is an artist, and artists are notorious for shortchanging themselves on sleep. From that perspective too 'he who keeps Israel will neither slumber or sleep'.

APPENDIX A

Concordance by fields

For words which appear in one of the lexical groups discussed in Chapter 2, poetic texts are indicated by italics. For *mškb*, occurrences treated with the *škb* group are enclosed in square brackets; the other occurrences are treated with the *mškb* group.

Word	Field	Total	Texts
'kl	S	14	Gen 19.3; 24.33bis,54; 26.30; 31.54; Lev 14.47; Judg 19.4,21; 1 Kgs 19.6; Isa 65.4; Ruth 3.3,7; Eccl 5.11
bṭḥ	S	3	Ezek 34.25; Hos 2.20; Job 11.18
bqr	S	18	Gen 20.8; 24.54; 26.31; 28.18; 32.1; 41.8; Num 22.13,21; Josh 3.1; 6.12,15; 8.10; Judg 19.5,8,27; 1 Sam 3.15; 1 Kgs 3.21; Hos 7.6
gg	S	3	Josh 2.8; 2 Sam 11.2; Ps 102.8
ḥdr	S	1	2 Sam 4.7
ḥzwn	S	1	Isa 29.7
ḥzywn	S	4	Job 4.13; 7.14; 20.8; 33.15
ḥlwm	S	25	Gen 20.3,6; 37.5,6,8,9bis,10; 40.5thrice; 41.7,15, 17,22; Judg 7.13bis,15; 1 Kgs 3.5,15; Isa 29.7; Job 7.14; 20.8; 33.15; Dan 2.1
ḥlm	S	18	Gen 28.12; 37.5,6,9bis,10; 40.5; 41.1,5,11,15,17, 22; Judg 7.13; Isa 29.8bis; Dan 2.1,3
	Z	10	Gen 40.5,8; 42.9; Deut 13.2,4,6; Jer 23.25; 29.8; Joel 3.1; Ps 126.1
ḥrd	S	3	Lev 26.6; Job 11.19; Ruth 3.8
y'p	S	1	Judg 4.21
yṣw'	S	1	*Ps 132.3*
	D	1	*Job 17.13*
	I	2	*Gen 49.4*; 1 Chr 5.1
	N	1	*Ps 63.7*
yqṣ	DS	7	1 Kgs 18.27; Hab 2.19; Ps 35.23; 44.24; 59.6; 73.20; 78.65
	S	15	Gen 28.16; 41.4,7,21; Judg 16.14,20; 1 Sam 26.12; 1 Kgs 3.15; Isa 29.8bis; Jer 31.26; Ps 3.6; 17.15; 139.18; Prov 6.22
	D	6	2 Kgs 4.31; Isa 26.19; Jer 51.39,57; Job 14.12; Dan 12.2

	W	3	Gen 9.24; Joel 1.5; Prov 23.35
yšb	S	2	Ezek 34.25; Ps 91.1
yšn	DS	4	1 Kgs 18.27; *Ps 44.24; 78.65; 121.4*
	S	15	Gen 2.21; 41.5; Judg 16.19; 1 Sam 26.7,12; 1 Kgs 3.20; 19.5; *Isa 5.27*; Ezek 34.25; *Hos 7.6; Ps 3.6; 4.9; Prov 4.16; Cant 5.2; Eccl 5.11*
	D	6	*Jer 51.39*,57; *Ps 13.4; Job 3.13; Cant 7.10; Dan 12.2*
kswt	S	2	Exod 22.26; Job 24.7
lylh	S	37	Gen 20.3; 31.40; 32.14,22,23; 40.5; Exod 12.30; Num 22.8,19,20; Josh 4.3; 8.9,13; Judg 16.3; 1 Sam 26.7; 2 Sam 17.16; 19.8; 1 Kgs 3.5,19; Isa 29.7; Hos 7.6; Ps 91.5; Job 4.13; 7.3; 20.8; 27.20; 30.17; 33.15; Prov 31.15; Ruth 3.2,8,13; Cant 3.8; Eccl 2.23; 8.16; Esth 6.1; Neh 2.12
lyn	AS	5	Zeph 2.14; Ps 59.16; Job 39.9,28; 41.14
	S	45	Gen 19.2bis; 24.23,25,54; 28.11; 31.54; 32.14,22; Num 22.8; Josh 3.1; 4.3; 6.11; 8.9; Judg 18.2; 19.4,6,7,9bis,10,11,13,15bis,20; 20.4; 2 Sam 17.8, 16; 19.8; 1 Kgs 19.9; Isa 10.29; 65.4; Jer 14.8; Ps 91.1; Job 24.7; 31.32; Ruth 1.16bis; 3.13; Cant 7.12; Neh 4.16; 13.20,21; 1 Chr 9.27
	M	2	2 Sam 12.16; Joel 1.13
	Z	19	Exod 23.18; 34.25; Lev 19.13; Deut 16.4; 21.23; Isa 1.21; 21.13; Jer 4.14; Zech 5.4; Ps 25.13; 30.6; 49.13; 55.8; Job 17.2; 19.4; 29.19; Prov 15.31; 19.23; Cant 1.13
mṭh	S	3	2 Sam 4.7; *Prov 26.14; Cant 3.7*
	B	10	Gen 47.31; 48.2; 49.33; 1 Sam 19.13,15, 16; 2 Kgs 1.4,6,16; 2 Chr 24.25
	D	4	2 Sam 3.31; 1 Kgs 17.19; 2 Kgs 4.21,32
	I	1	Ezek 23.41
	N	2	1 Kgs 21.4; *Ps 6.7*
	W	1	Amos 6.4
	Z	8	Exod 7.28; 1 Sam 28.23; 2 Kgs 4.10; 11.2; *Amos 3.12*; Esth 1.6; 7.8; 2 Chr 22.11
msb	W	1	*Cant 1.12*
mṣʿ	S	1	*Isa 28.20*
mškb	S	7	[2 Sam 4.5],7,11; 11.2,13; *Job 7.13; 33.15*
	B	5	Exod 21.18; 2 Sam 13.5; 1 Kgs 1.47; *Ps 41.4; Job 33.19*
	D	3	*Isa 57.2; Ezek 32.25*; 2 Chr 16.14
	I	14	*Gen 49.4*; [Lev 18.22; 20.13; Num 31.17, 18,35; Judg 21.11,12]; *Isa 57.7,8*,[8]; [Ezek 23.17];

			Prov 7.17; Cant 3.1
	N	6	*Hos 7.14; Mic 2.1; Ps 4.5; 36.5; 149.5*; Eccl 10.20
	Z	11	Exod 7.28; Lev 15.4,5,21,23,24,26bis; 2 Sam 17.28; 2 Kgs 6.12; *Prov 22.27*
mtq	S	1	Eccl 5.11
ndd	S	4	Gen 31.40; Isa 38.15; Job 20.8; Esth 6.1
nwḥ	S	1	Eccl 5.11
nwm	DS	2	*Ps 121.3,4*
	AS	1	*Isa 56.10*
	S	1	*Isa 5.27*
	D	2	*Nah 3.18; Ps 76.6*
nwmh	W	1	*Prov 23.21*
'wr	S	3	Zech 4.1bis; Cant 5.2
'yn	S	6	Gen 31.40; Ps 132.4; Job 27.19; Prov 6.4; 20.13; Eccl 8.16
'yp	S	1	Isa 5.27
'lh	S	1	Ps 132.3
'p'p	S	2	Ps 132.4; Prov 6.4
'ṣl	S	3	Prov 6.9; 24.30; 26.14
'ṣlh	S	1	Prov 19.15
'rb	S	2	Jer 31.26; Prov 3.24
'rś	S	2	*Ps 132.3; Job 7.13*
	B	1	*Ps 41.4*
	D	2	Deut 3.11bis
	I	2	*Prov 7.16; Cant 1.16*
	N	1	*Ps 6.7*
	W	1	*Amos 6.4*
	Z	1	*Amos 3.12*
pḥd(v)	S	1	Prov 3.24
pḥd(n)	S	2	Ps 91.5; Cant 3.8
p'm	S	3	Gen 41.8; Dan 2.1,3
	N	1	Ps 77.5
	Z	1	Judg 13.25
pqḥ	S	2	Job 27.19; Prov 20.13
ṣlm	S	1	Ps 39.7
qwm	S	26	Gen 24.54; 32.14,23; Exod 12.30; Num 22.13,21; Deut 6.7; 11.19; Judg 16.3; 19.27; 1 Sam 3.6,8; 2 Sam 11.2; 1 Kgs 3.21; 19.5,7,8; Jonah 1.6; Ps 127.2; Job 7.4; Prov 6.9; 31.15; Ruth 3.14; Cant 5.5; Eccl 12.4; Neh 2.12
rdm	S	6	Judg 4.21; Jonah 1.5,6; *Prov 10.5*; Dan 8.18; 10.9
	D	1	*Ps 76.7*

rḥṣ	S	3	Gen 19.2; 24.32; Judg 19.21
ślmh	S	3	Exod 22.25,26; Deut 24.13
šḥr	S	2	Gen 19.15; Josh 6.15
škb	AS	2	*2 Sam 12.3; Isa 56.10*
	S	59	Gen 19.4; 28.11,13; Exod 22.26; Lev 14.47; 26.6; Deut 6.7; 11.19; 24.12,13; Josh 2.1,8; Judg 16.3; 1 Sam 3.2,3,5bis,6,9bis,15; 26.5bis,7bis; 2 Sam 4.5,7; 11.9,13; 1 Kgs 3.19,20; 19.5,6; 2 Kgs 4.11; *Isa 51.20; Hos 2.20; Jonah 1.5; Mic 7.5; Ps 3.6; 4.9; 57.5; Job 7.4; 11.18; 27.19; 30.17; Prov 3.24bis; 6.9,10,22; 24.33*; Ruth 3.4bis,7,8, 13,14; Eccl 2.23; *4.11*
	B	6	2 Sam 13.5,6,8; 1 Kgs 1.2; 2 Kgs 9.16; *Ps 41.9*
	D	64	Gen 47.30; Deut 31.16; *Judg 5.27*; 2 Sam 7.12; 1 Kgs 1.21; 2.10; 3.20; 11.21,43; 14.20,31; 15.8,24; 16.6,28; 17.19; 22.40,51; 2 Kgs 4.21,32; 8.24; 10.35; 13.9,13; 14.16,22,29; 15.7,22,38; 16.20; 20.21; 21.18; 24.6; *Isa 14.18; 43.17; 50.11*; Ezek 31.18; *32.19,21,27,28*,29,30,31; *Ps 88.6; Job 3.13; 7.21; 14.12; 20.11; 21.26; Lam 2.21*; 2 Chr 9.31; 12.16; 13.23; 16.13,14; 21.1; 26.2,23; 27.9; 28.27; 32.33; 33.20
	I	55	Gen 19.32,33bis,34bis,35bis; 26.10; 30.15,16; 34.2,7; 35.22; 39.7,10,12,14; Exod 22.15,18; Lev 15.18,24bis,33; 18.22; 19.20; 20.11,12,13,18,20; Num 5.13,19; Deut 22.22bis,23,25bis,28,29; 27.20,21,22,23; 28.30; 1 Sam 2.22; 2 Sam 11.4,11; 12.11,24; 13.11,14; *Isa 13.16; Jer 3.2;* Ezek 23.8; *Zech 14.2*
	M	4	2 Sam 12.16; 13.31; 1 Kgs 21.27; *Jer 3.25*
	N	1	1 Kgs 21.4
	W	3	*Amos 6.4; Prov 23.34bis*
	Z	18	Lev 15.4,20,24,26; *Num 23.24; 24.9*; 2 Sam 8.2; 2 Kgs 4.34; *Isa 14.8*; Ezek 4.4bis,6,9; *Ps 68.14; Job 38.37; 40.21*; Ruth 3.4,7
škm	S	16	Gen 19.2; 20.8; 26.31; 28.18; 32.1; Josh 3.1; 6.12,15; 8.10,14; Judg 19.5,8,9; Ps 127.2; Prov 27.14; Cant 7.13
šlwm	S	3	Lev 26.6; Ezek 34.25; Ps 4.9
šmš	S	4	Gen 15.12; 28.11; Exod 22.25; Deut 24.13
šnh	S	21	Gen 28.16; 31.40; Judg 16.14,20; *Isa 38.15*; Jer 31.26; Zech 4.1; *Ps 90.5; 127.2; 132.4; Prov 3.24; 4.16; 6.4,9,10; 20.13; 24.33; Eccl 5.11; 8.16*; Esth 6.1; Dan 2.1

	D	4	*Jer 51.39*,57; *Ps 76.6; Job 14.12*
šqd	S	2	Ps 102.8; 127.1
šqṭ	S	1	Job 3.26
šth	S	7	Gen 24.54; 26.30; Judg 19.4,21; 1 Kgs 19.6; Ruth 3.3,7
tnwmh	S	5	*Ps 132.4; Job 33.15; Prov 6.4,10; 24.33*
trdmh	S	7	Gen 2.21; 15.12; 1 Sam 26.12; *Isa 29.10; Job 4.13; 33.15; Prov 19.15*

APPENDIX B

Sleep field collocations

Collocations are listed under each word involved; texts are listed only at the first occurrence, thus, e.g., texts for the collocation *lyn* / *'kl* are listed under *'kl* / *lyn*.

Word	Word	Freq	Texts
'kl	*lyn*	6	Gen 19.2-3; 24.54; 31.54; Judg 19.4,20-21; Isa 65.4
	škb	5	Gen 19.3-4; Lev 14.47; 1 Kgs 19.6; Ruth 3.3-4,7
bw'	*šmš*	4	Gen 15.12; 28.11; Exod 22.25; Deut 24.13
bṭḥ	*škb*	2	Hos 2.20; Job 11.18
bqr	*lylh*	5	Num 22.8-13,19-21; Josh 8.9-10,13-14; Hos 7.6
	škm	7	Gen 20.8; 26.31; 28.18; 32.1; Josh 3.1; 6.12; 8.10
	qwm	5	Gen 24.54; Num 22.13,21; Judg 19.27; 1 Kgs 3.21
ḥzywn	*ḥlwm*	3	Job 7.14; 20.8; 33.15
	lylh	3	Job 4.13; 20.8; 33.15
	mškb	2	Job 7.13-14; 33.15
	trdmh	2	Job 4.13; 33.15
ḥlwm	*ḥzywn*	3	
	ḥlm	9	Gen 37.5,6,9bis,10; 40.5; 41.15; Judg 7.13; Dan 2.1
	yqṣ	2	Gen 41.7; 1 Kgs 3.15
	mškb	2	Job 7.13-14; 33.15
ḥlm	*ḥlwm*	9	
	yqṣ	6	Gen 28.12-16; 41.1-4,5-7,17-21; Isa 29.8bis
	p'm	2	Gen 41.5-8; Dan 2.1
ḥrd	*škb*	3	Lev 26.6; Job 11.18-19; Ruth 3.8
yqṣ	*ḥlwm*	2	
	ḥlm	6	
	yšn	3	Judg 16.19-20; 1 Sam 26.12; Ps 3.6
	šnh	4	Gen 28.16; Judg 16.14,20; Jer 31.26
yšn	*yqṣ*	3	
	škb	4	1 Sam 26.7; 1 Kgs 19.5; Ps 3.5; 4.9
	šlwm	2	Ezek 34.25; Ps 4.9

	šnh	3	Judg 16.18-20; Prov 4.16; Eccl 5.11
	trdmh	2	Gen 2.21; 1 Sam 26.12
lylh	*bqr*	5	
	ḥzywn	3	
	lyn	8	Gen 32.14,22; Num 22.8; Josh 4.3; 8.9; 2 Sam 17.16; 19.8; Ruth 3.13
	ndd	2	Gen 31.40; Esth 6.1
	pḥd	2	Ps 91.5; Cant 3.8
	qwm	4	Exod 12.30; Judg 16.3; Prov 31.15; Neh 2.12
	*šk*b	3	1 Kgs 3.19; Job 30.17; Eccl 2.23
	šnh	3	Gen 31.40; Eccl 8.16; Esth 6.1
lyn	*'kl*	6	
	lylh	8	
	qwm	4	Gen 24.54; 32.14,22-23; Num 22.8-13
	rḥṣ	3	Gen 19.2; 24.23-32; Judg 19.20-21
	škb	2	Gen 28.11; Ruth 3.13
	škm	8	Gen 28.11-8; 31.54–32.1; Josh 6.11-12; 8.9-10; Judg 19.4-5,7-8,9; Cant 7.12-13
	šth	3	Gen 24.54; Judg 19.4,20-21
mškb	*ḥzywn*	2	
	ḥlwm	2	
ndd	*lylh*	2	
	šnh	3	Gen 41.40; Isa 38.15; Esth 6.1
'yn	*'p'p*	2	Ps 132.4; Prov 6.4
	pqḥ	2	Job 27.19; Prov 20.13
	šnh	4	Gen 31.40; Ps 132.4; Prov 6.4; Eccl 8.16
'p'p	*'yn*	2	
	tnwmh	2	Ps 132.4; Prov 6.4
'ṣl	*škb*	2	Prov 6.9-10; 24.30-33
	šnh	2	Prov 6.9-10; 24.30-33
	tnwmh	2	Prov 6.9-10; 24.30-33
'rb	*šnh*	2	Jer 31.26; Prov 3.24
pḥd	*lylh*	2	
p'm	*ḥlm*	2	
pqḥ	*'yn*	2	
qwm	*bqr*	5	
	lylh	4	
	lyn	4	
	škb	7	Deut 6.7; 11.19; Judg 16.3; 1 Sam 3.5-6,6-8; Job 7.4; Ruth 3.14
rḥṣ	*lyn*	3	
śmlh	*škb*	2	Exod 22.26; Deut 24.13
	šmš	2	Exod 22.26; Deut 24.13

škb	*'kl*	5	
	bṭḥ	2	
	ḥrd	3	
	yšn	4	
	lylh	3	
	lyn	2	
	'ṣl	2	
	qwm	7	
	śmlh	2	
	šlwm	2	Lev 26.6; Ps 4.9
	šmš	2	Exod 22.25-26; Deut 24.13
	šnh	5	Gen 28.11-16; Prov 3.24; 6.9,10; 24.33
	šth	3	1 Kgs 19.6; Ruth 3.3-4,7
	tnwmh	2	Prov 6.10; 24.33
škm	*bqr*	7	
	lyn	8	
šlwm	*yšn*	2	
	škb	2	
šmš	*bw'*	4	
	śmlh	2	
	škb	2	
šnh	*yqṣ*	4	
	yšn	3	
	lylh	3	
	ndd	3	
	'yn	4	
	'ṣl	2	
	'rb	2	
	škb	5	
	tnwmh	4	Ps 132.4; Prov 6.4,10; 24.33
šth	*lyn*	3	
	škb	3	
tnwmh	*'p'p*	2	
	'ṣl	2	
	škb	2	
	šnh	4	
trdmh	*ḥzywn*	2	
	yšn	2	

APPENDIX C

Other field collocations

As noted in the text, only vocabulary appearing in the sleep field was checked for collocations in these other fields.

C.1. *Death field collocations*

Here the restriction on collocations listed has been relaxed slightly to include *'wlm*, *'wr*, and *'m-'bty-*. These additional elements appear in chart 4.1, but not chart 2.6.

Word	Word	Freq	Texts
yqṣ	*yšn*	3	Jer 51.39,57; Dan 12.2
	qwm	2	Isa 26.19; Job 14.12 (?)
yšn	*yqṣ*	3	
	šnh	2	Jer 51.39,57
mṭh	*škb*	3	1 Kgs 17.19; 2 Kgs 4.21,32
'wlm	*šnh*	2	Jer 51.39,57
'wr	*qwm*	2	Isa 14.9; Job 14.12
'm- 'bty-	*škb*	40	Gen 47.30; Deut 31.16; 2 Sam 7.12; 1 Kgs 1.21; 2.10; 11.21,43; 14.20,31; 15.8,24; 16.6, 28; 22.40,51; 2 Kgs 8.24; 10.35; 13.9,13; 14.16, 22,29; 15.7,22,38; 16.20; 20.21; 21.18; 24.6; 2 Chr 9.31; 12.16; 13.23; 16.13; 21.1; 26.2,33; 27.9; 28.27; 32.33; 33.20
qwm	*yqṣ*	2	
	'wr	2	
	škb	2	Isa 43.17; Job 14.12
škb	*mṭh*	3	
	'm- 'bty-	40	
	qwm	2	
šnh	*yšn*	2	
	'wlm	2	

C.2. *Intercourse field collocations*

In this field *mškb* appears twice, first as a member of the *mškb* group, collocating with *qwm* and *lylh*, and second as a member of the *Yšn* group, collocating with *škb* (cf. §2.5 and chart 2.6).

Word	Word	Freq	Texts
lylh	*mškb*	2	Prov 7.9-17; Cant 3.1
	škb	3	Gen 19.33,34,35
mškb	*lylh*	2	
	qwm	2	2 Sam 11.2; Cant 3.1-2
mškb	*škb*	2	Lev 18.22; 20.13
qwm	*mškb*	2	
	škb	2	Gen 19.33,35
škb	*lylh*	3	
	mškb	2	
	qwm	2	

C.3. *Nocturnal activity field collocations*

Word	Word	Freq	Texts
lylh	*qwm*	2	Ps 119.62; Lam 2.19
ʿwr	*šḥr*	2	Ps 57.9; 108.3
qwm	*lylh*	2	
šḥr	*ʿwr*	2	

NOTES

Notes to Chapter 1

1. Unless otherwise noted, all Scripture citations are from the *Revised Standard Version*, hereafter RSV.

2. The references to sleep and waking in the individual complaints have received attention starting with Schmidt (1928), who attempted to establish that they reflected a cultic juridical Sitz. This thesis has been picked up by Beyerlin (1970) and Kraus (1978), and will be examined in Chapter 4 of this study.

3. Rudolph (1971, 341) suggests that 'wir das Motiv für den tiefen Schlaf in dem Gefühl der vermeintlichen Sicherheit finden, das ihm der bisherige günstige Verlauf seiner Reise gegeben hat'.

4. Ziegler's comment is suggestive here: 'Die Darstellung erinnert lebhaft an Ex 11f. und 14. Hier wie dort vernichtet Jahwe die Feinde Israels während der Nacht. Das Wirken Jahwes ist in Dunkel gehüllt; der Mensch soll nicht Zeuge des göttlichen Eingreifens sein. Erst am Morgen, wenn es hell wird, sieht er das Ergebnis: die Feinde liegen, von der Hand Gottes hingestreckt, tot am Boden' (1950, 287).

5. The *trdmh* which falls on Abraham (Gen 15) may belong here. It is discussed in Chapter 2. As an entry point to dreams in the Old Testament, see Ehrlich (1953).

6. Finkelstein (1968, 36) has suggested that implicit in Jacob's complaint is the charge that Laban did not supply appropriate clothing for him, as may have been customary in such arrangements. Much the same language as appears in the verse is used in Jer 36.30: 'Therefore thus says the Lord concerning Jehoiakim king of Judah, He shall have none to sit upon the throne of David, and his dead body shall be cast out to the heat by day and the frost by night'.

7. Where supplements have been added, in these too the entry is lacking.

8. An adjacent article by the same author treats 'sleep, deep' (*rdm* means only 'to be fast asleep').

9. Roland de Vaux ([1961] 1965, 1.182) briefly discusses the watches of the night, but this is as close as he comes to a discussion of sleep.

10. Oepke's 'Sleep in the OT and Judaism' is often cursory: 'The Israelite, too, values sleep for its refreshing and revitalizing power (Jer. 31.26) . . . Not to sleep by night is a mark of the faithful and diligent servant (Gn. 31.40)' (1965, 434).

11. The English translation of this volume has not yet appeared.

12. The volumes of the revised *International Standard Bible Encyclopedia*

and in the supplementary series to the *Dictionnaire biblique* which would contain 'sleep' are forthcoming as of 1984.

13. Thomson notes that other readings of Ps 127.2 are possible, but does not offer a defense of his reading. Nor is the notion of what constitutes divine intervention spelled out, although from his later remarks (1955, 432) it appears to be in the dual causality school.

14. While the focus remains on the Old Testament, in some cases the Old Testament preserves evidence for understandings which would not have been shared by the writers.

Notes to Chapter 2

1. Lutzeier takes this notion to be equivalent to Coseriu's use of field value and Schwarz's use of sense domain (1982, 11-12).

2. Barr (1961, 109) may be consulted for a more polemical articulation of the same methodological position.

3. 'A subdivision of an act in a dramatic presentation in which the setting is fixed and the time continuous' (Morris [1969] 1982).

4. Gen 25.29, 30; Judg 8.4, 5; 1 Sam 14.28, 31.

5. Isa 29.8; 32.2[?]; Ps 63.2; 143.6[?]; Job 22.7; Prov 25.25.

6. GKC §72t, Joüon ([1923] 1965, §80k) and KB emend to either a verbal or adjectival form of *y'p*, while BDB assigns it to *'yp*. Since the form can be explained as a regular CîC form colored by the guttural (cf *wayyāšet, wayyāben, wayyāreb,* and GKC §22h for guttural influence), and since the perfect also appears (Jer 4.31), there seems little need to emend. Driver (1957, 74) proposed relating the form to Syriac *'w/yp*, from which is formed *'āftā* 'swooning, spasm', and, encouraged by LXX (A) *apeskarisen* and (B) *eskotōthē*, seeing here the meaning 'to twitch convulsively'. Although this is an interesting suggestion, the same form occurs in three other similar contexts (1 Sam 14.28, 31; 2 Sam 21.15) in which Driver's suggestion would not be appropriate, and thus relating the form to these specific senses of the Syriac seems a less economic solution.

7. *kšl, nwm, yšn*, Isa 5.27; *rdm*, Judg 4.21; *mškb* [??], 2 Sam 17.28-29; *šnt 'rbh* [?], Jer 31.25-26.

8. Pairs ordered in order of appearance; texts cited after Herdner 1963 [hereafter *CTA*], and Virolleaud 1968 cited as *Ug V*, followed by text and line numbers: *ḥlm/ḏrt* 6.3.4-5, 10-11; 14.1.35-36; 3.150-51; 6.296-97; *yšn/nhmmt* 14.1.31-32; *ndy/lyn* 17.1.5-6, 16; *ndy/'ly* 17.1.4-5, 15; *nhmmt/qmṣ* 14.1.34-35; *n'mt/šnt Ug V* 2.R12; *'ly/škb* 17.1.5-6, 15; *škb/'ly* 5.5.19-21; *škb/qmṣ* 14.1.34-35; *šnt/nhmmt* 14.1.33-34; *šnt/škb* 14.1.33-34. Of these, *yšn/nhmmt* and *Yšn/škb* were previously noted by Dahood as occurring in both Ugaritic and Biblical Hebrew (1972, 215). Likewise, *yšn/nhmmt/škb* and *nhmmt . . . ḥlm* (Dahood 1975, 14).

9. They include Ps 127.2, Eccl 5.11; Ps 3.6; 4.9; Gen 28.16 for *Yšn*, Isa 56.10; Nah 3.18; Isa 5.27; Ps 121.3, 4 for *Nwm*, and Gen 2.21; 15.12; Jonah 1.5, 6 for *Rdm*.

10. In regard to possible cognates for *rdm*, Dahood suggests that Ebla evidences a cognate with Hebrew *Rdm*, citing the equation of Sumerian *ma-mu* 'night, dream' with *ra-da-mu* (published in Materiali epigrafici di Ebla 1, no. 1263 rev 6.7-8), a suggestion which—Dahood claims—Pettinato subsequently accepted (1982, 7 n. 12).

11. *hregkō* 'snore' in Judg 1.5, 6; *katanussō* passive 'to be pricked at heart; to lie in a deep slumber' in Dan 10.9 [Theodotion].

12. *UT* 416, *WUS* 141. The evidence is slim here, but I would follow KB in recognizing two roots, and suggest that the expected Aramaic **ytn* has been edged out by *ytn* 'to give'.

13. It is arguable that the other two cases are weak counterexamples. Judg 16.19, in which Samson is put to sleep prior to being shaved, is the one case of a pi'el *yšn*, which might be construed as the human counterpart to the divine use of the *trdmh*. And 1 Sam 26.5-12, in which David steals the sleeping Saul's spear and jar, does contain a reference to the *trdmt yhwh* (v. 12).

14. For 1 Sam 3.2-3 I follow McCarter's suggestion (1980, 98) that the first clause of v. 3 places the action before dawn.

15. Alternately, *ky-nsk 'lykm yhwh rwḥ trdmh* in Isa 29.10.

16. Von Rad's observation is apropos here: 'At a particularly important place, the story-tellers love to point to an intervention of Jahweh's which occurred at a definite point in time, and yet decided the whole affair. Thus in I Sam. xxvi a deep sleep which Jahweh caused to come over Saul and his men favoured David's enterprise' (1962, 51-52). Less convincingly, Dahood: 'Why God should intervene in an incident in which he is otherwise not mentioned has not been satisfactorily explained, and one suspects that in *tardēmat yhwh*, *yhwh* merely serves as a superlative to stress the depth of the sleep that permitted David and his men to operate undetected' (1974, 391). But Dahood is correct in observing that Prov 19.15 tells against a blanket statement that *trdmh* is used for divinely influenced sleep (1974, 392). We have here taken the course of working from the characteristic uses of *Rdm* and concluded that Prov 10.5 (but not necessarily Prov 19.15!) is anomalous.

17. *BHS* suggests *yšnw* for *yšknw*, which the RSV follows here.

18. In the growing literature on parallel pairs the effect of switching the order has not been adequately addressed. One proposal regarding one possible effect of switching the order is offered by Gevirtz. He notes that the Ugaritic pair *'rbt* / *ḥln* is switched when Baal reverses his decision on their presence in his house (*CTA* 4.5.126-27; 7.17-19), and then juxtaposes this reversal with another: 'When, therefore, Isaac came to bless Esau, employing the same fixed parallelism that he had employed in his benediction over Jacob, "dew of heaven" // "fatness of earth", it may well have been tradition

that had prescribed the inversion of phrases. Nevertheless, it does not appear possible to ignore the implication that the author of this passage, by his skillful use of tradition in reversing the parallelism, may have intended thereby to reverse the blessing as well' (1963, 40). And Dahood takes up the question of pair reversal: 'One can find at least a score of cases where the order of the Ugaritic "fixed pairs" is reversed . . . When the Biblical poets reversed the Ugaritic sequence a plausible reason can often be assigned for the reversal, such as the requirements of chiasmus or syllable count' (1972, 77-78). As evidence Dahood cites the (Ugaritic) *p* / *špt* 'mouth' / 'lip' as used in Prov 18.6-7, *dbr* / *šd* 'field' / 'steppe' and *šd* / *mdbr* 'field' / 'steppe' as used in Joel 1.19-20, and *lb* / *kbd* 'heart' / 'liver' as used in Anat 2.25-26 (all examples of reversal for chiasmus' sake). A bibliography on parallel pairs could be built by beginning with the following: Avishur (1971, 1975, 1976), Boling (1960), Craigie (1971), Dahood (1972, 1975), Fisher (1972, 1975), Gevirtz (1963), Held (1957), and Watson 'Reversed word-pairs in Ugaritic poetry' [forthcoming in *Ugarit-Forschungen*].

19. Gemser (1963, 87) suggests 'der Rausch nach der Ausschweifung'.

20. *'prywn* in Cant 3.9 is not included in this section. For discussion, see Pope (1977, 441-43).

21. Ivory, Amos 6.4; gold and silver, Esth 1.6.

22. This suggestion is at least as old as Michaelis (Driver 1902, 53). It rests, first, on the use of *'rs* (Aramaic) for 'bier' and a similar occurrence in a Palmyrene bilingual text, second, on the Transjordanian megaliths (Cheyne and Black 1899-1903, 1.510). This evidence alone is not particularly strong, and thus Driver's judgment that the suggestion 'is little more than conjectural' (1902, 53) is understandable. Nevertheless, Driver concludes: 'Thus it is not impossible that the giant relic shown at Rabbah was a sarcophagus; though, as this meaning of *'rś* is uncertain, it is better to suppose that what was really a sarcophagus was popularly called a "bed"' (1902, 54). But see below.

23. Amos 6.4; Cant 1.16.

24. 1 Kgs 21.4; 2 Kgs 1.4, 6, 16; Amos 6.4; Cant 3.7; 2 Chr 24.25.

25. 2 Sam 11.2; 1 Kgs 1.47. But these are weaker examples than the other texts, which portray times in the Solomonic and following periods.

26. *mṭh* in 2 Kgs 1.4, 6, 16; *'rś* in Ps 132.3.

27. In poetry, when two words appear in parallel, and one of them is a word only occurring in poetry, that word does not necessarily function as the B-word. Thus *mṭh*/*'rś* Amos 6.4; Ps 6.7 and *mškb*/*yṣw'* Gen 49.4, but *'rś*/*mškb* Ps 41.4; Job 7.13; Prov 7.16-17.

28. Tomback 1978, and now two more from Kition, (*mṣbt*) *'l mškb* . . . and *'l mškb nḥtnm l'lm*, in Teixidor 1979, 132.

29. Source identifications follow Noth (1972).

30. The *mṭh*/*mškb* breakdown may be seen easily in table 3.1, ch. 3 §2.a.

Notes to Chapter 3

1. Also 1 Sam 9.25 [LXX]. The references to grass growing on roof tops (2 Kgs 19.26 // Isa 37.27) suggests that sleeping on roofs might have been more comfortable than one would first think. Noth comments, 'The roof... could be used for living quarters (Isa. 22.1) or for sleeping space, especially in the hot season of the year, as they still do. There flax could be spread to dry (Josh. 2.6). The roof could support an upper chamber... probably built at a corner of the roof, made of clay walls... and sticks... The strength of house foundations occasionally allows the conclusion that there was a complete upper storey' (1966, 153).

2. Compare the derivation of English 'chamberlain'. Salonen notes 'in Mari war das *bīt majjāli* ein wichtiger Palastraum in der Administration' (1963, 143).

3. Dalman [1928-42] 1964, 7.79 suggests that in these 'die Schlafgeräte aufbewahrt werden, wohl, um nachts in anderen Räumen aufgeschlagen zu werden'. This room is used to hide Joash and his nurse, and thus the suggestion that the phrase refers to a storage area rather than to a more heavily-used area is reasonable.

4. For Israelite houses, Aharoni (1982), Shiloh (1970, 1978), and Yeivin (1954) are the most useful general sources. The briefer treatments in Beebe (1968), Callaway (1983) and Davey (1977) may also be consulted. For Bronze Age domestic and temple architecture, see Ben-Tor (1973) and Herzog (1980) together with literature there cited.

5. It is, however, absent in van den Born 1968 [*Bibel-lexikon*], Broshi 1962 [*Encyclopaedia Biblica*], Fohrer 1962 [*Biblisch-historisches Handwörterbuch*], Galling 1937 [*Biblisches Reallexikon*], Ludwig 1959 [*Calwer Bibellexikon*], Mare 1979 [*International Standard Bible Encyclopedia*, revised], Weippert 1977 [*Biblisches Reallexikon*, revised].

6. Callaway's informal discussion of an eleventh-century BC home in Kh. Raddana does include the suggestion that 'For family socializing... they would line up shoulder to shoulder on a bench-like ledge built of stone along the base of the house wall', but no ledge is illustrated in the house plans, and it plays no part in his description of where people slept (1983, 45). And Davey (1977, 34) reconstructs a four-room house with a small rear room supplied with two wooden (!) benches.

7. As an example of the material beyond the scope of this discussion, the following dictum may be noted: 'Eight things cause a diminuation of seed, namely, salt, hunger, scalls, weeping, sleeping on the ground, lotus, cucumbers out of season, and bloodletting below, which is as bad as any two' (*b. Giṭṭin* 70a).

8. The Bronze Age bed will be discussed in the context of Palestinian burials. The Persian bed, recovered from Tomb 650 at Tell el-Far'a, is published in Petrie (1930) and Iliffe (1935). The frame (now totally

decomposed) was covered with bronze, had 'turned' legs, with cross-pieces on the short ends. As Iliffe (who was responsible for cleaning the pieces after they were published) reports, the initial report was mistaken in reconstructing the bed with the heaviest part on the ground rather than at the top (1935, 184). Neither Petrie nor Iliffe provides measurements for the reconstructed bed.

9. However, the difference in status between the parties in the two narratives and the lack of the entire clause containing the mention of the bed in Genesis 24 should be noted.

10. Omitted are therefore those occurrences of *mškb* identified as non-spatial in Chapter 2, as well as Og's *'rś* in Deut 3.

11. McCullough notes that the 'beds of ivory' of Amos 6.4 appear also in the tribute Hezekiah sent to Sennacherib (*ANET*, 288; 1962, 373).

12. This verse is set as prose in the RSV.

13. So, e.g., Gese (1962, 427) and Wolff (1977, 197). Recently Mittmann (1976, 151-52) has proposed identifying vv. 13-14 as an insertion, with vv. 12 + 15 as the original unit.

14. For discussion, often with bibliography, see Gese (1962), Mittmann (1976), Ruldolph (1973), Wolff (1977).

15. Rudolph (1973, 157) follows Fraenkel's judgment (*Die aramäischen Fremdwörter im Arabischen*, 1886, 40, 288) that the Arabic word is derived from Greek.

16. Accepted by Deller (1964), Wolff (1977, 196), and noted in KB.

17. But Mittmann cites another Akkadian text (K 2411.16-19) which he interprets as follows: 'Die Angaben könnten kaum eindeutiger sein. *amar(t)u* konstituiert die Langseite, *pūtu* die Breitseite des Bettkastens, beide als Konstruktionselemente, nicht im Sinne der geometrischen Dimensionen' (1976, 156). Thus the probable sense of Mittmann's earlier statement is that if *pūtu* referred to one of the short ends, it would be the head end that it would refer to. Sumerian and Akkadian text designations appear in 'Abbreviations'.

18. Reproduction in Barnett, *The Nimrud Ivories*, 1975, 130. Both the medium and the uncertain provenance argue against taking this as direct evidence for a Syro-Palestinian type.

19. Published in Tufnell (1953, pl. 29, no. 21). The model is from Tomb 1002, which Tufnell identifies as 8th century (1953, 230). Measurments are not provided, and it should be noted that Tufnell labels it a 'couch'.

20. Barnett reflects the uncertainty: 'the panels . . . appear to have formed the backs of thrones . . . or perhaps beds' (1982, 53).

21. I owe the reference to Galling (1937, 109); translation by Lichtheim (1973, 232-33).

22. Mittmann summarizes: 'Ein Spezifikum des ägyptischen Bettes ist die Form der Beine, die, anfänglich Rinderbeinen nachgebildet, seit der 3. Dynastie zunehmend und seit Beginn des Neuen Reiches regelmässig die

Gestalt von Löwenbeinen erhielten. Diese Konstanz erklärt sich offenkundig aus der zeremoniellen Rolle des Bettes als Totenbahre, deren thereomorpher Charakter aus apotropäischen Gründen noch stärker ausgeprägt war . . ' (1976, 159). The question of whether there was a separate class of funerary couches is disputed. Compare Fischer (1977, 768) and Baker (1966, 108).

23. Ranging from 1.46 : 1 (fig. 17, 1) to 1.65 : 1 (fig. 18, 1).

24. Stern (1982) argues that at present there are no examples of Jewish or Samaritan tombs in Palestine datable to the fifth or fourth centuries BC. For surveys of burial practices in Palestine see Callaway (1963), Meyers (1970), Rahmani (1981-82). What is still lacking is a convenient summary which includes information about the relative proportion of different sorts of burials for each of the periods in question.

25. Stiebing lists the following sites: Gezer Caves 2 I and 27 I, Jericho tombs A 13 and K 2, and Ophel Tombs 2 and 3. MacAlister does not list a platform for cave 27 I (1912, pl. 13.9); but a number of enclosed platforms (irregular) are described for cave 2 I (1912, 1.74). In addition, platforms are indicated for caves 3 I and 30 II (1912, pl. 13.7,11). The platforms in Jericho tombs A 13 and K 2 are very irregular, and in fact are listed as being Proto-Urban (Kenyon *et al.* 1960, 48; 1965, 9). For the second Ophel tomb discussed, Vincent notes: 'The little rock-hewn ledge on which the corpse had long ago been laid had been somewhat carefully levelled by the use of a curious concrete made of beaten clay. Its length was 1 mètre 70, and its breadth varied from 80 to 90 centimètres . . . I incline to the belief that it was stretched upon its left side, with the head pointing south-west, and the knees slightly bent' (1911, 25). Vincent does not provide a description of another ledge.

26. Primary, jar, anthropoid coffin, 'bathtub' and other coffin burials, massive secondary burials, pyre burials, and urn burials.

27. Pyre, pit, grave, cist-grave, and cave.

28. Type 1: characteristically primary burial in a grave or cist grave with a 'bowl' pottery pattern; type 2: characteristically massive secondary burial in cave with 'lamp-1' pottery pattern; type 3: characteristically massive secondary burial in cave with 'lamp-2' pottery pattern; type 4: characteristically massive secondary burial in cave with 'juglet-1' pottery pattern.

29. Megiddo 1090 (Loffreda 1968, 269) and Gezer 28 (MacAlister 1912, pl. 59.12).

30. Abu Gosh 1, 2, 3 (Cooke 1923-24, 115), Beth Shemesh 2, 4, 5, 6, 7, 8, 14, 16 (MacKenzie 1912-13, pl. 5, 8, 9, 10; Grant 1931, 10), Lachish 105, 106 (Tufnell 1953, pl. 125), Tell en Nasbeh 3, 15 (McCown 1947, 102, 123).

31. Beth Shemesh 7 is not included because the ledges appear only on the side.

32. Abu Gosh 1, 2, 3 (Cooke 1923-24, 115), Beth Shemesh 3, 4, 5, 6, 7, 8, 14, 16 (MacKenzie 1912-13, pl. 6, 8, 9, 10; Grant 1931, 10), Lachish 105, 106, 109, 6006 (Tufnell 1953, 189, 248, pl. 125), Tell en Nasbeh 15 (McCown 1947, 123).

33. Abu Gosh 1, 2, 3 (Cooke 1923-24, 115), Beth Shemesh 2, 3, 4, 5, 6, 7, 8 (MacKenzie 1912-13, pl. 5, 6, 8-10), Lachish 6006 (Tufnell 1953, 248).

34. A potential complication in the use of this evidence is Ussishkin's suggestion that the architecture is Phoenician, citing parallels in Asia Minor, Cypress, and Armenia (1970, 46).

35. All dimensions provided by the authors for resting-places are cited here. The third cave (the Garden Tomb!) is reported to have undergone major modifications during the Byzantine period.

36. Without references, Hughes also offers the following means (rounding here to the nearest centimeter): Nippur male, 168 cm, female, 151 cm, Mycenaean male, 159 cm, Cephallenian male, 163 cm, Early Iron Age Greek male, 161 cm.

37. An indication of the relative social equality between creditor and debtor assumed by the formulation in Deuteronomy is the prohibition against the *creditor* himself sleeping in the garment.

38. Josephus, perhaps reading *kbd*, offered the following: 'Next she made up the bed as for a sick person and put a goat's liver beneath the covers; and when at daybreak her father sent to fetch David, she told those who came for him that he had been attacked by illness during the night, and she showed them the bed all covered up, and by the quivering of the liver which shook the bedclothes convinced them that what lay there was David gasping for breath' (*Antiquities* 6.217).

39. An indication of the material available for the post-Biblical period is provided by the following quotation: 'Another used to say: When love was strong, we could have made our bed on a sword-blade; now that our love has grown weak, a bed of sixty [cubits] is not large enough for us' (*b. Sanhedrin* 7a). And Preuss ([1923] 1978, 493) notes that *b. Qiddušin* 4.14 is evidence for the practice of (unmarried) men sleeping together.

40. Stephan records that contemporary Palestinian shepherds 'have a siesta from the fourth to the ninth hour of the day' (1921, 205). I owe the reference to Pope (1977, 329).

41. References in Gunkel ([1929] 1968, 572).

42. Some emend *mškbwtm* in both cases. Thus for Hos 7.14 Rudolph (1966, 152) suggests *'l-mšknwtm* on the grounds that the activity is public. Kraus (1978, 1145) and others read *mšpḥwtm*. The juxtaposition of the two verses suggests rather that the word be retained as is.

43. Andersen and Freedman (1980, 474) attempt to leave even this question open by suggesting that the initial *wl'* could govern both clauses in the first half of the verse.

44. Both here and in Hos 7.14 and Ps 4.5 Dahood assumes a private life setting for uses of the bed which are equally—or more—likely to be public.

Notes to Chapter 4

1. The relative infancy of the field is indicated by the fact that it was in 1982 that 'a team of Harvard University scientists has identified a naturally occurring human substance that appears to play a role in initiating deep sleep' (Los Angeles Times Service 1982, 7).

2. For an introduction to these and other issues, see Hartmann (1973).

3. These translations are employed below for the Babylonian Talmud and Midrash Rabbah respectively. In the following quotations (both for Hebrew and other Semitic languages), when additional text is provided in English to establish the context, it is either enclosed in square brackets or the non-English text is inserted into the English text. The Midrash Rabbah is cited as [Book]. *R.*; other midrashim are cited as *Midr.* [Book].

4. Eliade is of interest here: 'Since Hypnos is brother to Thanatos, we see why, in Greece as in India and in Gnosticism, the act of 'awakening' had a 'soteriological' meaning (in the broadest sense of the word). Socrates awakens those who talk with him, even though against their will. 'How tyrannical you are, Socrates!', Callicles exclaims (*Gorgias*, 505d). But Socrates is perfectly conscious that his mission to wake people is divine . . . 'As you will not easily find another like me, I would advise you to spare me. I dare say that you may feel irritated *at being suddenly awakened when you are caught napping*; and you may think that if you were to strike me dead as Anytus advises, which you easily might, then you would *sleep on for the remainder of your lives*, unless God in his care of you gives you another gadfly' (*Apology* 30e; Eliade 1963, 337).

5. The malady, now read *'di'u'*, although sometimes equated in lexical lists with Sumerian *sag.gig* 'headache', is suspected to refer to a more serious disease, perhaps malaria; cf. *CAD 'di'u'*.

6. See also the incantation added as a postscript to Adapa (K 8214) dated by Liagre-Böhl to the neo-Assyrian period, where a description of illness includes the following lines: 'Wenn dieser [Mensch nun bei Tag oder Nacht] / An Schüttelfrost leidet / [Und an sein Lager gefesselt] / Den süssen Schlaf muss entbehren' (Liagre-Böhl 1959, 428).

7. Because hard work is necessary for a good night's sleep? Or, more likely in the context, because he does not have many goods to worry about?

8. The RSV here follows the LXX.

9. Further research or discoveries will be necessary to clarify how much this difference in distribution is simply due to the Old Testament (and Egyptian!) examples coming primarily from wisdom literature.

10. If so, interpretation via the Arabic *'urūq* 'veins' would be quite unlikely. Pope (1973, 219, 223) notes a variety of interpretive options.

11. 1922, 106. Bezold does not, however, cite texts, and one wonders whether his examples were prosaic or poetic.

12. Other examples are *Odyssey* 1.363—repeated a number of times during the poem—and 10.91.

13. Such a soul is sometimes, but not uniformly, referred to as an 'external soul'.

14. I owe the reference to Nilsson ([1952] 1964, 54).

15. In addition to these references, Ehrlich (1956, 134-35) and Thomson (1955, 424-25) may be consulted.

16. This midrash is preserved in a similar form in *Eccl. R.* 10.23. And an additional saying along these lines is cited by Thomson (1955, 429) from Weber's *System der Altsynagogalen Palästinischen Theologie*, 1880, p. 222. Gaster ([1969] 1975, 2.838) notes that 'Ishtar' assumes the form of a bird for intelligence purposes in the Hittite 'Tale of Elkuniršа'. For a possible parallel in a different direction, one of the activities attributed to demons is that 'they make the secrets of the couch as clear as day' (*CT* 16 43.41, trans. Thompson [1903, 187]).

17. For the Elijah and Elisha cycle, see Fohrer (1972, 221-22). For Ezek 13, see Zimmerli (1979, 297) together with the literature he cites. For Frazer's interpretation of the women's activity as soul-hunting, see Gaster ([1969] 1975, 2.615-17). Gaster also understands the reference to the *npš* 'going out' in Cant 5.6 to reflect belief in an external soul ([1969] 1975, 2.813).

18. This understanding is represented by the targums and Symmachus (Anderson [1972] 1981, 2.911).

19. In addition to the material presented here, there is also material lying nearby which has not been included. Alongside the question of the meaning of sleep language for death in the New Testament, there have been proposals for theologically appropriate use of this language for death (Bailey 1964, with bibliography). For the use of sleep language in conjunction with death in the Qur'ân, see Schreiner (1977), Smith (1979) and Thomson (1955, 425-26) with references there cited. And from Deir 'Alla we find *tškb.mškby.'lmyk* 'You will sleep the sleep of death' (2.11; Hoftijzer and van der Kooij 1976, 174, 180).

20. Cited from Kees, *Zeitschrift für ägyptische Sprache und Altertumskunde* 74 (1938): 78f.

21. Cited from Otto, *Die biographischen Inschriften der ägyptischen Spätzeit*, 1954, 193.

22. The Badarian civilization is taken by the authors to be a phase of the pre-dynastic period before Petrie's first phase (Early/Amratian).

23. 'O King, mighty in waking and great in sleeping, for whom sweetness is sweet, raise yourself, O King, for you have not died' (Faulkner 1969, 154).

24. For the following citations from Gilgamesh: translit. Thompson (1930); trans. *ANET* 89-99. The first text is Old Babylonian, the remainder are from the Nineveh recension.

25. In line 147 Speiser reads *ša-mu-ti sur-*[*ri i-mu-tu*].

26. 'The sleep at night is like this world, and the awakening of the morning is like the world to come . . . The awakening in the morning is like the future world . . . To a man who awakens out of his sleep in like manner will the dead awake in the future world' (Thomson 1955, 430).

27. While in most cases the identification of these texts is unproblematic, such is not the case with Cant 7.10b: *dwbb śpty yšnym*. The text is often emended on the basis of the LXX, Syriac, and Vulgate to read 'gliding over lips and teeth' (RSV), an emendation adopted in Pope (1977, 641). Provisionally, the Masoretic text [hereafter MT] is followed here, primarily on the strength of rabbinic traditions such as *Cant. R.* 7.10, *Ṣemaḥot* 8.4 (both cited above), and *Midr. Ps* 30.3.

28. Driver (1962) covers some of the same material, but does not significantly advance the discussion.

29. And Alfrink's studies are reflected in de Vaux's discussion (1961) 1965, 1.59.

30. While *qwm* is used frequently in the human sleep activity field (26x), *'wr* only 3x and *rgz* not at all.

31. Fohrer (1972, 220) takes v. 11b to be the result of the denial of 'honorable burial'.

32. Helpful on Sheol in general are Eichrodt (1967, 2.211-13), Kaufmann ([1960] 1972, 311), Ringgren (1966, 243), Tromp (1969, 186-87), and Vermeule (1979, 29).

33. Likewise, sleep is included in the list of things 'which in large quantities are harmful but in small quantities are beneficial' (*b. Giṭṭin* 70a).

34. Here we have learned from Wolff's treatment of sleep and rest: 'Good sleep becomes the mark of the man who lives in the rhythm of Yahweh's giving and calling. Rest manifests the art of living, that is to say the wisdom whose crowning characteristic is the fear of Yahweh' (1974a, 134).

35. A structuralist reading of these three texts would not necessarily cut completely across their intentionalities. The situation would, of course, be simpler if any of these texts had employed *'wr* ('Under the apple tree I awakened you' [Cant 8.5a; cf. Pope 1977, 386, 663]).

Notes to Chapter 5

1. While vulnerability and receptivity to divine communication consistently emerge as dominant themes when sleep is mentioned, they do not occur together. Of course, vulnerability in general is a concern often addressed in dreams, but at least in the Old Testament the treatment of dreams in situations of vulnerability is sometimes heavily ironic. Joseph dreams of ruling his brothers in the same chapter in which he is sold into slavery (Gen 37). A Midianite soldier is given a dream portending defeat for

the benefit of his eavesdropping opponent (Judg 7). YHWH's promise of protection to Jacob—which could have been narrated with a straight face—is used to develop further Jacob's portrait as a hard bargainer (Gen 28).

2. Text and translation lines g-i Landsberger (1968, 100-101). The relationship between this sequence and the lines from an Old Babylonian version are unclear: *ši-ta-am ša i-li a-na-ku ek-mé-ku* 'Des Schlafes der Götter bin ich beraubt' (von Soden 1959, 216).

3. 'In deorum templis ad dormiendum se prosternebant, quia certis ritibus atque caeremoniis effectis animoque bene praeparato atque prorsus in res devinas converso verisimillimum erat illum per somnium apparitūrum esse deum in cuius templo incubant' (Ehrlich 1953, 13).

4. Ehrlich distinguishes between the text and its possible prehistory: 'In unserem alttestamentlichen Texte ist von Inkubation nicht die Rede, doch mag auf der kanaanäischen Stufe der Erzählung vielleicht an eine solche gedacht worden sein' (1953, 32).

5. Pope (1973, 263-64) suggests 'strength' for *zmrwt*, citing Arabic *dmr* and Exod 15.2; 2 Sam 23.1; Isa 12.2; 25.5; Ps 118.14. This makes excellent sense in light of v. 9, although why *blylh*? If song, particularly cultic song (Loewenstamm 1969), then celebration of deliverance might be envisioned. But neither of these helps make sense of v. 11. Perhaps Elihu is simply not particularly coherent here (cf. Andersen [1976, 255-58]), but if vv. 10-11 are taken together, 'songs' is probably more appropriate, and the picture is more individualistic. But what wisdom (v. 11) has to do with help (v. 9) remains unclear. Fohrer comments: 'Dass dieser Gott "in der Nacht Lobgesänge gibt", hängt damit zusammen. Denn der Mensch, der auf Gott vertraut, empfindet die Lobgesänge, die diesem Vertrauen entspringen, als von Gott geschenkt. Er singt sie in der "Nacht", die die Tiefe seiner Not und seines Unglücks abbildet (vgl Jes 17,14; Ps 30,6), wie umgekehrt die erhoffte Hilfe Gottes mit dem Morgen verbunden wird (vgl Jes 17,14; Ps 46,6; 90,14; 143,8). Der Glaubende bedrängt Gott also nicht, sondern gibt ihm im Hymnus recht, und preist seine gnädige Hilfe, auf die er vertrauensvoll wartet' (1963, 476).

6. This is, of course, begging a major question, and is one of the points at which Beyerlin will attempt to strengthen Schmidt's case.

7. Schmidt subsequently changed his judgment on this verse: 'Previously . . . I associated this with 3.6 and 5.4 . . . and referred to an ordeal at the awakening of the accused, which the following curse here on the slanderer seemed to justify. But the tone of this psalm, especially the immediately preceding verse, makes this impossible' (1934, 244; tm).

8. Schmidt's Pss 4, 5, 7, 17, 26, 27, 57 plus Pss 3, 11, 23, 63. Pss 31 and 142 appear in Schmidt's list, but not Beyerlin's.

9. As Hasel (1970, 470) has noted, the evidence is at best ambivalent on this point.

10. Psalms 9–10, 12, 25, 54, 55, 56, 59, 62, 64, 86, 94, 140, 142, 143.

11. 'It is important that the oath is the only thing which the accused says in the ceremonial of the ordeal procedure' (Preuss 1933, 139; tm).

12. Begrich's 'Das priesterliche Heilsorakel' (*ZAW* 52 [1934] : 84) is cited in support.

13. *KAI* reads *l'pt'*. The initial *l* either marks the vocative (Cross and Saley) or is the [directive] preposition ('towards', i.e. 'against'; *KAI*, Caquot, Zevit). On the basis of the not unreasonable assumption that the three addressees correspond to the three representations, *l't'* is emended to *l'pt'* 'Flyer(s)' by Cross and Saley, and Caquot. The following *'lt* may be read either as 'goddess(es)' (Cross and Saley, *KAI*) or 'pact' (Caquot).

14. Baker provides brief descriptions of Bes and Thoeris in the context of his description of the Sitamun chair (18th Dynasty) decorations: 'Partly human in form, he [Bes] has the tail, mane and ears of a lion, and he was regarded as a potent protector against the tangible terrors of life, such as snakes, and also the intangible. Sometimes he is shown wearing a panther skin, sometimes a kilt, and he is often portrayed dancing and beating a tambourine or wielding knives . . . the hippopotamus goddess [Thoeris], almost always shown standing and pregnant—the patroness of women in childbirth. In spite of their formidable appearances these were friendly gods who guarded the household and especially watched over sleeping people' (1966, 65-66).

15. For a general treatment of protective and menacing spirits, see Contenau (1947). In addition to the texts cited here, cf. also those cited in ch. 4 §1.b above.

16. Translation line 19 from *CAD* '*majālu*'; cf. Thompson 1903, 128-29.

17. For a description of the ritual, see, conveniently, Lambert (1957). Text and translation below are Borger's; variants are not indicated.

Notes to Chapter 6

1. For which see Dossin (1935), Oppenheim (1959), and Seux (1976, 243-50, 375-77, 475-77) together with literature there cited.

2. Oppenheim describes in detail the process of feeding the gods in the morning and evening, but makes no mention of any need to awaken them (1964, 188-89).

3. Translit. and trans. provided by Langdon (1909, 18-19) are *ûma ša ni-it-ti la i-du-u* 'Spirit that knows not . . '; I have been unable to identify the source of the suggested emendation. Of Huwawa it is also said that he knows not sleep (*ANET*, 79), so this may be a literary *topos*.

4. Lambert and Millard 1969, from which both text and translation are taken. For more recent works, see bibliography in Oden 1981.

5. The first two times preserved both in the Old Babylonian (1.358-59; 2.1.7-8) and in the Assyrian (rev. 4 [3],7-8,40-41); the third time in a Neo-

Late Babylonian text (rev. 1.2-3).

6. Lines 8, 56, 81, 134, 245 in the composite text, whose numbers Kutscher prefixes with '*'.

7. As in the *balag* to Dumuzi, TCL 15 no. 8, 130: 'Der Herr, der unstete, bis wann liegt er?' (Frank 1939, 96).

8. Kutscher interpreted the 'false' sleep in terms of its temporal character—it is false because Enlil will awaken. But subsequent waking is part of the definition of sleep. The *balag*s cited by Cohen suggest rather that the sleep is false in the same sense that one is 'out of the office' at convenient moments. Does this usage perhaps reflect a practice of telling petitioners that the king was sleeping long after he had risen from his siesta? Under either interpretation it is difficult to be certain of what Nergal's 'false sleep' implies.

9. Texts which speak of YHWH resting, such as Exod 20.11, have not been included because words used for sleep and words used for rest are not used in the same context (one needs to go to Job's description of the grave [3.13] to find an exception to this!). Jer 1.12, by virtue of its use of *šqd*, is a good candidate for inclusion, and will be discussed below in the context of Ps 121. Ps 7.7, 'Arise, O Lord, in thy anger, / lift thyself up against the fury of my enemies; / awake, O my God; thou hast appointed a judgment' is a borderline case because the verbs employed (*qwm*, *'wr*) do not unambiguously mark prior sleep (as does *yqṣ*).

10. Jacobsen (1961) provided an extremely suggestive study of the phenomena captured by the symbol 'Tammuz'. And one implication of this study is that the middle term between this fertility god and national disaster is the human king who, having played Tammuz's role in the cult, is now carried off by the foe. In this respect the study is complementary to Gurney's (1962), a summary of the role of Tammuz/Dumuzi, cast primarily in the form of refuting Frazer's hypothesis which took Tammuz as one exemplar of a widespread dying and rising god pattern. While Inanna might in some moods be content to leave matters there (Tammuz dying but not rising), Gestinanna would not, and her annual descent to the netherworld for the sake of her brother (see Jacobsen 1976, 61) seriously qualifies Gurney's conclusions. More recently, Kramer in a series of articles (1980, 1982a, 1982b, 1983) has pursued the question via the *topos* of the weeping goddess, which may appear as 'the multi-faceted Inanna mourning her spouse Dumuzi who had been carried off bound and fettered to the Nether World—a tragic fate that served as a metaphor for the death of the king and the destruction of the Sumerian cities and temple' (1982a, 141).

11. The Sumerian text, K 3356, titled 'Lament to Tammuz and Innini' by Langdon, contains the following line: 'Oh shepherd that sleepest, thou that liftest thyself up, how long (?) thou that art estranged . . ' (1913, 98).

12. Outside of 'Ishtar's descent to the netherworld', the question of responsibility for Dumuzi's fate is not often raised (Lambert 1983, 214). But

'the Father', whom Kramer identifies as Enki, appears to play a role in a lament by Lisin (Kramer 1982b, 142), and the neo-Babylonian lament edited by Lambert (1983) contains the line 'Bel has deprived me of my consort, my beloved spouse' (line 23; 1983, 213), which Lambert takes as evidence of sectarian strife.

13. Evidence for Baal's annual sleep appears subsequently, and has been discussed by de Vaux (1941). It consists of a reference in Menander (preserved in Josephus), an inscription from Ammon, and a number of Phoenician inscriptions. Menander recorded that Eirōmos 'was the first to celebrate the awakening of Heracles in the month of Peritius' (*Antiquities* 8.5.3 §146). As this month in the Macedonian calendar corresponds to the beginning of spring, the most likely interpretation of this practice is that it refers not to a daily awakening, but to the awakening after a long winter's sleep (de Vaux 1941, 19). And it may be this activity—or a daily activity—which is reflected in the title *mqm 'lm* in the inscriptions.

14. Particular gods, especially the sun god, might be spoken of as sleepless, so also those who made the nights miserable.

15. 'Johanan the high priest did away with the Avowal concerning the Tithe. He too made an end also of the "Awakeners" and the "Stunners". Until his days the hammer used to smite in Jerusalem, and in his days none needed to inquire concerning *demai*-produce' (*m. Ma'aśer Šeni* 5.15; trans. Danby 1933, 82). Neusner (1971, 1.161) does not propose a date for this, but suggests, 'The pericope . . . may represent the form of the pre-Houses-materials. Those materials were redacted at Yavneh'. And the saying is picked up and commented upon in the Babylonian Talmud: '*He also abolished the wakers*. What does "wakers" mean?—Reḥabah said: The Levites used daily to stand upon the dais and exclaim, 'Awake, why sleepest Thou, O Lord?' He said to them, Does, then, the All-Present sleep? Has it not been stated, 'Behold, He that keepeth Israel shall neither slumber nor sleep!' But so long as Israel abides in trouble and the Gentiles are in peace and comfort, the words "Awake, why sleepest Thou, O Lord?" [should be uttered]' (*b. Soṭa* 48a). The editors gloss: 'Since his reign was blessed with peace and prosperity, he felt it was unnecessary for the Levites to use the words'.

16. The references in the Old Testament to other gods sleeping could be assigned to a number of these types, and this is perhaps an indication that other ways of analyzing the data are possible. I would be inclined to identify Hab 2.19 as an example of the first type (diurnal) and 1 Kgs 18.27 as an example of the fourth type. In light of the comparative material the dilemma the priests of Baal were in comes through more clearly: if the god is asleep, he must be awakened. And loud noises do wake up gods. But the Egyptian practice of waking the gods up carefully and the Mesopotamian *topos* of *ḫubūrum* suggests that this tactic too has its drawbacks. Also in regard to this incident, Schüpphaus, picking up on the temporal note in v. 27 ('And at

noon'), suggests that Elijah may be suggesting that Baal is taking a siesta (1982, 1035). This would add another type of divine sleep which has not been encountered elsewhere.

17. And different places in life would be implied as well by primary or secondary uses of these lamentations.

18. Cf. Ps 78.60. The case of Ps 44 is less clear; I am here following Beyerlin (1976).

19. In fact, the texts use rather finely graded language. In one case there is a direct question: why do you sleep? (Ps 44.24) In one case a psalm narrates YHWH's awakening 'as from sleep' (Ps 78.65). In the remaining cases one calls on YHWH to awaken (Ps 35.23; 59.5b-6), or describes YHWH as awakening, if the MT in Ps 73.20 is followed.

20. For anthropomorphism in general, Bromiley's contribution to the revised *International Standard Bible Encyclopedia* (1979, 137) is useful.

WORKS CITED

Abercrombie, J.R.

1979 'Palestinian Burial Practices from 1200 to 600 B.C.E.'. Ph.D. diss., University of Pennsylvania.

Aharoni, Y. (ed.)

1973 *Beer-sheba I*. Tel Aviv: Tel Aviv University.

1982 *The Archaeology of the Land of Israel*. Philadelphia: Westminster Press.

Aistleitner, J.

1974 *Wörterbuch der ugaritischen Sprache*. Berlin: Akademie-Verlag.

Albright, W.F.

1941-43 'The Excavation of Tell Beit Mirsim. Vol. 3. The Iron Age'. *AASOR* 21-22.

Alfrink, B.

1943 'L'expression *šākab 'im 'ăbôtâyw*'. *OTS* 2 106-18.

1948 'L'expression *ne'ĕsap 'el-'ammâyw*'. *OTS* 5 118-31.

Andersen, F.I.

1976 *Job*. Tyndale Old Testament Commentaries. Downers Grove: Inter-Varsity Press.

Andersen, F.I. and D.N. Freedman.

1980 *Hosea*. AB 24. Garden City: Doubleday.

Anderson, A.A.

[1972] 1981 *Psalms*. 2 vols. NCB. London: Marshall, Morgan & Scott. Reprint. Grand Rapids: Eerdmans.

Aristotle

Works. 23 vols. Loeb Classical Library.

Avishur, Y.

1971 'Pairs of Synonymous Words in the Construct State (and in Appositional Hendiadys) in Biblical Hebrew'. *Semitica* 2 17-81.

1975 'Word Pairs Common to Phoenician and Biblical Hebrew'. *UF* 7 13-47.

1976 'Studies in Stylistic Features Common to the Phoenician Inscriptions and the Bible'. *UF* 8 1-22.

Bailey, R.E.

1964 'Is "Sleep" the Proper Biblical Term for the Intermediate State?' *ZNW* 55 161-67.

Baker, H.

1966 *Furniture in the Ancient World*. New York: Macmillan.

Baldinger, R.

1968 'La synonymie: problèmes sémantiques et stylistiques'. In *Probleme der Semantik*, ed. W.T. Elwert, Zeitschrift für französische Sprache und Literatur Beiheft, n.s., 1, 41-61.

Ball, C.J.

1922 *The Book of Job*. Oxford: Oxford University Press.

Balz, H.

1972 '*hypnos ktl*'. In *Theological Dictionary of the New Testament*. ed. G. Kittel, VIII, 545-56. 10 vols. Grand Rapids: Eerdmans.

Barkay, G. and A. Kloner.
1976 'Burial Caves North of the Damascus Gate, Jerusalem'. *IEJ* 26 55-57.

Barnett, R.
1982 *Ancient Ivories in the Middle East*. Qedem 14. Jerusalem: The Hebrew University of Jerusalem.

Barr, J.
1960 *Theophany and Anthropomorphism in the Old Testament*. VTSup 7, 31-38.
1961 *The Semantics of Biblical Language*. Oxford: Oxford University Press.
1968 'The Image of God in the Book of Genesis'. *BJRL* 51 11-26.

Barrois, A.G.
1939 *Manuel d'archéologie biblique*. 2 vols. Paris: Editions Auguste Picard.

Bauer, T., B. Landsberger, and F.H. Weissbach
1933 'Lexikalisches Archiv'. *ZA* 41 216-36.

Baumgartner, W.
1917 *Die Klagegedichte des Jeremia*. Giessen: Töpelmann.

Beebe, H.
1968 'Ancient Palestinian Dwellings'. *BA* 31 38-58.

Ben-Tor, A.
1973 'Plans of Dwellings and Temples in Early Bronze Age Palestine'. *EI* 11 92-98. [Hebrew]

Beyerlin, W.
1970 *Die Rettung der Bedrängten in den Feindpsalmen der Einzelnen auf institutionelle Zusammenhänge untersucht*. FRLANT, 99. Göttingen: Vandenhoeck & Ruprecht.
1976 'Innerbiblische Aktualisierungsversuche'. *ZThK* 73 446-60.

Bezold, C.
1922 'Zum babylonisch-assyrischen Wörterbuch'. *ZA* 34 105-12.

Boling, R.G.
1960 '"Synonymous" Parallelism in the Psalms'. *JSS* 5 221-55.

Bonnet, H.
1952 *Reallexikon der ägyptischen Religionsgeschichte*. Berlin: de Gruyter.

Borger, R.
1967 'Das dritte "Haus" der Serie *bīt rimki* (VR 50-51, Schollmeyer HGŠ NR 1)'. *JCS* 21 1-17.

Born, A. van den.
1968 'Bett'. In *Bibel-lexikon*, 2nd edn, ed. H. Haag and A. van den Born. Zürich: Benziger Verlag, 207-208.

Braus, K.
1806 *Biblisches universal Lexicon*. 2 vols. Augsburg: Matthias Riegers.

Bright, J.
1965 *Jeremiah*. AB 21. Garden City: Doubleday.

British Museum. Dept. of Egyptian and Assyrian Antiquities.
1896 *Cuneiform Texts from Babylonian Tablets, etc., in the British Museum*. London: The Trustees.

Bromiley, G.W.
1979 'Anthropomorphism'. In *The International Standard Bible Encyclopedia*. rev. edn, ed. G.W. Bromiley, 4 vols. Grand Rapids: Eerdmans, I, 136-39.

Broshi, M.
1962 '*mittâ*'. In *Encyclopaedia Biblica*, ed. U. Cassuto *et al.*, IV, Jerusalem: Bialik Institute, 832-34.

Brown, F., S.R. Driver, and C.A. Briggs
1951 *A Hebrew and English Lexicon of the Old Testament*. Oxford: Oxford University Press.

Brunton, G., and G. Caton-Thompson.
1928 *The Badarian Civilization and Predynastic Remains near Badari*. BSAE 46. London: British School of Archaeology in Egypt.

Buck, A. de.
1939 *De Godsdienstige Opvatting van den Slaap*. Ex Oriente Lux, Mededeelingen en Verhandelingen 4.

Buis, P.
1966 'Les formulaires d'Alliance'. *VT* 16 394-411.

Bussby, F.
1934 'A Note on *šēnā'* in Ps. CXXVII 2'. *JTS* 35 306-307.

Buttrick, G.A. (ed.)
1962 *Interpreter's Dictionary of the Bible*. 4 vols. Nashville: Abingdon.

Cagni, L.
1969 *L'epopea di erra*. Studi Semitici 34. Università di Roma: Instituto di studi del vicino oriente.
1977 *The Poem of Erra*. SANE 1/3. Malibu: Undena.

Callaway, J.A.
1963 'Burials in Ancient Palestine'. *BA* 26 74-96.
1983 'A Visit with Ahilud'. *BARev* 942-53.

Calmet, A.
1722 *Dictionnaire historique, critique, chronologique, géographique et littéral de la Bible*. 2 vols. Paris: Emery, Saugrain, Pierre Martin.
1730 *Dictionnaire historique, critique, chronologique, géographique et littéral de la Bible*. 2 vols. with 2 supplementary vols. Paris: Emery, Saugrain, Pierre Martin.

Calvin, J.
1949 *Commentary on the Book of Psalms*. 5 vols. Repr. Grand Rapids: Eerdmans.

Caquot, A.
1973 'Observations sur la première tablette magique d'Arslan Tash'. *Journal of the Ancient Near Eastern Society of Columbia University* 5 45-52.

Caquot, A., M. Sznycer, and A. Herdner
1974 *Textes ougaritiques: introduction, traduction, commentaire*. Littératures anciennes du Proche-Orient 7. Paris: Editions du Cerf.

Cheyne, T., and S. Black (eds.)
1899–1903 *Encyclopaedia Biblica*. 4 vols. New York: Macmillan.

Childs, B.S.
1971 'Psalm Titles and Midrashic Exegesis'. *JSS* 16 137-50.

Clay, A. (ed.)
1912-23 *Babylonian Records in the Library of J. Pierpont Morgan*. 4 vols. New York: Privately Printed.

Cohen, M.
balag-compositions. SANE 1/2 Malibu: Undena.

Collinson, W.E.
1939 'Comparative Synonymics: Some Principles and Illustrations'. *Transactions of the Philological Society*, 54-77.
Contenau, G.
1947 *La magie chez les Assyriens et les Babyloniens*. Paris: Payot.
Cooke, F.
1923-24 'The Site of Kiriat Jearim'. *AASOR* 5 105-20.
Corswant, W.
1960 *A Dictionary of Life in Bible Times*. New York: Oxford University Press.
Coseriu, E. and H. Geckeler
1974 'Linguistics and Semantics'. In *Current Trends in Linguistics*, ed. T. Sebeok, 12 103-74. 14 vols. The Hague: Mouton Pubs.
Cowley, A.E.
1910 *Gesenius' Hebrew Grammar as Edited and Enlarged by the Late E. Kautzsch*. 2nd edn. Oxford: Oxford University Press.
Craigie, P.C.
1971 'Parallel Word Pairs in the Song of Deborah (Judges 5)'. *Journal of the Evangelical Theological Society* 20 15-22.
1976 *The Book of Deuteronomy*. NICOT. Grand Rapids: Eerdmans.
Cross, F.M., Jr, and R.J. Saley
1970 'Phoenician Incantation and a Plaque of the Seventh Century B.C. from Arslan-Tash in Upper Syria'. *BASOR* 197 42-49.
Dahood, M.
1965 *Psalms I*. AB 16. Garden City: Doubleday.
1970 *Psalms III*. AB 17A. Garden City: Doubleday.
1972 'Ugaritic-Hebrew Parallel Pairs'. In *Ras Shamra Parallels* 1, ed. L.R. Fisher. AnOr 49. Rome: Pontifical Biblical Institute, 71-382.
1974 'Hebrew-Ugaritic Lexicography, 12'. *Biblica* 55 381-93.
1975 'Ugaritic-Hebrew Parallel Pairs'. In *Ras Shamra Parallels* 2, ed. L.R. Fisher. AnOr 50. Rome: Pontifical Biblical Institute, 1-33.
1982 'Eblaite and Biblical Hebrew'. *CBQ* 44 1-24.
Dalman, G.
[1928-42] *Arbeit und Sitte in Palästina*. 7 vols. Gütersloh: Gütersloher Verlagshaus.
1964 Reprint. Hildesheim: Georg Olms.
Danby, H.
1933 *The Mishnah*. Oxford: Oxford University Press.
Davey, C.
1977 'Domestic Architecture of the Old Testament'. *Buried History* 13 21-37.
Delekat, L.
1967 *Asylie und Schutzorakel an Zionheiligtum*. Leiden: Brill.
Delitzsch, F.
[1867] 1970 *Biblical Commentary on the Psalms*. 3 vols. Biblical Commentary on the Old Testament. 25 vols. Reprint. Grand Rapids: Eerdmans.
Deller, K.
1964 Review of *Die Möbel des Alten Mesopotamien*, by A. Salonen. *Or* n.s. 33 99-103.
Dever, W.G.
1969 'Iron Age Epigraphic Material from the Area of Khirbet el-Kôm'. *HUCA* 40 139-204.

Dodds, E.R.

1951 *The Greeks and the Irrational*. Sather Classical Lectures 25. Berkeley: University of California Press.

Dillmann, A.

1865 *Lexicon Linguae Aethiopicae*. Leipzig: Weigel.

Donald, T.

1963 'The Semantic Field of "Folly" in Proverbs, Job, Psalms and Ecclesiastes'. *VT* 13 285-92.

Donner, H., and W. Röllig

1971 *Kanaanäische und aramäische Inschriften*. Wiesbaden: Otto Harrassowitz.

Dossin, G.

1935 'Prières auz "dieux de la nuit" (AO 6769)'. *RA* 32 179-87.

Dothan, M.

1971 'Ashdod II–III'. *'Atiqot* English series 10.

Driver, G.R.

1957 'Problems of Interpretation in the Heptateuch'. In *Mélanges Bibliques Rédigés en l'honneur de André Robert*. Travaux de l'institut Catholique de Paris 4. Paris: Bloud & Gay, 66-76.

1962 'Plurima mortis imago'. In *Studies and Essays in Honor of A.A. Newman*, ed. M. Ben-Horin *et al.* Leiden: Brill, 137-43.

Driver, S.R.

1902 *Deuteronomy*. 3rd edn. International Critical Commentary. Edinburgh: T. & T. Clark.

Duhm, B.

[1922] 1968 *Das Buch Jesaia*. 5th edn. Göttingen: Vandenhoeck & Ruprecht.

Eager, G.

1915 'Bed, Bedchamber, Bedstead'. In *The International Standard Bible Encyclopedia*, ed. J. Orr, 5 vols. Chicago: Howard-Severance, I, 421-23.

Easton, B.

1915 'Sleep'. In *The International Standard Bible Encyclopedia*, ed. J. Orr. 5 vols. Chicago: Howard-Severance, IV, 2817.

Eichrodt, W.

1967 *Theology of the Old Testament*. 2 vols. Philadelphia: Westminster Press.

Ehrlich, E.L.

1953 *Der Traum im Alten Testament*. BZAW 73.

1956 'Der Traum im Talmud'. *ZNW* 47 133-45.

Eissfeldt, O.

[1965] 1972 *The Old Testament*. New York: Harper & Row.

Eliade, M.

1963 'Mythologies of Memory and Forgetting'. *HR* 2 329-44.

1978 *A History of Religious Ideas*. Vol 1. *From the Stone Age to the Eleusinian Mysteries*. Chicago: University of Chicago Press.

Emerton, J.A.

1974 'The Meaning of *šēnā'* in Psalm CXXVII:2'. *VT* 24 15-31.

Epstein, I.

1948 *The Babylonian Talmud*. 35 vols. London: Soncino Press.

Erman, A.

1894 *Life in Ancient Egypt*. London: Macmillan.

[1927] 1966 *The Ancient Egyptians*. New York: Harper & Row.

Fairbairn, P. (ed.).

[1891] 1957 *Fairbairn's Imperial Standard Bible Encyclopedia*. 6 vols. Repr. Grand Rapids: Zondervan.

Falkenstein, A.

1931 *Die Haupttypen der sumerischen Beschwörung*. LSS n.s. 1. Leipzig: J.C. Hinrichs.

Faulkner, R.O.

1969 *The Ancient Egyptian Pyramid Texts*. Oxford: Oxford University Press.

Finkelstein, J.J.

1968 'An Old Babylonian Contract and Genesis 31.38f.'. *JAOS* 88 30-36.

Firth, J.R.

[1951a] 1957 'General Linguistics and Descriptive Grammar'. *Transactions of the Philological Society*. Reprint. *Papers in Linguistics 1934-51*, London: Oxford University Press, 216-28.

[1951b] 1957 'Modes of Meaning'. In *Essays and Studies*. Reprint. *Papers in Linguistics, 1934-51*, London: Oxford University Press,, 190-215.

Fischer, H.G.

1977 'Bett'. In *Lexikon der Aegyptologie*, ed. W. Helck and E. Otto. 3 vols. to date. Wiesbaden: Otto Harrassowitz, I, 767-68.

1979 'Kopfstütze'. In *Lexikon der Aegyptologie*, ed. W. Helck and E. Otto. 3 vols. to date. Wiesbaden: Otto Harrassowitz, III, 686-93.

Fisher, L. (ed.)

Ras Shamra Parallels, 1. AnOr 49, Rome: Pontifical Biblical Institute.

1975 (ed.). *Ras Shamra Parallels*, 2. AnOr 50. Rome: Pontifical Biblical Institute.

Fohrer, G.

1962 'Bett'. In *Biblisch-historisches Handwörterbuch*, ed. B. Reicke and L. Rost. 3 vols. Göttingen: Vandenhoeck & Ruprecht, I, 235-36.

1963 *Das Buch Hiob*. KAT 16. Gütersloh: Gütersloher Verlagshaus (Gerd Mohn).

1972 *History of Israelite Religion*. Nashville: Abingdon Press.

Frank, C.

1939 *Kultlieder aus dem Ischtar-Tamūz-Kreis*. Leipzig: Otto Harrassowitz.

Freedman, H., and M. Simon (eds.)

1939 *Midrash Rabbah*. Translated by H. Freedman *et al.* 10 vols. London: Soncino Press.

Frei, H.

1974 *The Eclipse of Biblical Narrative*. New Haven: Yale University Press.

Friedlander, G. (trans.)

1965 *Pirqê de Rabbi Eliezer*. 2nd edn. New York: Hermon.

Fritz, V. and A. Kempinski

1976 'Vorbericht über die Ausgrabung auf der *Ḫirbet el-Mšāš* 3. Kampagne 1975'. *ZDPV* 92 83-104.

Frohnmeyer, K.

1959 'Schlaf, schlafen, schlummern'. In *Calwer Bibellexikon*. 5th edn. ed. T. Schlatter. Stuttgart: Calwer Verlag, 1175.

Galling, K.

1937 *Biblisches Reallexikon*. HAT. Tübingen: J.C.B. Mohr (Paul Siebeck).

Gardiner, A.H.
1935 *Hieratic Papyri in the British Museum*. 3rd series: *Chester Beatty Gift*. 2 vols. London: British Museum.

Gaster, T.H.
[1969] 1975 *Myth, Legend, and Custom in the Old Testament*. 2 vols. Repr. New York: Harper & Row.

Gelb, I.J. *et al.* (eds.)
1956 *The Assyrian Dictionary*. 14 vols. to date. Chicago: The Oriental Institute.

Gemser, B.
1955 'The *rîb*-Pattern in Hebrew Mentality'. *VTSup 3* 120-37.
1963 *Sprüche Salomos*. HAT. 2nd edn. Tübingen: J.C.B. Mohr (Paul Siebeck).

Gese, H.
1962 'Kleine Beiträge zum Verständnis des Amosbuches'. *VT* 12 417-38.

Gevirtz, S.
1963 *Patterns in the Early Poetry of Israel*. Studies in Ancient Oriental Civilization 32. Chicago: University of Chicago Press.

Gnuse, R.
1982 'A Reconstruction of the Form-critical Structure in 1 Samuel 3'. *ZAW* 94 379-89.

Goldin, J.
1955 *The Fathers according to Rabbi Nathan*. Yale Judaica Series 10. New Haven: Yale University Press.

Gordon, C.H.
1965 *Ugaritic Textbook*. AnOr 38. Rome: Pontifical Biblical Institute.

Grant, E.
1931 *Ain Shems Excavations (Palestine) 1928-1929-1930-1931, Part 1*. Biblical and Kindred Studies 3. Haverford: Haverford College.

Greenfield, J.C.
1962 'Studies in Aramaic Lexicography, 1'. *JAOS* 82 290-99.
1969 'Some Glosses on the Keret Epic'. *EI* 9 60-65.

Gunkel, H.
[1910] 1977 *Genesis*. Göttingen: Vandenhoeck & Ruprecht.
[1929] 1968 *Die Psalmen*. Göttingen: Vandenhoeck & Ruprecht.

Gunkel, H. and J. Begrich
1933 *Einleitung in die Psalmen*. Göttingen: Vändenhoeck & Ruprecht, 1933.

Gurney, O.R.
1956 'The Sultantepe tablets. 3, The Tale of the Poor Man of Nippur'. *AnSt* 6 145-64.
1962 'Tammuz Reconsidered'. *JSS* 7 147-60.

Gwaltney, W.C., Jr
1983 'The Biblical Book of Lamentations in the Context of Near Eastern Lament Literature'. In *Scripture in Context II*, ed. W.W. Hallo *et al.*, Winona Lake: Eisenbrauns,191-211.

Halliday, M.A.K.
1966 'Lexis as a Linguistic Level'. In *In memory of J.R. Firth*, ed. C.E. Bazell *et al.*, Longman's Linguistics Library. London: Longmans, Green & Co., 148-62.

Hamp, V.
1972 'Der Herr gibt es den Seinen im Schlaf, Ps 127,2d'. In *Wort, Lied und Gottesspruch: Beiträge zu Psalmen und Propheten. Festschrift für Joseph Ziegler*, ed. J. Schreiner. Forschung zur Bibel 2. Würzburg/ Stuttgart: Echter Verlag and Katholisches Bibelwerk, 71-79.

Hartman, L.F., and A.A. DiLella
1978 *The Book of Daniel*. AB 23. Garden City: Doubleday.

Hartmann, E.
1973 *The Functions of Sleep*. New Haven: Yale University Press.

Hasel, G.
1970 Review of *Die Rettung der Bedrängten in den Feindpsalmen der Einzelnen auf institutionelle Zusammenhänge untersucht*, by W. Beyerlin. *JBL* 89 470-72.

Hastings, J. (ed.)
1903 *A Dictionary of the Bible*. 5 vols. New York: Charles Scribner's Sons.

Haupt, P.
1881-82 *Akkadische und sumerische Keilschrifttexte nach den Originalen im Britischen Museum*... Leipzig: J.C. Hinrichs.

Held, M.
1957 'Studies in Ugaritic Lexicography and Poetic Style'. Ph.D. diss., Johns Hopkins University.

Herdner, A.
1963 *Corpus des tablettes en cunéiformes alphabétiques découvertes à Ras Shamra-Ugarit de 1929 à 1939*. Mission de Ras Shamra 10. Paris: Librairie Orientaliste Paul Geuthner.

Herzog, Z.
1980 'A Functional Interpretation of the Broadroom and Longroom House Types'. *Tel Aviv* 7 82-89.

Hesiod
1970 *The Homeric Hymns and Homerica*. Loeb Classical Library.

Higger, M. (ed.)
1969 *Treatise Semaḥot*. Jerusalem: Makor.

Hoftijzer, J. and G. van der Kooij
1976 *Aramaic Texts from Deir 'Allā*. Leiden: Brill.

Holman, C.M.
1970 'Analysis of the Text of Psalms 139'. *Biblische Zeitschrift* 14 37-71, 198-227.

Homer
1961 [1951] *The Iliad of Homer*. Trans. R. Lattimore. Chicago: University of Chicago.
1968 [1965] *The Odyssey of Homer*. Trans. R. Lattimore. New York: Harper & Row.

Honeyman, A.M.
1939 'The Pottery Vessels in the Old Testament'. *Palestine Exploration Quarterly* 71 76-90.

Horne, L.
1983 'Recycling an Iranian Village: Ethnoarchaeology in Baghestan'. *Archaeology* 36 16-20.

Hossfeld, F.-L., and I. Meyer
1974 'Der Prophet vor dem Tribunal'. *ZAW* 86 30-50.

Hughes, D.R.
1965 'Human Bones. i. Report on Metrical and Non-metrical Aspects of EB-MB and MBA Human Remains from Jericho (1957-8 Excavations)'. In *Excavations at Jericho*. Vol. 2. *The Tombs Excavated in 1955-8*, ed. K.M. Kenyon. Jerusalem: British School of Archaeology.

Huré, C.
1715 *Dictionnaire universal de l'Ecriture Sainte*. 2 vols. Paris: Godard.

Iliffe, J.
1935 'A Tell Fār'a Tomb Group Reconsidered'. *Quarterly of the Department of Antiquities in Palestine* 4 182-86.

Jacobsen, T.
1961 'Towards the Image of Tammuz'. *HR* 1 189-213.
1976 *The Treasures of Darkness*. New Haven: Yale University Press.

Jastrow, M.
[1903] 1967 *A Dictionary of the Targumim, the Talmud Babli and Yerushalmi, and the Midrashic Literature*. Reprint. Brooklyn: P. Shalom .

Jenni, E.
1978a *''āb'. Theologisches Handwörterbuch zum Alten Testament*, ed. E. Jenni. Munich: Chr. Kaiser I, 1-17.
1978b *'bḥn'. ibid.*, 272-75.

Jolles, A.
1916 'Hypnos'. In *Paulys Realencyclopädie der klassischen Altertumswissenschaft*, ed. G. Wissowa. 24 vols. Stuttgart: J.B. Metzler.

Josephus, F.
Works. 9 vols. Loeb Classical Library.

Joüon, P.P., S.J.
[1923] 1965 *Grammaire de l'hébreu biblique*. Rome: Pontifical Biblical Institute.

Kaufmann, Y.
[1960] 1972 *The Religion of Israel*. New York: Schocken Books.

Kees, H.
1933 'Aegypten'. In *Handbuch der Altertumswissenschaft*, ed. W. Otto, 12 vols. Munich: C.H. Beck III, 1.3.1.

Kennedy, J.
1898 *Studies in Hebrew Synonyms*. London: Williams & Norgate.

Kenyon, K.
1970 *Archaeology in the Holy Land*. 3rd edn. New York: Praeger.

Kenyon, K. *et al.*
1960 *Excavations at Jericho*. Vol. 1. *The Tombs Excavated in 1952-4*. Jerusalem: British School of Archaeology.
1965 *Excavations at Jericho*. Vol. 2. *The Tombs Excavated in 1955-8*. Jerusalem: British School of Archaeology.

Kitto, J. (ed).
1857 *The Cyclopaedia of Biblical Literature*. 10th edn. 2 vols. New York: Ivison & Phinney.

Knudtzon, J.A.
1910 *Die El-Amarna-Tafeln*. VAB 2. 2 vols. Leipzig: J.C. Hinrichs.

Köcher, F., and A.L. Oppenheim
1957 'The Old-Babylonian Omen Text VAT 7525'. *AfO* 18 62-77.

Koehler, L., and W. Baumgartner
1953 *Lexicon in veteris testamenti libros*. 2nd edn. Leiden: E.J. Brill.
1967– *Hebräisches und aramäisches Lexikon*. 3rd edn. 3 parts to date. Leiden: E.J. Brill.

Kramer, S.N.
1972 *Sumerian Mythology*. rev. edn. Philadelphia: University of Pennsylvania Press.
1980 'The Death of Dumuzi'. *AnSt* 30 5-13.
1982 BM 98396: A Sumerian Prototype of the Mater-Dolorosa'. *EI* 16 141-46.
1982 'Lisin, the Weeping Goddess'. In *Zikir Sumim*, ed. G. van Driel *et al.* Leiden: Brill, 133-44.
1983 'The Weeping Goddess'. *BA* 46 69-80.

Kraus, H.-J.
1972 [1967] 'Der lebendige Gott'. In *Biblisch-theologische Aufsätze*. Neukirchen-Vluyn: Neukirchener Verlag, 1-36.
1978 *Psalmen*. 5th edn. 2 vols. BKAT. Neukirchen-Vluyen: Neukirchener Verlag.

Kutscher, R.
1975 *O Angry Sea (a-ab-ba hu-luh-ha)*. Yale Near Eastern Studies 6. New Haven: Yale University Press.

Labat, R.
1935 *Le poème babylonien de la création (Enūma eliš)*. Paris: Librairie d'Amérique et d'Orient, Adrien-Maisonneuve.

Lambert, W.G.
1957 Review of *Studies on the Assyrian Ritual and Series bît rimki* by J. Laessoe. *BO* 14 227-30.
1959-60 'Three Literary Prayers of the Babylonians'. *AfO* 19 47-66.
1960 *Babylonian Wisdom Literature*. Oxford: Oxford University Press.
1983 'A Neo-Babylonian Tammuz Lament'. *JAOS* 103 211-16.

Lambert, W.G., and A.R. Millard
1969 *Atra-ḫasīs*. Oxford: Oxford University Press.

Landes, G.M.
1967 'The Kerygma of the Book of Job'. *Interpretation* 21 3-31.

Landsberger, B.
1968 'Zur vierten und siebenten Tafel des Gilgamesch-Epos'. *RA* 62 128-35.

Langdon, S.
1909 *Sumerian and Babylonian Psalms*. Paris: Librairie Orientaliste Paul Geuthner.
1913 *Babylonian Liturgies*. Paris: Librairie Orientaliste Paul Geuthner.

Lewis, I.M.
1971 *Ecstatic Religion*. Harmondsworth: Penguin.

Liagre-Böhl, F.
1949 'Hymne an Nergal, den Gott der Unterwelt'. *BO* 6 165-70.
1959 'Die Mythe vom weisen Adapa'. *Die Welt des Orients* 2 416-31.

Lichtheim, M.
1973 *Ancient Egyptian Literature*. Vol. 1. *The Old and Middle Kingdoms*. 3 vols. Berkeley: University of California Press.
1976 *Ancient Egyptian Literature*. Vol. 2: *The New Kingdom*. 3 vols. Berkeley: University of California Press.

Lindblom, J.
1942 'Bemerkungen zu den Psalmen I'. *ZAW* 59 1-13.
1961 'Theophanies in Holy Places in Hebrew Religion'. *HUCA* 32 91-106.

Loewenstamm, S.E.
1969 'The Lord is My Strength and My Glory'. *VT* 19 464-70.

Loffreda, P.
1968 'Typological Sequences of the Iron Age Rock-cut Tombs in Palestine'. *Liber Annuus* 18 244-87.

Los Angeles Times Service.
1982 'Body Chemical Called Sleep Inducer'. *New Haven Register* May 14, p. 7.

Ludwig, W.
1959 'Bett'. In *Calwer Bibellexikon*, ed. T. Schlatter. Stuttgart: Calwer Verlag, 151.

Lutzeier, P.R.
1982 'The Notion of Lexical Field and its Applications to English Nouns of Financial Income'. *Lingua* 56 1-42.

Lyons, J.
1966 'Firth's Theory of "Meaning"'. In *In Memory of J.R. Firth*, ed. C.E. Bazell *et al.* Longman's Linguistics Library. London: Longmans, Green & Co., 288-302.
1977 *Semantica.* 2 vols. Cambridge: Cambridge University Press.

Lys, D.
1959 *Nèphèsh.* Etudes d'histoire et de philosophie religieuses, publiées sous les auspices de la Faculté de théologie protestante de l'Université de Strasbourg 50. Paris: Presses universitaires de France.

MacAlister, R.A.S.
1912 *The Excavation of Gezer 1902-1905 and 1907-1909.* 3 vols. London: J. Murray.

Machinist, P.
1983 'Rest and Violence in the Poem of Erra'. *JAOS* 103 221-26.

MacKenzie, D.
1912-13 *Excavations at Ain Shems (Beth-Shemesh).* Palestine Exploration Fund Annual.

Malkiel, Y.
1974 Review of *Zur Wortfelddiskussion: Untersuchungen zur Gliederung des Wortfeldes "alt-jung-neu" im heutigen Französisch*, by H. Geckeler. *Foundations of Language* 12 271-85.

Mallowan, M.E.L.
1966 *Nimrud and its Remains.* 3 Vols. New York: Dodd, Mead.

Mandelkern, S.
1971 *Veteris Testamenti Concordantiae.* Repr. Jerusalem: Schocken.

Mare, W.H.
1979 'Bed'. In *The International Standard Bible Encyclopedia.* Rev. edn, ed. G.W. Bromiley. 2 vols. to date. Grand Rapids: Eerdmans, I, 445-47.

Marquet-Kraus, J. (ed.)
1949 *Les fouilles de 'Ay (et-Tell) 1933-1935.* Bibliothèque théologique et historique 45. Paris: Librairie Orientaliste Paul Geuthner.

Mazar, A.
1976 'Iron Age Burial Caves North of the Damascus Gate'. *IEJ* 26 1-8.

McCarter, P.K., Jr.
1980 *I Samuel.* AB 8. Garden City: Doubleday.

McClintock, J. and J. Strong (eds.)
1894-96 *Cyclopaedia of Biblical, Theological, and Ecclesiastical Literature.* 12 vols. New York: Harper.

McCown, C.
1947 *Tell-en-Nasbeh*. Vol. 1: *Archaeological and Historical Results*. Berkeley: Palestine Institute of the Pacific School of Religion.
McCullough, W.S.
1962 'Bed'. In *Interpreter's Dictionary of the Bible*, ed. G.A. Buttrick. 4 vols. Nashville: Abingdon I, 372-73.
McGrath, E.
1983 'Schooling for the Common Good'. *Time*, Aug. 1, 66-67.
Meyers, E.M.
1970 'Secondary Burials in Palestine'. *BA* 33 2-29.
Milgrom, J.
1981 'Sancta Contagion and Altar/City Asylum'. *VTSup* 32 278-310.
1983 'Of Hems and Tassels'. *BARev* 9 61-65.
Mittmann, S.
1976 'Amos 3,12-15 und das Bett der Samarier'. *ZDPV* 92 149-67.
Montet, P.
1958 *Everyday Life in Egypt in the Days of Ramesses the Great*. London: Edward Arnold.
Moor, J.C. de.
1971 *The Seasonal Pattern in the Ugaritic Myth of Ba'lu according to the Version of Ilimilku*. AOAT 16. Neukirchen-Vluyn: Neukirchener Verlag.
Morenz, S.
1973 *Egyptian Religion*. Ithaca: Cornell University Press.
Morris W. (ed.)
1969 *The American Heritage Dictionary of the English Language: New College Edition*. Boston: Houghton Mifflin.
Mowinckel, S.
1961 [1921] *Psalmenstudien 1. Awän und die individuellen Klagepsalmen*. Repr. Amsterdam: Schippers.
Murtonen, A.
1958 *The Living Soul: A Study of the Meaning of the Word naefaeš in the Old Testament Hebrew Language*. StudOr 23/1.
Neusner, J.
1971 *The Rabbinic Traditions about the Pharisees before 70*. 3 vols. Leiden: Brill.
Nicholson, E.W.
1974 'The Interpretation of Exodus 24.9-11'. *VT* 24 77-97.
Nilsson, M.P.
[1952] 1964 *A History of Greek Religion*. 2nd edn. New York: W.W. Norton.
Nöldeke, T.
1886 Review of *Prolegomena eines neuen hebräisch-aramäischen Wörterbuchs zum Alten Testament*, by F. Delitzsch. *Zeitschrift der Morgenländischen Gesellschaft* 40 718-43.
Noth, M.
1966 *The Old Testament World*. Philadelphia: Fortress.
1972 *A History of Pentateuchal Traditions*. Englewood Cliffs: Prentice-Hall.
Oates, D.
1959 'Fort Shalmaneser—an Interim Report'. *Iraq* 21 98-129.

Oden, R.A.
1981 'Divine Aspirations in Atrahasis and Genesis 1–11'. *ZAW* 93 197-216.

Oehman, S.
1953 'Theories of the "Linguistic Field"'. *Word* 9 123-34.

Oepke, A.
1965 '*katheudō*'. In *Theological Dictionary of the New Testament*. ed. G. Kittel. 10 vols. Grand Rapids: Eerdmans, III, 432-37.

Ogle, M.B.
1933 'The Sleep of Death'. *Memoirs of the American Academy in Rome* 11 81-117.

Oppenheim, A.L.
1956 *The Interpretation of Dreams in the Ancient Near East*. Transactions of the American Philosophical Society, n.s., 46/3.
1959 'A New Prayer to the "Gods of the Night"'. *Studia biblica et orientalia 3, Oriens antiquus*. Analecta Biblica 12. Rome: Pontifical Biblical Institute, 282-301.
1964 *Ancient Mesopotamia*. Chicago: University of Chicago Press.

Orr, J. (ed.)
1915 *The International Standard Bible Encyclopedia*. 5 vols. Chicago: Howard-Severance.

Pedersen, J.
1926-40 *Israel, its Life and Culture*. 4 vols. in 2. London: Oxford University Press.

Petrie, W.M.F.
1927 *Objects of Daily Use*. BSAE 42. London: British School of Archaeology in Egypt.
1930 *Beth Pelet I*. BSAE 48. London: British School of Archaeology in Egypt.

Pettinato, G.
1966 'Die Bestrafung des Menschengeschlechts durch die Sintflut'. *Or* 37 165-200.

Plato
1963 *Plato*, ed. E. Hamilton and H. Cairns. Bollingen Series 71, Princeton: Princeton University Press.

Polzin, R.
1976 *Late Biblical Hebrew: Toward an Historical Typology of Biblical Hebrew Prose*. Harvard Semitic Monographs 12. Missoula: Scholars.

Pope, M.H.
1973 *Job*. 3rd edn. AB 15. Garden City: Doubleday.
1977 *Song of Songs*. AB 7C. Garden City: Doubleday.

Preuss, J.
[1923] 1978 *Julius Preuss' Biblical and Talmudic Medicine*. New York: Sanhedrin Press.

Preuss, R.
1933 'Das Ordal im alten Israel'. *ZAW* 51 121-40, 227-55.

Price, I.M.
1927 *The Great Cylinder Inscriptions A and B of Gudea*. New Haven: Yale University Press.

Pritchard, J. (ed.)
1969 *Ancient Near Eastern Texts relating to the Old Testament*. 3rd edn with supp. Princeton: Princeton University Press.

Rad, G. von
1962 *Old Testament Theology*. Vol. 1. *The Theology of Israel's Historical Traditions*. New York: Harper & Row.
1966 *Deuteronomy*. OTL. Philadelphia: Westminster Press.
Rahmani, L.Y.
1982 'Ancient Jerusalem's Funerary Customs and Tombs. Parts 1-4'. *BA* 44 (1981) 171-77, 229-36; 45 43-53, 109-19.
Rawlinson, H.C.
1891 *The Cuneiform Inscriptions of Western Asia*. Vol. 4: *A Selection from the Miscellaneous Inscriptions of Assyria*. 2nd edn. London: R.E. Bowler.
Reicke, B.
1966 'Schlaf'. In *Biblisch-historisches Handwörterbuch*, ed. B. Reicke and L. Rost. 4 vols. Göttingen: Vandenhoeck & Ruprecht, III, 1699.
Reisner, G.
1896 *Sumerisch-Babylonische Hymnen*. Berlin: Spemann.
Reisner, I.
1979 *Der Stamm ʿbd im Alten Testament*. BZAW 149. Berlin: de Gruyter.
Richards, K.
1971 Review of *Die Rettung der Bedrängten in den Feindpsalmen der Einzelnen auf institutionelle Zusammenhänge untersucht*, by W. Beyerlin. *CBQ* 33 95-96.
Ringgren, H.
1966 *Israelite Religion*. Philadelphia: Fortress.
Robertson, D.A.
1972 *Linguistic Evidence in Dating Early Hebrew Poetry*. SBL Dissertation Series 3. Missoula: Scholars.
Robinson, E. (ed.)
1832 *Calmet's Dictionary of the Holy Bible*. Boston: Crocker & Brewster.
Rudolph, W.
1966 *Hosea*. KAT 13/1. Gütersloh: Gütersloher Verlagshaus (Gerd Mohn).
1971 *Joel, Amos, Obadja, Jona*. KAT 13/2 Gütersloh: Gütersloher Verlagshaus (Gerd Mohn).
1973 'Schwierige Amosstellen'. In *Wort und Geschichte*, ed. H. Gese and H.P. Rüger. AOAT 18. Kevelaer, Butzon & Bercker, 157-62.
1975 *Micha, Nahum, Habakuk, Zephanja*. KAT 13/3. Gütersloh: Gütersloher Verlagshaus (Gerd Mohn).
Saggs, H.W.F.
1974 'External Souls in the Old Testament'. *JSS* 19 1-12.
Salonen, A.
1963 'Die Möbel des Alten Mesopotamien'. *Annales Academiae Scientiarum Fennicae*, series B, 127.
Sauren, H., and G. Kestmont.
1971 'Keret, Roi de ḫubur'. *UF* 3 181-221.
Saussure, F. de.
[1915] 1966 *Course in General Linguistics*. ed. C. Bally, A. Sechehaye, and A. Riedlinger. New York: McGraw-Hill.
Sawyer, J.F.A.
1972 *Semantics in Biblical Research*. Studies in Biblical Theology, 2nd series, 24. Naperville: Alec R. Allenson.

1973 'Hebrew Words for the Resurrection of the Dead'. *VT* 23 218-34.
1980 'Types of Prayer in the Old Testament'. *Semantics* 7 131-43.

Scharfstein, Z.
1964 *'oṣar hamillim wĕhanniwim* (Thesaurus of words and phrases). 3rd edn. Tel Aviv: Hoza'ath Shîloh.

Schechter, S. (ed.)
1967 *Aboth de Rabbi Nathan*. New York: Feldheim.

Schenkel, D.
1869 *Bibel-lexikon*. 5 vols. Leipzig: Brockhaus.

Schilling, O.
1968 'Schlaf'. In *Bibel-Lexikon*. 2nd edn, ed. H. Haag Einsiedeln: Benzinger Verlag, 1539.

Schmidt, H.
1928 *Das Gebet des Angeklagten im Alten Testament*. BZAW 49.
1934 *Die Psalmen*. HAT. Tübingen: J.C.B. Mohr (Paul Siebeck).

Schollmeyer.
1912 *Sumerische-babylonische Hymnen und Gebete an Šamaš, I.* Paderborn: F. Schöningh.

Schott, S.
1958 'Eine Kopfstütze des Neuen Reiches'. *Zeitschrift für ägyptische Sprache und Altertumskunde* 83 141-44.

Schreiner, S.
1977 'Die Analogie von Schlaf und Tod im Koran'. *Kairos* 19 116-23.

Schüpphaus, J.
1982 *yšn*. In *Theologisches Wörterbuch zum Alten Testament*, ed. G.J. Botterweck and H. Ringgren. 3 vols. to date. Stuttgart: W. Kohlhammer, III, 1032-35.

Seux, M.-J.
1976 *Hymnes et prières aux dieux de Babylonie et d'Assyrie*. Littératures anciennes du proche-orient. Paris: Editions du Cerf.

Shiloh, Y.
1970 'The Four-room House'. *IEJ* 20 180-90.
1978 'Elements in the Development of Town Planning in the Israelite City'. *IEJ* 28 36-51.

Sinclair, J. McH.
1966 'Beginning the Study of Lexis'. In *In Memory of J.R. Firth*, ed. C.E. Bazell *et al.*, Longman's Linguistics Library. London: Longmans, Green & Co., 410-30.

Smend, R.
1906 *Die Weisheit des Jesus Sirach. Hebräisch und deutsch*. Berlin: G. Reimer.

Smith, J.I.
1979 'The Understanding of *nafs* and *rūh* in Contemporary Muslim Consideration of the Nature of Sleep and Death'. *Muslim World* 69 151-62.

Soden, W. von
1959 'Beiträge zum Verständnis des babylonischen Gilgameš-Epos'. *ZA* 53 209-35.
1965-81 *Akkadisches Handwörterbuch*. Wiesbaden: Otto Harrassowitz.
1981 'Zum hebräischen Wörterbuch'. *UF* 13 157-64.

Speiser, E.A.
1951 'The Semantic Range of *dalāpu*'. *JCS* 5 64-66.
Spence, N.C.W.
1961 'Linguistic Fields, Conceptual Systems, and the *Weltbild*'. *Transactions of the Philological Society*, 87-106.
Stephen, S.H.
1921 'Modern Palestinian Parallels to the Song of Songs'. *Journal of the Palestine Oriental Society* 2 1-80.
Stern, E.
1982 *Material Culture of the Land of the Bible in the Persian Period 538–332 B.C.* Warminster: Aris & Phillips.
Stiebing, W.H. Jr
1970 'Burial Practices in Palestine during the Bronze Age'. Ph.D. diss., University of Pennsylvania.
Strack, H.L.
1929 *Hebräisches Vokabularium in grammatischer und sachlicher Ordnung*. 12th edn, ed. A. Jepsen. Munich: C.H. Beck.
Tawil, H.
1980 ''Azazel the Prince of the Steepe'. *ZAW* 92 43-59.
Taylor, C. (ed.)
1799-1801 *Calmet's Great Dictionary of the Holy Bible*. 3 vols. London: Taylor.
Teixidor, J.
1967– 'Bulletin d'épigraphie sémitique'. *Syria* 43–.
Thompson, J.A.
1980 *The Book of Jeremiah*. NICOT. Grand Rapids: Eerdmans.
Thompson, R.C.
1903 *The Devils and Evil Spirits of Babylonia*. Vol. 1. *Evil Spirits*. London: Luzac.
1904 *The Devils and Evil Spirits of Babylonia*. Vol. 2. *Fever Sickness and Headache*. London: Luzac.
1903 *The Epic of Gilgamesh*. Oxford: Oxford University Press.
Thomson, J.G.S.S.
1955 'Sleep: An Aspect of Jewish Anthropology'. *VT* 4 421-33.
Thureau-Dagan, F.
1921 *Rituels accadiens*. Paris: Leroux, 1921.
Tomback, R.S.
1978 *A Comparative Semitic Lexicon of the Phoenician and Punic Languages*. SBL Dissertation Series 32. Missoula: Scholars.
Tromp, N.J.
1969 *Primitive Conceptions of Death and the Nether World in the Old Testament*. Biblica et orientalia. Rome: Pontifical Biblical Institute.
Tufnell, O.
1953 *Lachish*. Vol. 3. *The Iron Age*. The Wellcome–Marston Archaeological Research Expedition to the Near East 3. London: Oxford University Press.
Ullmann, S.
1972 'Semantics'. In *Current Trends in Linguistics*, ed. T. Sebeok. 14 vols. The Hague: Mouton 9, 343-94.
Unger, E.
1931 *Babylon*. Berlin: de Gruyter.

Ussishkin, D.
1970 'The Necropolis from the Time of the Kingdom of Judah at Silwan, Jerusalem'. *BA* 33 34-46.

Vaux, R. de
1941 'Les prophètes de Baal sur le Mont Carmel'. *Bulletin du Musée de Beyrouth* 5 7-20.
[1961] 1965 *Ancient Israel*. 2 vols. New York: McGraw-Hill.

Vermeule, E.
1979 *Aspects of Death in Early Greek Art and Poetry*. Sather Classical Lectures 46. Berkeley: University of California Press.

Vincent, H.
1911 *Underground Jerusalem*. London: Horace Cox.

Virolleaud, C.
1968 'Les nouveaux textes mythologiques et liturgiques de Ras Shamra (XXIVe Campagne 1961)'. In *Ugaritica 5*, by J. Nougayrol, E. La Roche, C. Virolleaud, C.F.A. Schaeffer, Bibliothèque archéologique et historique 80. Mission de Ras Shamra 16. Paris: Imprimerie Nationale, 545-606.

Watson, P.J.
1979 *Archaeological Ethnography in Western Iran*. Viking Fund Publications in Anthropology, 57. Tucson: University of Arizona Press.

Webb Associates (ed.)
1978 *Projected 1985 Body Size Data*. NASA Reference Publication 1024. Washington: NASA Scientific and Technical Information Office.

Weippert, H.
1977 'Möbel'. In *Biblisches Reallexikon*. 2nd edn, ed. K. Galling. Tübingen: J.C.B. Mohr (Paul Siebeck), 228-32.

Weiser, A.
1962 *The Psalms*. OTL. Philadelphia: Westminster Press.

Widengren, G.
1955 *Sakrales Königtum im Alten Testament und im Judentum*. Stuttgart: W. Kohlhammer.

Wijsenbeek-Wijler, H.
1978 *Aristotle's Concept of Soul, Sleep and Dreams*. Amsterdam: Adolf M. Hakkert.

Wilcke, C.
1969 *Das Lugalbandaepos*. Wiesbaden: Otto Harrassowitz.

Wilson, R.R.
1980 *Prophecy and Society in Ancient Israel*. Philadelphia: Fortress.

Winer, G.
1847 *Biblisches Realwörterbuch*. 3rd edn. 2 vols. Leipzig: Moritz Schafer.

Witzel, P.M., O.M.F.
1935 *Tammuz-Liturgien und Verwandtes*. AnOr 10. Rome: Pontifical Biblical Institute.

Wolff, H.W.
1974a *Anthropology of the Old Testament*. Philadelphia: Fortress.
1974b *Hosea*. Hermeneia. Philadelphia: Fortress.
1977 *Joel and Amos*. Hermeneia. Philadelphia: Fortress.
1980 *Dodekapropheton*. BKAT 14, fasc. 12. Neukirchen-Vluyn: Neukirchener Verlag.

Yeivin, S.

1954 '*binyān*'. In *Encyclopaedia Biblica*, ed. U. Cassuto *et al*. 8 vols. Jerusalem: Bialik Institute, II, 179-263.

Young, E.

1970 *Analytical Concordance to the Bible*, rev. W.B. Stevenson. Grand Rapids: Eerdmans.

Zevit, Z.

1977 'A Phoenician Inscription and Biblical Covenant Theology'. *IEJ* 27 110-18.

Ziegler, J.

1950 'Die Hilfe Gottes "am Morgen"'. In *Alttestamentliche Studien: F. Nötscher zum 60. Geburtstag gewidmet*, ed. H. Junker and J. Botterweck, BBB 1. Bonn: Peter Hanstein.

Zimmerli, W.

1979 *Ezekiel*. Hermeneia. Philadelphia: Fortress.

INDEXES

INDEX OF OLD TESTAMENT REFERENCES

INDEX OF AUTHORS

JOURNAL FOR THE STUDY OF THE OLD TESTAMENT

Supplement Series

1 I, HE, WE AND THEY:
A LITERARY APPROACH TO ISAIAH 53
D.J.A. Clines

*2 JEWISH EXEGESIS OF THE BOOK OF RUTH
D.R.G. Beattie

*3 THE LITERARY STRUCTURE OF PSALM 2
P. Auffret

4 THANKSGIVING FOR A LIBERATED PROPHET:
AN INTERPRETATION OF ISAIAH CHAPTER 53
R.N. Whybray

5 REDATING THE EXODUS AND CONQUEST
J.J. Bimson

6 THE STORY OF KING DAVID:
GENRE AND INTERPRETATION
D.M. Gunn

7 THE SENSE OF BIBLICAL NARRATIVE I:
STRUCTURAL ANALYSES IN THE HEBREW BIBLE (2nd edition)
D. Jobling

*8 GENESIS 1-11: STUDIES IN STRUCTURE AND THEME
P.D. Miller

*9 YAHWEH AS PROSECUTOR AND JUDGE:
AN INVESTIGATION OF THE PROPHETIC LAWSUIT (RIB PATTERN)
K. Nielsen

10 THE THEME OF THE PENTATEUCH
D.J.A. Clines

*11 STUDIA BIBLICA 1978 I:
PAPERS ON OLD TESTAMENT AND RELATED THEMES
Edited by E.A. Livingstone

12 THE JUST KING:
MONARCHICAL JUDICIAL AUTHORITY IN ANCIENT ISRAEL
K.W. Whitelam

13 ISAIAH AND THE DELIVERANCE OF JERUSALEM:
A STUDY OF THE INTERPRETATION OF PROPHECY
IN THE OLD TESTAMENT
R.E. Clements

14 THE FATE OF KING SAUL:
AN INTERPRETATION OF A BIBLICAL STORY
D.M. Gunn

15 THE DEUTERONOMISTIC HISTORY
M. Noth

16 PROPHECY AND ETHICS:
ISAIAH AND THE ETHICAL TRADITIONS OF ISRAEL
E.W. Davies

17 THE ROLES OF ISRAEL'S PROPHETS
D.L. Petersen

18 THE DOUBLE REDACTION OF THE DEUTERONOMISTIC HISTORY
R.D.Nelson

19 ART AND MEANING: RHETORIC IN BIBLICAL LITERATURE
Edited by D.J.A. Clines, D.M. Gunn, & A.J. Hauser

20 THE PSALMS OF THE SONS OF KORAH
M.D. Goulder

21 COLOUR TERMS IN THE OLD TESTAMENT
A. Brenner

22 AT THE MOUNTAIN OF GOD:
STORY AND THEOLOGY IN EXODUS 32-34
R.W.L. Moberly

23 THE GLORY OF ISRAEL:
THE THEOLOGY AND PROVENIENCE OF THE ISAIAH TARGUM
B.D. Chilton

24 MIDIAN, MOAB AND EDOM:
THE HISTORY AND ARCHAEOLOGY OF LATE BRONZE AND IRON AGE JORDAN AND NORTH-WEST ARABIA
Edited by J.F.A. Sawyer & D.J.A Clines

25 THE DAMASCUS COVENANT:
AN INTERPRETATION OF THE 'DAMASCUS DOCUMENT'
P.R. Davies

26 CLASSICAL HEBREW POETRY:
A GUIDE TO ITS TECHNIQUES
W.G.E. Watson

27 PSALMODY AND PROPHECY
W.H. Bellinger

28 HOSEA: AN ISRAELITE PROPHET IN JUDEAN PERSPECTIVE
G.I. Emmerson

29 EXEGESIS AT QUMRAN:
4QFLORILEGIUM IN ITS JEWISH CONTEXT
G.J. Brooke

30 THE ESTHER SCROLL: THE STORY OF THE STORY
D.J.A. Clines

31 IN THE SHELTER OF ELYON:
ESSAYS IN HONOR OF G.W. AHLSTRÖM
Edited by W.B. Barrick & J.R. Spencer

32 THE PROPHETIC PERSONA:
JEREMIAH AND THE LANGUAGE OF THE SELF
T. Polk

33 LAW AND THEOLOGY IN DEUTERONOMY
J.G. McConville

34 THE TEMPLE SCROLL:
AN INTRODUCTION, TRANSLATION AND COMMENTARY
J. Maier

35 SAGA, LEGEND, TALE, NOVELLA, FABLE:
NARRATIVE FORMS IN OLD TESTAMENT LITERATURE
Edited by G.W. Coats

36 THE SONG OF FOURTEEN SONGS
M.D. Goulder

37 UNDERSTANDING THE WORD:
ESSAYS IN HONOR OF BERNHARD W. ANDERSON
Edited by J.T. Butler, E.W. Conrad & B.C. Ollenburger

38 SLEEP, DIVINE AND HUMAN, IN THE OLD TESTAMENT
T.H. McAlpine

39 THE SENSE OF BIBLICAL NARRATIVE II:
STRUCTURAL ANALYSES IN THE HEBREW BIBLE
D. Jobling

40 DIRECTIONS IN BIBLICAL HEBREW POETRY
Edited by E.R. Follis

41 ZION, THE CITY OF THE GREAT KING:
A THEOLOGICAL SYMBOL OF THE JERUSALEM CULT
B.C. Ollenburger

42 A WORD IN SEASON: ESSAYS IN HONOUR OF WILLIAM McKANE
Edited by J.D. Martin & P.R. Davies

43 THE CULT OF MOLEK:
A REASSESSMENT
G.C. Heider

44 THE IDENTITY OF THE INDIVIDUAL IN THE PSALMS
S.J.L. Croft

45 THE CONFESSIONS OF JEREMIAH IN CONTEXT:
SCENES OF PROPHETIC DRAMA
A.R. Diamond

46 THE BOOK OF THE JUDGES: AN INTEGRATED READING
B.G. Webb

47 THE GREEK TEXT OF JEREMIAH:
A REVISED HYPOTHESIS
S. Soderlund

48 TEXT AND CONTEXT:
OLD TESTAMENT AND SEMITIC STUDIES FOR F.C. FENSHAM
Edited by W. Claassen

49 THEOPHORIC PERSONAL NAMES IN ANCIENT HEBREW
J.D. Fowler

50 THE CHRONICLER'S HISTORY
M. Noth

51 DIVINE INITIATIVE AND HUMAN RESPONSE IN EZEKIEL
P. Joyce

52 THE CONFLICT OF FAITH AND EXPERIENCE IN THE PSALMS:
A FORM-CRITICAL AND THEOLOGICAL STUDY
C.C. Broyles

53 THE MAKING OF THE PENTATEUCH:
A METHODOLOGICAL STUDY
R.N. Whybray

54 FROM REPENTANCE TO REDEMPTION:
JEREMIAH'S THOUGHT IN TRANSITION
J. Unterman

55 THE ORIGIN TRADITION OF ANCIENT ISRAEL:
THE LITERARY FORMATION OF GENESIS AND EXODUS 1–23
T.L. Thompson

56 THE PURIFICATION OFFERING IN THE PRIESTLY LITERATURE:
ITS MEANING AND FUNCTION
N. Kiuchi

57 MOSES: HEROIC MAN, MAN OF GOD
G.W. Coats

58 THE LISTENING HEART: ESSAYS IN WISDOM AND THE PSALMS
IN HONOR OF ROLAND E. MURPHY, O. CARM.
Edited by K.G. Hoglund

59 CREATIVE BIBLICAL EXEGESIS:
CHRISTIAN AND JEWISH HERMENEUTICS THROUGH THE CENTURIES
B. Uffenheimer & H.G. Reventlow

60 HER PRICE IS BEYOND RUBIES:
THE JEWISH WOMAN IN GRAECO-ROMAN PALESTINE
L.J. Archer

* Out of print